Education and industry in the nineteenth century

Education and industry in the nineteenth century:
The English disease?

G. W. Roderick
M. D. Stephens

Longman
London and New York

Longman Group Limited London

*Associated companies, branches and representatives
throughout the world*

*Published in the United States of America
by Longman Inc., New York*

First published 1978

British Library Cataloguing in Publication Data

Roderick, Gordon Wynne
    Education and industry in the nineteenth
    century.
    1. Education – Great Britain – History –
    19th century
    I. Title   II. Stephens, Michael Dawson
    370'.941   LA631.7   77–30741

ISBN 0–582–48719–6

Printed in Great Britain by Richard Clay (The Chaucer Press) Ltd, Bungay, Suffolk

Contents

Foreword

In Rolt's splendid account of 'Victorian Engineering', the central chapter bears the title 'High Noon in Hyde Park'. The caption of course refers to the Great Exhibition of 1851 which symbolised perhaps the greatest period of engineering achievement which this country has known. The manifest enthusiasm which the exhibition engendered was equalled only by the quality of invention which it reflected. After High Noon, however, there usually follows a period which at best exhibits a mellowness, passing quickly into an evening which can sometimes be unconscionably chilly.

As many of our more careful historians have recorded, the signs of evening were already apparent long before the century was out – although few contemporary writers could have foreseen that it was still a comparative summer and that the full rigours of winter in economic terms would take almost a further century to make themselves fully apparent. Whilst Albion in general remained perfidious in the eyes of those abroad, a besetting complacency reigned at home. It is true that the social conscience of the nation was awakening, and in human terms we were progressing rapidly. The same was unfortunately not true of our industrial and economic development.

In many ways there was not the pressure to stimulate us to self criticism for, buttressed by a great empire with access to copious supplies of cheap raw materials, we were capable of performing well as a trading nation. Even this apparently fortunate state might not have pertained had it not been for our having been leaders in the industrial revolution which allowed us to parade our successes with such modest ostentation in 1851. Taken together, however, this happy combination of circumstances brought economic prosperity and discouraged all but the most perceptive from indulging in self-criticism.

Observers of events in Germany or America would have noticed a different state of affairs, for having started somewhat later in their industrial development, they were not only unencumbered by an inheritance of already dating processes, but there was an urgency to catch up and to compete. Thus by the end of the century the beginnings of mass production were well in evidence abroad whilst at home our productivity remained low and our attitudes to investment in new machinery were, to say the least, conservative.

A full analysis of the factors which conditioned national progress at that period would draw attention to a variety of influences not apparent in the rather superficial summary picture given in these paragraphs, though one of the most intriguing was that of educational attitudes. The effects of educational policy on national development are always difficult to evaluate because of the long time-scale necessary to determine whether a change in philosophy has been significant or not. Even given time enough, the true scientist would find the task daunting because of the many other changes in context which might have determined events. It is however always of interest to contrast attitudes to education and to do so in the nineteenth century in the context of industrial development leads to some inescapable conclusions.

Whereas technological education could have been seen to exist in France in the middle of the eighteenth century and in Germany shortly afterwards and while the basic idea of *wissenschaft* (which embodies the idea of learning coupled with research) was the accepted basis of nineteenth century German higher education, it was only towards the end of the century that science, let alone technology, began to establish itself within the British system and that minds were beginning to be sharpened by exposure to the art and techniques of systematic research. By contrast, we had remained dedicated to an education based on the classics and, whatever the virtues of classical education, we lacked the education and training at a professional level needed to match our continental rivals in industry.

This situation was to have particularly serious consequences in the present century – for there remains little evidence to suggest that we had been lacking in natural inventiveness and, whilst in the early stages of the industrial revolution invention alone was often enough, the later stages required a different breed of personnel to translate the basic ideas of invention into marketable products. We did not educate such people and it is also worth noting in passing that, almost without exception, our greatest contributions to invention were made by people who had not seen the inside of a British University.

Even if our problem had been clearly diagnosed, it is doubtful whether it would have been widely recognised, for when science education at last arrived it was accepted almost without question that a proper education for a 'gentleman' must be of a classical nature, while science was seen as something principally suited to the lower classes. This attitude still persists to a degree even today, and is one of the reasons why many of our best educated people still eschew the challenge of industrial production. Research has now some respectability – but the persistence of disesteem is clearly demonstrated by the ratios of graduate personnel in research to those in production in Britain and Germany. In 1973 the ratio was about 3:2 in the UK, whilst in Germany it was 1:7!

The status of the engineer and the ways in which he is used and regarded in industry is clearly an important factor in industrial success. The roots of our problem are mainly to be found in the nineteenth century and it is this which makes this study of the subject a matter of such importance. It is to be hoped that those who choose to pursue it will be stimulated to recognise the errors of the past and ensure that we do not continue to perpetuate them in the future.

The High Noon of the High Summer of 1851 was a remarkable period for Britain, and although summers recur at regular periods, they can be of variable quality. The area of education and training is one of the factors which can be of the greatest importance in determining that quality and it behoves us to seek to chart a new course in order to ensure that High Noon returns as soon as possible to this country.

Geoffrey Sims
19 December 1977

Acknowledgements

The authors are most grateful to Mrs Mary Wells, Miss Margaret Smith, Miss Julie Conlon and Miss Sylvia Stephens for so patiently typing various parts of the manuscript.

Chapter 1

The national ethos in the 1850s: Britain leads

On the first of May 1851 Queen Victoria opened the Crystal Palace Exhibition. The Great Exhibition was the pinnacle of the previous eighty years or so of English industrial life, the Industrial Revolution. The Exhibition heralded 'the opening of the Golden Age of Victorianism in the proper and essential meaning of the word'.[1] It was a manifestation also of 'a public recognition of the material progress of the age and the growing power of man over the physical world'.[2]

The spirit engendered by the Exhibition, in particular by Britain's success in the award of medals, was 'buoyant, optimistic and arrogant'.[3] The background to this national wave of optimism and euphoria was a growing material prosperity and 'a level of industrial production and foreign trade which set England far ahead of all other countries'. This mood 'which almost seems to have been born in 1851' lasted for the next twenty years, at the end of which period the foreign trade of the United Kingdom was more than that of France, Germany and Italy together and four times that of the United States. Britain was reaping the rich advantages of the lead gained by reason of political stability, of the Industrial Revolution and of native inventiveness. 'Material progress seemed as by some new law of nature, to have been showered without stint on a people who rated industriousness, business efficiency and private enterprise among the major virtues.'[4]

In 1851 Britain was almost exactly at mid-point of the period during which it is claimed she was the 'workshop of the world'.[5] The Great Exhibition of that year had been made possible by the Industrial Revolution which enabled Britain to rise 'to a position of global influence and power, unparalleled by any of its relative size before or since'[6] and to lead the world in the supply of manufactured goods, machinery and textile goods, particularly the latter. Indeed, the term Industrial Revolution itself is almost inseparable from that of cotton for it was the cotton industry which 'was the pacemaker of industrial change'[7] and which pioneered the mass demand for British goods. The cotton industry and the factory system in general owed its phenomenal rate of growth to 'inexhaustible supplies of cheap labour'[8] and to the ready availability of coal – Britain in 1870 still mined more coal than did Germany, France and the United States combined. But although the Industrial Revolution is firmly associated in the public mind with cotton it 'was by no means only cotton, or Lancashire or even textiles and cotton lost its primacy within it after a couple of generations'.[9] Nevertheless, the extent of the export of cotton goods was a significant psychological determinant in conditioning national attitudes in the second half of the nineteenth century.

The principal British exports during the nineteenth century were cotton goods, iron and steel, coal and machinery. In 1845 cotton and wool exports were valued at £35 million and accounted for some 79 per cent of British exports.[10] By 1880 textile exports had increased to £95 million at a time when iron and steel, coal and machinery amounted to £45 million. Textiles, therefore, still accounted for some 70 per cent of the main export earnings.[11] In 1907 the net value of the output of cotton goods was £45 million at a time when coal was £106 million, engineering £50 million, iron and steel £30 million and shipbuilding £21 million.[12] The favourable positions of coal, textiles and shipbuilding in the United Kingdom masked the effect of changes in international trade following new inventions and technologies, increasing demands for goods and the opening up of new markets. Two industries to come to the fore in the final quarter of the century were the chemical and electrical industries. As export earners these compared unfavourably with the earnings of traditional industries, and attention consequently still focused on the success of the latter. This success obscured the fact that the newly emerging industries were far more dependent on systematic technology and scientific research; in Britain both the chemical and electrical industries relied to a considerable extent on trained German and American manpower. Furthermore, in a period of intense competition for world markets traditional industries were equally dependent on the implementation of scientific discoveries and technological innovations.

But in 1851 this was very much in the future. At that time against a background of impressive performances of British industry and spectacular engineering triumphs everywhere to be seen – in ship-building, in railway transport, in canals and bridge building – the elation, jubilation and complacency were excusable. The spectacular successes of the previous eighty years conditioned thinking and thus determined attitudes towards education, to the role of the state and to the conduct of industrial affairs.

The pioneers of the Industrial Revolution had been untutored, lacking formal education, products of the ancient tradition of British craftsmanship – men such as Crompton, Smeaton, Bramah and Maudslay. The Industrial Revolution it seemed owed little to education systems or to direct action from the state. The key issue in education at the turn of the century was related to the spread of education for the 'lower orders'. In this the influence of religion was dominant. The aim was to produce a God-fearing, law-abiding and industrious work-force; sober, honest, literate citizens imbued with a sense of duty. The conviction grew during the first quarter of the century that with increasing industrialisation there was a need for the industrial worker, described as a 'mechanic' or 'artisan', to have a knowledge of science related to his industrial practice. Consequently, technical education from its origins became associated in the public mind with the education of the artisan, the philosophy of middle-class education meanwhile being firmly based on the principles of the Christian religion and on a knowledge of classics. Training of the mind and formation of character were paramount objectives of the private schools and grammar schools, largely the preserve of the middle and upper classes, and these objectives were to be attained by instruction in classics and the Christian religion. Many of the schools served as 'feeders' to the ancient universities of Oxford and Cambridge which themselves provided a general liberal education centred on the classics. Such an education was appropriate both for the 'gentleman' and the 'professional' man, for whom it served as a cultural foundation leading to further education in law, theology or medicine.

Thus the commonly held belief that the Industrial Revolution owed little to the ancient universities or to the grammar schools or to education in its formalised setting was justified in general terms. But that a knowledge of some science was widely diffused among industrialists in the late eighteenth and early nineteenth centuries is evident: there were several sources from which this could be obtained: itinerant lecturers, literary and philosophical societies, the Royal Institutions and the Dissenting Academies.[13] Nevertheless the Industrial Revolution clearly owed little to educational systems for such did not really exist. At mid-century the prevailing philosophy was that Britain owed her success to national character and qualities, to her craftsmen and engineers, well-endowed with native ability. These, allied to daring entrepreneurship and unfettered individualism, had brought Britain to the top. What indeed was owed to education? Why should things not continue as before?

Such arguments conveniently overlooked the part played by natural resources, geographical factors and the advantages of being a powerful maritime and commercial nation. Even in the atmosphere of the general euphoria surrounding the Great Exhibition one critic, Lyon Playfair, dared to draw attention to such things. Sir Lyon Playfair (1818–98, first Baron Playfair) was educated at St Andrews University, later taking a PhD in chemistry under von Liebig at Giessen University. After holding posts at the Royal School of Mines and Edinburgh University he entered Parliament as member for the Scottish universities in 1868. He was one of the first scientific men of affairs, becoming Postmaster-General and Vice-President of the Council of Education. In the past, he pointed out, the ready availability of cheap natural resources had been in Britain's favour, but in future the development of transport and communications systems would tend to cancel out differences in natural resources. The race would, therefore, go to the nation which commanded the greatest scientific skill. Playfair's introductory lecture on the occasion of the opening of the Government School of Mines in 1851 was a prophetic warning. In it he declared that 'as surely as darkness follows the setting of the sun, so surely will England recede as a Manufacturing nation, unless her industrial population become much more conversant with science than they are now'.[14] Playfair later toured the Continent at the request of HRH Prince Albert in order to study technical education at first hand. On his return he complained that in England there was 'an overweening respect for practice and a contempt for science. In this country we have eminent "practical men" and eminent "scientific men" but they are not united and generally walk in paths wholly distinct.'[15] Thus did Playfair put his finger on the weakness of England's position. Despite the impressive performances of her industries in winning medals, England was one of the few major competing countries without an organised system of technical education. Until that time England had a clear start in the industrial field but Playfair sounded the alarm bells of industrial competition. At the time the rival to be watched was France, for America and Germany were some way behind; when industrial competition reached its greatest intensity during the final quarter of the century England's rivals had become America and Germany.

Following Playfair's critical observations the feeling gradually grew that without systematic instruction and scientific research the industry of the United Kingdom would be overtaken by those of other countries. Thanks to Playfair the Great Exhibition became a turning point in that it marked the beginnings of state intervention in the affairs of science, technology and industry. As well as being a tangible embodiment of the national belief in the idea of progress and a natural order of increasing material prosperity the Exhibition led to an enhanced status for science and technology.

Self-help versus state intervention

Samuel Smiles's *Self-Help* which appeared in 1859 sold 20,000 copies that year and another 130,000 during the next thirty years. It was quickly succeeded by Smiles's other works with similar themes: thrift, character and duty. They formed

a veritable catalogue of Victorian 'virtues'. This long series of smug lay sermons on the virtues of industry and honesty, connecting always the practice of such virtue with the reward of material prosperity, is the shoddiest side of the mentality of the time. It was the instructive creed of the prosperous industrialists and businessmen whose ethics now dominated English manners as they dominated English economic life.[16]

The views of the often maligned Smiles came within a tradition of self-help and self-improvement which goes back to the end of the eighteenth century, a tradition which grew out of the Industrial Revolution and nonconformity. The concept of self-improvement was 'intellectual rather than purely moral improvement, though the two are of course usually linked, and it implies improvement undertaken by an individual of his own set purpose, in his own time, and often at the cost of some effort of sacrifice'.[17]

The origins of self-improvement owed much to Wesley's influence. Wesley believed that even the most poorly endowed had a duty to seek self-improvement; idleness was a sin from which Man could be saved by self-improvement. Although Methodism or even religion was not the only force inspiring an individual towards self-improvement it was a powerful influence the strength of which can be gauged from the following accounts by Cornish miners who were thus inspired. One such was John Williams of St Just, a poet-miner, who wrote

I was working eight-hour shifts, and when after the forenoon shift I should go up a little after 2 pm – I had to go to school with my dirty face and hands because I could not stay to go home to wash. I studied very hard and gained knowledge of arithmetic, mensuration, geometry, algebra, conic sections, and the specific gravities of substance. When I left school I continued my studies at home and commenced the study of trigonometry, land surveying and mine surveying. I put my money to buy books, and in a few years I had a decent library.[18]

Another miner who rose from Methodist class leader to local preacher and then to Minister wrote of his youth:

During lonely walks we exercised ourselves in questions of science, history, theology, etc. having only one end in view – self-improvement. We had no bookseller nearer than Penzance, seven miles distant; many a time did we walk thither for the purpose of getting a book or hearing a lecture on philosophy and walk home again.[19]

Self-improvement was held out as a text for workmen by employers for through it a well-disciplined work-force could be achieved. Linked to this individual approach went an upsurge of mutual improvement. It underlay the formation of book clubs and libraries, literary and philosophical societies, debating societies, scientific societies, lyceums and athenaeums. Later 'mutual improvement' classes were a common feature of mechanics' institutes. At a time when state and municipal action was lacking the philosophies of self and of mutual improvement were of benefit to the progress of science and industry. Faraday attended mutual improvement classes in his formative years and many scientists, engineers and industrial leaders were self-educated men who had been motivated by the spirit of improvement.

But the concept of self-help as advocated by Smiles went beyond the idea of mere self-improvement; it was antipathetic to state involvement in the affairs of the individual. One must not look to outside sources to provide learning opportunities, the answer lay rather in 'self-culture' through diligence and 'persevering effort'.[20] Many of those who advocated the virtue of self-help were at the same time anti-state at the very time when the need for state and municipal intervention was becoming increasingly evident.

Herbert Spencer was one outspoken opponent of state interference. He regarded the state as an enemy of man's evolutionary progress, his views being embodied in such work as *State Education Self Defeating* (1851) and *Man Versus the State* (1884). J. W. Hudson who carried out the first major survey of adult educational institutions in the United Kingdom later wrote: 'On the whole the experience of the past is proof of the danger of government interference – while it affords conclusive evidence of the superior and enduring value of voluntary effort.'[21]

Such attitudes were shared by those in positions of power and authority. Robert Lowe, the instigator of 'payment-by-results' when Chancellor of the Exchequer, expressed the view: 'I hold it as our duty not to spend public money to do that which people can do for themselves.'[22] This became a cardinal principle of government spending in education.

The belief in individualism and the dislike of state interference and of centralised administration were widespread. There was a fear, too, that state support would lead inevitably to state control.

On the Continent, on the other hand, the principle of state support was widely accepted. The phenomenal advance of education in all the German states was in fact based on extensive state and municipal support. Matthew Arnold at the end of the century found little evidence to suggest that in consequence of this education in Germany had been seriously damaged by state control. Earlier, following a survey of schools and colleges in Germany in 1868, he had written:

Our dislike of authority and our disbelief in science have combined to make us leave our school system . . . to take care of itself as best it could. Under such auspices, our school system has very naturally fallen all into confusion; . . . it has done and does nothing to counteract the indisposition to science which is our great intellectual fault.[23]

In Arnold's view there were two great obstacles which 'oppose themselves to our consulting foreign experience with profit'. One was 'our notion of the state as an alien, intrusive power in the community, not summing up and representing the action of individuals, but thwarting it' and the other 'our high opinion of our own energy and prosperity'.[24]

The dislike of state interference was finally dispelled and overcome only by the fear of losing that prosperity. In the face of increasing intensity of foreign competition for goods and markets the state gradually and reluctantly intervened in educational affairs.

Industrial competition and the later Victorians

The Great Exhibition had been a great stimulus to the promotion of science and technology; likewise the fear of industrial competition acted as a spur. The truth of Playfair's prophetic warning in 1851 became increasingly evident during the final quarter of the nineteenth century, when against a background of intensifying national rivalry in industry and trade a great debate raged around the importance of science and technical education and the need for government intervention. The task of educating the nation in the realities of the situation begun by Playfair in the 1850s was carried on by a scientific lobby whose foremost spokesman was Thomas Huxley.

Official public recognition of the danger facing the country was conceded by the Royal Commission on Scientific Instruction and the Advancement of Science under the chairmanship of the Duke of Devonshire (hereinafter referred to as the Devonshire Commission). As early as the 1870s at a time when it could fairly be claimed that Britain was still leading the world, the Commission alluded to the danger of falling behind in the competitive race, impressed no doubt by the constant reiteration of this theme by witness after witness from industry and education. 'Much has to be done', it said, 'which will require continuous efforts on the part of the administration unless we are content to fall behind other nations in the encouragement which we give to pure science, and as a consequence to minimise the danger of losing our pre-eminence in regard to its applications.'[25] From that time on public speeches by statesmen and industrialists, and annual reports of educational bodies, all testified to the growing awareness of the impact of foreign competition.

The proselytising activities of men such as Playfair and Huxley, aided by worried industrialists such as the German born William Siemens and Isaac Lowthian Bell, the Cleveland iron manufacturer, helped to change the climate of opinion in England and so overcame both the apathy of the establishment towards science and technology and at the same time the laissez-faire policies which were rooted in a dislike of state interference. Speaking at the opening of Sir Josiah Mason's Science College (later Birmingham University) in 1880 Thomas Huxley declared

This College appears to be an indication that we are reaching the crisis of the battle. . . . In the last century combatants were champions of ancient literature and modern literature; but some thirty years ago, the contest became complicated by the appearance of a third army, ranged around the banner of physical science. I am not aware that anyone has the authority to speak in the name of this new host. For it must be admitted to be somewhat of a guerilla force, composed largely of irregulars, each of whom fights pretty much for his own hand.[26]

He pointed out that in the past practical men had believed that 'rule of thumb' methods were adequate as we had achieved prosperity by the use of such methods. In the future they would be totally inadequate, he argued, for the progress of arts and manufactures: 'We may take it for granted that in the opinion of those best qualified to judge, the diffusion of thorough scientific education is an absolutely essential condition of industrial progress.'[27]

The corner-stone of the arguments against the inclusion of science in educational institutions was the belief that the sciences had no part in liberal education and did not enable an individual to become cultured. 'How often have we been told,' complained Huxley,

that the study of physical science is incompetent to confer culture. In the belief of the majority of Englishmen culture is obtainable only by a liberal education and a liberal education is synonymous with one form of literature, that of Greek and Roman antiquity. The man who has learned Latin and Greek, however little, is educated, while he who is versed in other branches of knowledge is no more than a respectable specialist.[28]

Huxley drew attention to the government's almost obsessional interest in technical instruction for the artisan, in which field 'the Government is already doing a great deal', and its neglect of university education and of the promotion of research. Whilst advocating the need for pure science he conceded that 'it could not be converted into the most modest bread and cheese. Britain whose immense wealth and prosperity hang upon the thread of applied science is far behind France and another of the greatest wants of our times is the proper support and encouragement of original research.'[29]

The overwhelming case for scientific research was very much the concern, too, of George Gore, an industrial chemist who earned his living by chemical analysis and had set up his own private Institute for Scientific Research in Birmingham. As a witness to the Devonshire Commission he described himself as a researcher in physics and chemistry. His radical views appeared in a book entitled *The Scientific Basis of National Progress*. He began this work with the statement:

There is uneasiness at present respecting our ability to maintain our position in the race of progress and as our future success as a nation is based largely on science, it is desirable to call attention to the great public importance of new scientific knowledge and the means of promoting its development. By the neglect of scientific investigation, we are sacrificing our welfare as a nation. Present knowledge only enables us to maintain our present state. National progress is the result of new ideas, and the chief source of new ideas is *original research*.[30]

Scientific research was the key to the future according to Gore:

New knowledge is new power is a maxim which scientific discovery has impressed upon us. . . . The time is near when this nation will be compelled by the injurious consequences arising from its neglect of scientific research to acquire a knowledge of the relations of science to national existence and welfare, and to adopt some means of encouraging discovery. . . . England will be compelled, by the necessities of human progress and the advance of foreign intellect, to determine and recognise the proper value of scientific research as a basis of progress. National superiority can only be maintained by being first in the race, and not by buying inventions of other nations.[31]

Like Huxley, Gore drew attention to the government's emphasis on technical education: 'The intense desire which exists in this country for "quick returns" has shown itself in the much greater readiness to aid technical education than to promote permanent progress by means of scientific research.'

An unexpected figure among this small band of reformers was Colonel Alexander Strange. Born in 1818, the son of Sir Thomas Strange, he was educated at Harrow and entered the Indian Army as a Royal Engineer. He had marked scientific ability and on returning to England in 1861 contributed papers to the British Association for the Advancement of Science and to the Royal Society, being elected a Fellow of the Society. In 1868 he presented a paper to the British Association at Norwich in which he persuasively argued that only the state could adequately support the advance of science and called for a chain of state-sponsored research institutes, a National Science Council and a Minister of Science. He developed his ideas further in papers to the British Association in 1871 entitled 'On Government Action in Science' and to the Society of Arts in 1872 on 'The Relation of the State to Science'.

As a witness to the Devonshire Commission, Strange, like Gore, pointed to the extent that the government was supporting geology and astronomy in the form of observatories, museums, botanic gardens and the Geological Survey. He advocated state endowment of the universities and for the provision of state science laboratories in physics, chemistry and metallurgy for: 'All science should be cultivated, even branches of science which do not appear to promise immediate advantage' for 'one cannot tell what branch now economically unproductive may not eventually lead to untold wealth'.[32]

Huxley in his writings pointed out that the country was engaged in a grim struggle for existence, in an industrial war of greater significance than were the military wars of the beginning of the century. He called the nation to organise itself for victory. In an address on technical education at Manchester in 1887 he provided a simple but perceptive analysis of the situation facing the country:

Let me call your attention to the fact that the terrible battle of competition between the different nations of the world is no transitory phenomenon, and does not depend upon this or that fluctuation of the market, or upon any condition that is likely to pass away. . . . We are at present in the swim of one of those vast moments in which, with a population far in excess of that which we can feed, we are saved from a catastrophe, through the impossibility of feeding them, solely by our possession of a fair share of the markets of the world. And in order that that fair share may be retained, it is absolutely necessary that we should be able to produce commodities which we can exchange with food-growing people, and which they will take, rather than those of our rivals, on the ground of their greater cheapness or their greater excellence. . . .

Our sole chance of succeeding in a competition, which must constantly become more and more severe, is that our people shall not only have the knowledge and the skill which are required, but that they shall have the will and the energy and the honesty, without which neither knowledge nor skill can be of any permanent avail.[33]

Unfortunately, much evidence suggested there was a conspicuous failure to organise collectively for such a victory. Britain's position relative to that of her competitors continued to give rise to concern until the outbreak of the First World War. British industry did not stagnate, for it doubled its output between 1870 and 1913, but in the world as a whole there was a fourfold increase. Furthermore,

whereas Britain in 1870 produced one-third of the world's output of manufactures, in 1913 it produced only one-seventh. In the early 1880s its manufacturing output was exceeded by that of the United States. In the first decade of the 20th century Germany also passed the British output of manufactures and increased their output a good deal faster than Britain did.[34]

German states, following the example of Prussia, had invested enormous sums in education, right through from primary schools to the universities. The principles underlying the German outlook were in direct contrast to those prevailing in England. Her entire education system was state sponsored and controlled. Great numbers of highly trained scientists and engineers were produced by excellent technical high schools which had no equivalent in England, and from a diversity of high level technical institutes specialising in various branches of technology. German zeal and thoroughness manifested itself in every sphere: in education, in industry, in research, in management, in salesmanship and in the ability to capture foreign markets. The impact of this was quickly felt as she overtook Britain's lead in the production of pig iron, steel, ferrous alloys and sulphuric acid, while she made the synthetic dyestuffs industry almost an all Germany industry.

Germany had by now replaced France as the bogy nation. Britain faced severe competition from her for markets, particularly in Mesopotamia, Brazil, Chile and Uruguay. As market after market fell into German hands 'there were times, particularly towards 1900, when foreign competition seemed to be a brooding menace rather than a bracing challenge and the familiar label "made in Germany" was used as the grimmest of forebodings'.[35]

An impression of how the Germans appeared to English minds at mid-century is found in the autobiography of Edmund Muspratt who in 1850 travelled in a leisurely fashion via Hull, Hamburg, Berlin, Dresden, Cassel and Marburg to study at Giessen university. 'We English', he said, 'looked upon the Germans as slow-going people, dreaming, and half asleep. We knew little and cared less for Germany, not knowing that education was gradually changing the German mind as their universities turned their attention to science.'[36]

Muspratt was the son of James Muspratt, who is credited with being the 'father' of the English heavy chemical industry. As a chemical manufacturer himself and a Pro-Chancellor of Liverpool University, Edmund Muspratt did much to guide its early academic fortune. The subject of industrial competition and its relation to higher education therefore was one on which he was qualified to speak with some authority. In his autobiography, published in 1917, he wrote:

Our statesmen and governing classes, who, if educated, had passed through our public schools, and Oxford and Cambridge, were unable to recognise or anticipate the enormous advantage Germany would obtain in commerce and industry by means of its higher education, but Cobden, Sir John Bowring and W. J. Fox, and many Radicals, were educational reformers, and, had their warnings been listened to, England at the present day would not have suffered from the competition of Germany in many industries.[37]

Muspratt belonged to that growing band who, taking Germany as the exemplar, prompted the government into action in the final quarter of the century. The numerous education commissions and ensuing legislation from 1870 onwards reflected the efforts of the Victorians to get to grips with the changing situation, to make up for the previous half-century of inactivity, to create some order out of the confused and chaotic state of education, to provide a measure of support for scientific and technical education and to provide the funds belatedly recognised as being essential for the support of education.

Chapter 2

Laying the foundations: Elementary education

Prior to mid-century education was largely in the hands of the voluntaryists; Church schools, dame schools, charity schools supplemented by Sunday schools made up the provision of schooling. Having been first in the field the Church bodies were anxious to preserve their dominant position, consequently the progress of a state system of education was hindered by the secular–religious power struggle for the control of education. Within the religious organisations themselves there was a sharp and bitter cleavage between the Established Church and the nonconformists.[1] Power blocs were not confined to the Church bodies; manufacturers and landowners too had their own economic interests to defend whenever the state attempted to bring forth new legislation requiring school attendance.

Between 1800 and 1840 there was a significant growth of schooling, indeed West[2] argues that there was an 'explosion' in the school population of the major towns in the 1830s. Brougham's Select Committee Report[3] in 1820 revealed that one in fourteen of the population was being schooled. This was attributable mainly to the energy of the ecclesiastical groups but also partly to the willingness of parents to pay fees; a survey by the Manchester Statistical Society in 1834 revealed that 80 per cent of school children's education in the City was being paid for entirely by parental fees. Brougham's survey found a considerable rate of growth, confirmed by Lord Kerry's official investigation in 1833 to 1835. Lord Kerry's Parliamentary Return of 1833 made the first attempt to calculate the proportion of eligible children actually receiving education. The ratio of children attending day schools to the total population was estimated by Kerry in 1833 to be 1 : 11. Between 1818 and 1833 the number of schools increased from 748,000 to 1,294,000 'without any intervention by the Government or public authorities'.[4] During the same period Sunday schools increased by over 225 per cent, that is double the growth rate of the day schools.

But such figures present an altogether too encouraging a picture of the quality of education provided. Speaking at the opening of the Mechanics' Institution School building in Liverpool in 1837 Sir Thomas Wyse MP said:

A large proportion of the youthful population . . . do not attend any school whatsoever. . . . the education given in those which are attended is of the worst description. The schools are few, and in the worst sites, and of the most wretched kind, the attendance fluctuating and for very limited periods, the teachers incompetent, sometimes profligate, miserably instructed and paid . . . the scholars, in most cases, doing little, and what they are doing ill.[5]

The Manchester Statistical Society's survey of Liverpool children between the ages of five and fifteen in 1834 produced the following picture: 244 dame schools, 195 common day schools, 50 charity schools, 143 private and boarding schools. The first two categories provided wretched accommodation for the poorer classes. The charity schools, which were supported by various denominations, also catered largely for the working classes; the private and boarding schools, on the other hand, were for the wealthier classes. Even in the private schools the quality of instruction was not high and the wealthier classes preferred to employ tutors or send their children away to select schools.

Wyse, as Chairman of the Central Society of Education set up in 1836, argued that the greatest defect of English education was the total lack of a national organisation. An early attempt had been made by Brougham when he introduced a Bill based on his enquiry into the 'education of the lower orders' but this did not progress very far. Pressure for state action increased during the 1820s, culminating in the petitioning of the government by widely representative groups and societies. The result was a government grant of £20,000 in 1833 earmarked for the 'erection of school houses'. This was a notable landmark in the history of English education for it represented the first intervention of the central state in the affairs of education. Such a step, however, was a long way behind continental practice where, influenced by Pestalozzi's ideas, German and Swiss states had established a system of popular schools based on compulsory attendance. The contrast with the key state of Massachusetts in America where an educational tradition was well established long before the beginning of the nineteenth century was even more dramatic.

By 1839 central government in England was giving £30,000 p.a. for education. Four-fifths of the grant went to the National Society founded by Bell in 1811 (its full title was the National Society for the Education of the Poor in the Principles of the Established Church), the remaining fifth went to the British and Foreign School Society founded in 1814 after six years existence as the Royal Lancastrian Society. Both societies based their school instruction on the catechism and a study of the Bible. Instruction was based on a monitorial system – nine- to ten-year-old monitors teaching less bright pupils in small groups. Whatever might have been the true statistical picture of schools nationally the growing conviction was that these societies were not meeting the growing demand for education. Under pressure the government appointed three select committees to study the question of school provision; statistical societies meanwhile collected a plethora of facts and figures. The outcome was the appointment in 1839 of a Committee of the Privy Council to consider 'all matters affecting the education of the people'.

A matter of major concern to the Committee of Privy Council was the poor training of teachers. It proposed a state training college; this aroused the customary storm of protest based on the familiar theme of who should control education, the Church bodies or the state? James Kay (Secretary to the Committee) and E. C. Tufnell took independent action by opening a private training college at Battersea. This move inspired the establishment of a number of diocesan training colleges, Norwich and Chester being the first in 1840. In the next five years twenty colleges were established. The weaknesses of the monitorial system had by now been long apparent and following a suggestion by Kay-Shuttleworth (as James Kay was known after his marriage) the government in 1846 initiated a pupil-teacher scheme. According to this scheme salaries of from £5 to £20 were offered to all those who were prepared to serve a five-year apprenticeship to teaching. Such pupil-teachers were to receive tuition of not less than ninety minutes a day from teachers who would in turn receive £5 a year. After five years a pupil-teacher would stand a 'fair chance', but no more, of being awarded a Queen's Scholarship which would go towards the cost of three years study at a training college. This comprehensive scheme required £100,000 to finance it. Despite the cries of the voluntaryists who deprecated such vast increases in state help, and of the Anglicans who resented being treated as equals with Dissenters and Catholics, the scheme was put into effect.

Kay-Shuttleworth argued that elementary education appeared far better on paper than it was in reality. Many children were taught nothing beyond elementary reading, and school attendance was low. Throughout the 1840s the Inspectors' Reports drew attention to irregularity of school attendance, the early withdrawal of children and half-time attendance. A number of Acts were passed and several Commissions were set up during the 1840s which had a positive and salutary bearing on the question of national elementary education. These included the Select Committee to inquire into Factory Acts (1841), and the Royal Commission 'to inquire into the conditions of children employed in mines and other occupations' (1842). This found that many children between the ages of three and six were employed for twelve hours a day. Chadwick's *Report on the Sanitary Conditions of the Labouring Population* in 1842 drew attention to the plight of the large cellar populations in the major cities and in 1843 the Poor Law Commissioners published their *Report on the Employment of Women and Children in Agriculture* according to which many children in poor areas were sent out to work at an early age.

The employment of children of elementary school age was a central issue, an obstacle to be overcome. In Nottingham for instance 'the lace industry needed an army of small boys': boys usually over twelve wound yarn on to bobbins and threaded the bobbins on to the machines; they also supplied power for the hand-drawn machines. Girls were employed at a very young age as threaders and winders or to 'embroider (or sew) the finished lace'. In his survey of schooling in Nottingham, Retford and Bingham in the nineteenth century Roger Smith concluded that 'an important reason explaining the differences in school attendance was the varying industrial structures and employment opportunities for children in the three districts'.[6]

A less familar example is provided from Cornwall where conditions in the mining areas were rather better than in other mining areas of the country, and certainly an improvement on the large cities such as Birmingham, Liverpool and Manchester. Yet the evidence relating to Cornwall presented to the Children's Employment Commission of 1842 was depressing. Children began work at the surface at about seven years of age and often started underground for a six to eight hour day at the age of eight. One mine manager told the Commissioners that 'the children are younger now than formerly. In the course of a month we send back many, thinking them too small for the work; they are brought by the mothers who complain that they cannot get bread for them.'[7]

Officially there were no holidays save Christmas Day and Good Friday. Certain periods of the year in particular made heavy demands on the time of the children employed at the surface in dressing ores. The period just before the sale of the ore was such a time when children often rose at 4 a.m. and were obliged to work from 6 a.m. to 8 p.m.[8] Though the children's clothing was adequate it invariably became wet and had to be worn throughout the long day, while the diet was often scanty and lacked nutritional value. In such hours and conditions of employment schooling tended to be neglected in the early years of life. To make up for this many turned to self-improvement and education in later life.

In 1858 Lord Derby's government set up a Commission under the chairmanship of the Duke of Newcastle 'to enquire into the state of Popular Education in England' (hereinafter referred to as the Newcastle Commission). The Commission found a confusing scene of industrial schools, dockyard schools, factory schools, orphan and ragged schools in addition to public and private day schools. These were administered by a variety of organisations, principal among which were the National Society and the British and Foreign School Society. Kay-Shuttleworth, giving evidence relating to Manchester schools, stated that 'it would be scarcely possible to conceive of schools and institutions more inefficient for the purposes for which they were intended'. Furthermore, he considered they were 'lamentably inadequate in numbers'.[9]

In certain areas of the country the existing provision of schools may well have been sufficient for those who desired schooling and those who were free to attend school. Such areas may have existed in Lancashire and Yorkshire. The Reverend J. S. Winder, the Assistant Commissioner for those two counties, posed the question 'Does education pay?' in his report to the Commissioners.

The answer [he said] justifies their apathy rather than the professions of educational enthusiasts. There are no doubt a few occupations, that of an overlooker of a mill, for example, for which writing and arithmetic are indispensable but the amount required is small. . . . but posts of this description are not the rewards of education as such, but of dexterity, honesty and industry. . . . As to the common occupations which absorb the mass of operatives – weaving and spinning, and hammering, mining and delving, driving coal carts etc . . . I could hear of no proof that the educated workman could either command a preference for employment, or earn higher wages than an uninstructed man. You are almost always told by employers that they prefer educated work people. I dare say they do . . . there is pretty unanimous testimony that the educated are much more pleasant to deal with, less bigoted, more flexible, more willing to adapt themselves to the changing circumstances of trade. But, man for man, the uneducated seem as valuable as the educated, in a commercial sense, at any rate they earn as much money, and are engaged quite as readily.[10]

In Rochdale and Bradford Winder found that poverty and apathy were widespread and were the cause of neglect of parents concerning the education of their children. 'Education', he said, 'is ordinarily looked on as a matter of secondary importance and made to give way to the convenience of interests of the moment without scruple or hesitation.'[11]

After a comprehensive survey the Newcastle Commission produced a six-volume report in 1861. It reported that the average attendance in schools was only 76 per cent, that one-third of pupils attended for less than 100 days in any year and that less than one-fifth stayed on after the age of ten. Despite these deplorable facts the Commission rejected compulsory attendance as 'neither desirable nor attainable'. Indeed a minority of the Commission considered that 'since the Government had no education duties except towards those whom destitution, vagrancy or crime casts upon its hands it would be advised to withdraw its help and give free course to the sense of duty and the benevolence which have spontaneously achieved great results in other directions'.[12]

The Commission recommended an annual Government grant of 4s 6d–6s 0d (22½–30p) for each pupil in a school run by a certificated teacher. It was their view that most teachers found difficulty in 'heavily devoting himself to the drudgery' of teaching the three Rs and preferred to teach more 'pretentious' and less useful subjects. In order to correct this tendency the Commission proposed a system of local government grant of 1 guinea–22s 6d for all pupils who attended 140 days and who made satisfactory progress in the three Rs.

Robert Lowe, the Vice-President of the Department of Education (this had replaced the Privy Council in 1856), rejected the concept of local grants but did make the teaching of the three Rs the cornerstone of elementary education. He accepted the recommendations of the Commissioners that passing examinations in the three Rs should be the requisite of a government grant. This to him was value for money, as he told the House of Commons: 'If this system is not cheap, I can promise it shall be efficient: if it is not efficient, it shall be cheap.' Unfortunately, government policy and action till the end of the century in all fields of education seemed to be more often activated by the concern for cheapness than for efficiency. Lowe's Revised Code of Regulations came into being in July 1861, and the slogan 'payment-by-results' became part of educational history.

In 1860 the various Minutes of the Committee of Council had been digested into a Code (the Code of 1860) and acting on this Report the Committee of Council framed the Revised Code of Minutes and Regulations for the future distribution of Parliamentary grant. The new government regulations of 1862 certainly achieved saving money. Six- to eleven-year-olds were now arranged in six standards. For each child there was a capitation grant, another grant of 4*s* 0*d* (20p) on school average attendance figures and yet a further grant of 8*s* (40p) on a pupil attending 200 morning or afternoon sessions and passing the three Rs. The next few years showed a steadily increasing school population and steady reduction in government spending. But this result was achieved only at the expense of all subjects other than the three Rs. Teaching too became mechanical and lifeless. Matthew Arnold in his Annual Report for 1867 commented: 'I find in schools in general if I compare them with their former selves, a deadness, a slackness, and a discouragement which are not the signs and accompaniment of progress – This change is certainly to be attributed to the school legislation of 1862.'[13]

Meanwhile voluntary efforts to build schools were often not keeping pace with the rapid increase in child population. In 1869 the Birmingham Education League was formed, with Joseph Chamberlain as Vice-Chairman; this began to rouse the whole country 'to a sense of our educational destitution'. The Department's own enquiries in Manchester, Birmingham, Leeds and Liverpool were producing evidence of a deterioration. They found that two-fifths of working-class children between the ages of six and ten were not at school at all, and that most were leaving before their tenth birthday. Inspectors reported that attendance, teaching efficiency and parental attitude were as bad as ever. All this evidence prompted the government to promote a new Bill under William Forster.

The objects of this Bill were to cover the country with 'good' schools and to get the parents to send their children to school. They were to be effected by the creation of school boards whose members were to be elected by ratepayers. The school boards would be allowed to raise a penny rate to provide funds for new school buildings which would fill the 'gaps' in the provision of schools. Forster proposed giving the Voluntary Societies a year's grace during which they would receive government grants for school building. Again the Bill was attacked by extremists on both sides. The Birmingham League resented public money being paid to denominational schools and the Church resented the fact that there would be only simple Bible teaching in board schools.

Forster's year of grace became six months, but the Bill went through with its major provisions unchanged and the result was soon apparent in terms of new schools. By 1880 about 3,500 new board schools and 6,000 new voluntary schools had been built.

Parents, 'unless necessitous', had still to pay 'school pence' and school attendance was not compulsory. Lord Sandon's Act of 1876 carried Forster's Act a stage further. It ordered school attendance committees to be appointed in those districts which had not yet elected school boards, and declared it to be the duty of parents to see that their children received 'efficient elementary instruction'. Sandon's Act was better in theory than in practice for magistrates and members of school boards who personally did not approve of the Act turned a blind eye to breakers of it. Consequently in 1880 Gladstone's second government passed a further Act which made it obligatory for all children between five years and ten years to attend school full-time, and no child could leave school or work half-time until he had reached the standard required by local by-laws. From 1880 it was possible therefore to claim that compulsory elementary education was a reality throughout Britain.

During the period 1860 to 1890 the main concern of national policy was to produce a literate society well versed in the three Rs. It has been commonly assumed that the Industrial Revolution and the subsequent movement of people into towns had led to low literacy rates between 1825 and 1840. Recent research suggests that the level of literacy was considerably higher than has been thought to be the case.[14] It is difficult to correlate literacy rates with the extent of school provision, and it is very likely that the unexpectedly high literacy rates during the first half of the nineteenth century owed more to Sunday schools and adult schools than to public day schools.

There was undoubtedly an increase in literacy rates during the second half of the century as indicated by the proportion of the population signing the marriage register,[15] but it is arguable whether such an increase can be attributable to the introduction of the school boards. 'Forster's Act', claims one critic

did not significantly hasten the spread of literacy. What it did was to ensure that the rate at which literacy had increased in the period 1851–71 would be maintained. Had the state not intervened at this point it is likely that the progress of literacy would have considerably slowed in the last quarter of the century, simply because illiteracy was by that time concentrated in those classes and those regions that were hardest to provide for under the voluntary system of education.[16]

Evening schools

The idea that the state should be responsible for every child attaining a minimum standard of school training and attainment was first accepted in England as a principle of public policy in 1876. That many children were not achieving minimum standards was evidenced by irregular attendance, lack of school provision and inspectors' reports. The principle of supplementing early schooling and of remedying defects had been adopted by the Sunday school and adult school movements at the end of the eighteenth century. By the middle of the nineteenth century evening schools and night schools had become an established part of the educational scene; they embraced Sunday schools, adult schools, classes held in free public libraries, mechanics' institutes and night schools under government inspection. In 1842 the Rev. R. S. Bailey established the Sheffield People's College which inspired F. D. Maurice to set up the London Working Men's College in 1853. Later Quintin Hogg created polytechnics in London.

The demand for evening classes was in fact a reflection of the lack of adequate day schooling of a desirable quality. Evening schools received official recognition in 1851 with the award of government grants which were subsequently increased in 1855 and 1858. Changes introduced in 1862 implied that the schools were now seen as a continuation of the day school work – in effect an elementary continuation school. Grant-aided work was confined to elementary instruction, and as a consequence attendances fell and did not rise again until the 1890s.

The Code of 1893 changed the old conception of evening schools; the maximum age limit was lifted and no pupil was compelled to take elementary subjects. School boards became free to put on instruction at a more advanced level. Many did so, particularly the London School Board. Other boards, for instance Birmingham and Manchester, had instituted a 7th Standard or a Higher Grade Board School in which advanced science instruction was grant-aided by the government Department of Science and Art. This inevitably created the dilemma as to whether evening schools were to be part of the elementary system or of further and higher education. It was resolved by the Cockerton Judgement of 1900 which found against the London School Board. A Minute of the Board of Education in 1901 stated that instruction which was conducted in a public elementary school had to be in accordance with the Education Acts, but the London School Board at the time was spending ratepayers' money on evening schools to teach advanced chemistry. The ruling of the Court went against the Board.

The Newcastle Commissioners classified evening schools in three categories: those taught by the masters of private day schools; classes attached to Sunday schools; classes connected with mechanics' institutes. J. S. Winder reported that 'the evening schools, which are the natural agents for diffusing secondary education, are almost entirely occupied in supplying the deficiency of primary education'. In his view there was 'very great difficulty in finding teachers for the evening classes. . . . For the higher instruction there is an absolute dearth of professional teachers of the right stamp; and this is no doubt, one of the principal weaknesses of the very languid demand for anything beyond the rudiments of knowledge.'[17]

That these schools were necessary, given the state of elementary education in the country generally, there can be no doubt, and that they did achieve a great deal of useful work in difficult and limiting conditions is without dispute. Evening schools were very much a 'second best', and their grave deficiencies were revealed by Michael Sadler, Professor of the History and Administration of Education at Manchester University in 1907. Before moving into the academic world Sadler had for many years been an Inspector of Schools and was therefore very knowledgeable about the country's evening schools. They were, he wrote,

in some respects little but a makeshift for what should have been done in elementary day schools. Much that was attempted in the evening schools would have been better done by a well-organised system of day schools. . . . Work has been wanting in thoroughness of intellectual discipline because of the lack of sound foundation of elementary knowledge.

They were victims of fluctuations of popular interest and insufficient funds. There was no legal compulsion to attend them and they left untouched large sections of the community. What could be said in their favour was that they 'offered opportunities to those with enough force of character and physical vigour'.[18]

At St Helens Sadler found that the work of the evening schools was unsystematic and unconnected. 'Industrial conditions', he wrote, 'are not altogether favourable to the efficiency of the evening schools. . . . A large proportion of the male population is employed in glassworks and collieries. Much of the labour is very heavy, while the three-shift system, which obtains in some of the works, makes attendance practically impossible for many of the boys and men.' At Manchester he could see more clearly than elsewhere 'the impossibility of creating a brand new system of evening schools without relation to the past. For a widespread desire for serious evening instruction is always of gradual growth, and until such a desire has been evolved, no skill in organisation can give success to evening schools.' In Manchester, as everywhere else in evening schools, 'one sees earnest faces and strained attention. It is unfortunately no unknown thing for students to come straight from work, where they have been kept too late to be able to go home to tea.' At Widnes, which Sadler conceded was exceptional,

one of the main conditions of success was ensured when the chief employers, to a great extent influenced by the example of the chemical firm of Brunner Mond and Co., agreed to make evening school attendance compulsory of their apprentices. The United Alkali Company make a condition that all apprentices between the ages of 14 and 18 shall attend classes on three evenings a week, their fees being paid by the Company. Apprentices over 18 will then be allowed to compete for scholarships entitling them to attend day technical classes on two afternoons without loss of wages at the Company's expense. The other manufacturers have followed this example.

But even at Widnes there were problems. 'One difficulty is the impossibility in the chemical industry of excusing boys from work before breakfast. Hence young boys have to begin work at 6 a.m. and attend classes up to 9.30 p.m. and are often tired and sleepy.'[19]

Despite the changes that had been effected in evening schools Sadler, writing in 1902, commented that

their effective energy is at present exceedingly low . . . much of the instruction given is very rudimentary, and, as a result, there can be little real grading of institutions. The continuation schools are largely devoted to the recovery of work which has been done once in the elementary schools. The continuation work proper intrudes into the commercial and technical centres and no small part of the instruction given in the municipal technical school is elementary both in name and in nature.[20]

Sadler's final judgement on evening schools was:

Thus alike in their excellence and their defects, the evening classes have borne the characteristic features of English educational organisation. Free in their development, vigorous in some of their achievements, and often well-adapted to the requirements of the persevering and the strong, they have been unsystematic in arrangement, weakened by defects in the early training of their pupils and from a national point of view, insufficiently adjusted to the needs of the rank and file.[21]

Whereas Thomas Huxley drew attention to the shortcomings of English educational provision for what he termed the 'officer class', Sadler was clearly concerned with the deficiencies of the continuation schools in serving the needs of the rank and file.

The question to be decided [he wrote] is whether we in England gain more through stimulating and rewarding the energy of the vigorous few by our voluntary system of continuation schools than is lost through our failure to raise the general average of trained and disciplined efficiency by means of compulsory attendance for all? The same question comes up in some form or other in every attempt to balance the advantages of what may broadly be distinguished as the English and German forms of educational organisation. The Germans make thriftier use of their average material than we succeed in doing. . . . Can we afford the waste which our lack of organisation entails?[22]

Elementary education in Massachusetts and Liverpool

Towards the end of the nineteenth century Sir Philip Magnus, a leading educationist, was able to write that 'our elementary education is systematically developed'.[23] This was a reasonable judgement to make in the 1880s after a half-century of government attempts to bring a measure of order and cohesion into elementary education. Such certainly was not the case during the previous eighty years or so. The deficiencies in the English system are brought out starkly when a comparison is made between elementary education in a single American state, Massachusetts, and an English industrial city, Liverpool.

Educational legislation began in Massachusetts as early as the seventeenth century, penalties being enacted for those who failed to comply with an obligation on parents and employers to see that their children and apprentices were taught English and a knowledge of the capital laws. The first free school in the state was formed at Boston in 1635; a little later came the requirement that towns with more than 500 householders should maintain two grammar schools and two 'writing schools'. In 1767 school districts were permitted to levy taxes to defray the charges of supporting schools. An Act of 1789 provided for the Instruction of Youth and for the Promotion of Good Education. It was stated of late eighteenth-century Massachusetts that 'such was the value generally attached to a good education that the towns continued to tax themselves to an amount much exceeding the exactions of the law'.[24]

The city of Boston provides a good example of the advances that had been made in Massachusetts by mid-century. In 1836 it maintained 88 schools open to children of all classes; of these 74 were primary schools with an average of between 30 and 50 pupils aged four to seven. It also maintained several separate grammar schools for boys and girls aged seven to sixteen with an average of 250 pupils in each. In addition there were two further schools: the English high school and the Latin grammar school. The Latin grammar school prepared pupils for the university while the high school provided instruction in mathematics, physics, natural history, moral philosophy and French.

An Act of 1837 established a State Board of Education and also legislated for teacher training by creating teacher training colleges (Normal Schools). By this time Massachusetts teachers' salary bill cost the state 465,000 dollars (equivalent to over £100,000). The Act also demonstrated the state's interest in the education of industrial employees by establishing that any child under the age of fifteen years who had not regularly attended a day school for at least three months of the year preceding his proposed employment could not be employed. This led industrialists to take initiatives to create their own schools – the Boston Manufacturing Company's response was to erect three schools.

The Returns for 1840[25] illustrate the progress of the Massachusetts Common School system. Out of a population of 700,000 some 150,000 pupils attended school, suggesting that education was extensive and widespread. It was, it seems, a justifiable boast of the state that 'the property of all is taxed for the education of all'. In 1840 the state had 2,378 male teachers and 3,928 female teachers. An average of 2.80 dollars was spent for each child between four and sixteen years of age, the cost of public-supported education being 514,490 dollars (£125,000) and that of private education 241,114 dollars (£60,000).

Massachusetts, with its tradition of generous public expenditure on education for all, had by the early nineteenth century developed an egalitarian approach to educational provision. A largely literate population shared a common educational inheritance. By 1850 Massachusetts had established a comprehensive state-supported system financed out of taxation. Such an education system did not appear in England until the latter part of the century.

Elementary education in Liverpool, dispite the intense civic pride of the City fathers, demonstrates all the weaknesses of a system allowed to grow without the guiding hand of central direction and adequate financial support.

The earliest school to be established in Liverpool was John Gosse's Free Grammar School established in 1515. By the end of the eighteenth century the school was leading a precarious existence, as the town council had merged the lands with which it was endowed into the general corporate estate, in return granting it a miserable annual subsidy. In consequence it was forced to close down in 1803. Meanwhile a second school, the Bluecoat Hospital School, had been founded in 1808 for the charitable upbringing and industrial training of poor children.

The real beginnings of popular education, however, were to be found in the Sunday schools founded following a religious revival at the end of the eighteenth century. The Corporation did not intervene until 1826 when the town council established two free elementary schools to take the place of the Free Grammar School. This initiative prompted the founding of several schools, some by individuals but most by denominations of various kinds. By the 1840s elementary school provision for a population of a quarter of a million was limited to two free corporation schools together with two free Church schools, in addition to some two dozen charity schools. Progress continued to be slow until the creation of the Liverpool School Board in 1871 following Forster's Act of 1870. Between then and 1900 the School Board built forty schools. The voluntary bodies, not to be outdone, increased their provision, so that by the end of the century voluntary schools still formed the major part of provision.

One of the most notable events in the development of elementary education in Liverpool was the establishment of a voluntary organis-ation – the Council of Education – in 1874 with the object 'to promote and encourage elementary education by every available means, including a system of scholarships,'[26] prizes and awards. Its membership was widely representative of Church bodies, industry and commerce. It thus cut across the interdenominational religious conflicts which be-devilled the progress of English education. In its fifth Annual Report it drew attention to the fact that 'much needs to be done to secure the regular attendance at school of a large number of children who ought to be but still are not under instruction'.

Low and irregular attendance at school was a feature of elementary education in Liverpool throughout most of the nineteenth century. Prior to the setting up of the Liverpool School Board the established figure for the population of school age (three to thirteen years) was 94,868. This figure excluded the 11,149 children of the middle and upper classes who either went away to school or were catered for by private tutors and small private schools. The accommodation available for the estimated school population was 76,813, considerably less than the 94,868 supposed to be in school. The average attendance at school in the year was 42,116, or 44 per cent of the established school population. This was the state of affairs that the Council of Education set out to remedy. It did so by a system of prizes and rewards of merit for school pupils and by conferring suitable honours and rewards upon head-masters and headmistresses whose schools had the greatest proportion of pupils in attendance. That the average attendance was increased to 85 per cent by 1900 owed much to the Council's activities.

Elementary education in Liverpool demonstrated all the weaknesses which characterised the national educational scene. Far too much reliance was placed on voluntary effort, and the late intervention of the state and municipal authority meant that education was in the hands of a variety of competing bodies; a cohesive and adequately funded system did not emerge until the School Codes of the 1860s and the Education Act of 1870. For a long time there was a considerable shortfall between the numbers on school rolls and the estimated number of children of school age who were supposed to be at school. Further, the attendance of those on school rolls was irregular due either to the poverty of parents who could ill-afford to lose the potential income of their children or to parental apathy. There were insufficient numbers of teachers, for many pupil-teachers were unable to proceed to training colleges because of lack of scholarships. It was fortunate that the night schools and evening classes were able to provide 'remedial' education for the countless many who missed out in early life. This was accentuated by the lack of scholarships to enable children to proceed to the fee-paying secondary schools. An educational ladder was not created until the end of the century, and in this respect the Council of Education referred to earlier adopted a pioneering role instituting a system of scholarships some ten years earlier than did the City Council.

Elementary education then in Liverpool provided a poor contrast with Massachusetts and with continental cities. It was an inadequate foundation for other agencies of secondary and higher education to build on, and these in Liverpool as elsewhere in the country were particularly affected by the poor state of preparedness of pupil entrants.

Science in the elementary schools

For a period following the Revised Code of 1862 the teaching of reading, spelling and arithmetic dominated the schools. Earlier, many teachers had taken a delight in teaching elementary science but as it no longer counted for grant purposes innovation and experimentation of this kind disappeared from the schools. The Inspectors' Reports of the 1860s give an impression of uniform mediocrity in the schools. It was a case of examining bald facts in order that children might pass the examinations in the three Rs necessary to earn a grant: 'If a nation can be stupefied by its schools then the Revised Code came near to the point of stupefying children.'[27]

Under Forster's administration a little was done to liberalise the curriculum by offering grants of not greater than 3s (15p) for efficiency in not more than two subjects, usually geography, history, algebra or geometry. In 1875 the new Code introduced the idea of 'specific subject' grants; a grant of 4s (20p) per subject was awarded for each day scholar in Standards IV to VI who passed a satisfactory examination in not more than two of these specific subjects which included mechanics, botany and animal physiology. Further progressive changes were introduced in the Code of 1882 which involved a still more elaborate scheme of grants: 'obligatory' subjects included the Three Rs and needlework; 'optional' subjects included singing, drawing, geography, history and elementary sciences; and 'specific' subjects included algebra, mechanics, chemistry, botany, principles of agriculture, Latin, French, and domestic economy but no pupil could be presented in more than two of these specific subjects.

Major reforms were introduced following the recommendations of the Cross Commission in 1888. This had been set up two years earlier by Lord Salisbury to examine the state of education. It produced two reports (a majority and a minority) both of which emphasised the importance of science teaching. The majority report called for the abolition of 'payment-by-results' but a minority on the Commission would not go that far and advocated modification of the scheme. Sir George Kekewith, Secretary of the Department of Education, put several of their recommendations into effect in the Code of 1890; he dealt the death blow to 'payment-by-results' by substituting a single grant based on average attendance instead of on examination successes in the Three Rs. He also introduced appropriate grants for manual work and elementary science which now counted towards school attendance. Navigation was added to the list of specific subjects which were further increased by the addition of horticulture in the following year.

Thus between 1870 and 1900 succesive changes in regulations had increased the options available in the schools, widened the curriculum and gradually substituted the development of interest, awareness and intelligence for rote learning. But it would be wrong to overemphasise the impact of these changes, particularly with regard to science. The optional and specific subjects comprised a long list of subjects of which only some were in the sciences. Few schools took up science teaching owing to the dearth of qualified teachers available and the inadequate science instruction given in the training colleges. Furthermore, science did not become a compulsory subject in schools until 1904. The 'teacher problem' was to remain for years to come. It was highlighted as the crucial issue by a Committee which sat under Sir J. J. Thomson in 1916.

'It is extremely desirable', it reported, 'that there should be a much larger number of teachers in elementary schools qualified to give instruction in science, and that all possible steps should be taken to increase the supply.'[28]

The impact of the gradual 'liberalising' of the School Code, in the sense of creating a broader curriculum which included the sciences, can be seen in Liverpool from 1870 onwards. The pressing need for science instruction, not so much in terms of its educational value but in order to increase the scientific aptitudes of the skilled industrial worker, was recognised by the School Board in 1873 when a special sub-committee set up to report on technical education observed that 'it is of great importance, from a national point of view, to impart at least the elements of sound scientific knowledge to the future artisans of this country in order, as far as possible, to qualify them to compete on equal grounds with the same classes in Continental countries'. The sub-committee recommended that 'systematised object lessons' be taught to all pupils in the first and second standards and elementary science teaching in higher standards. Under the new Code in operation these could be counted as 'discretionary' subjects. Whenever possible, science classes of a more advanced character were to be formed in the Board's evening schools. These classes were to be open to pupils from the public day elementary schools at a reduced fee. 'The adoption of this scheme', concluded the sub-committee, 'would . . . tend to impart to the children, the future artisans of this country, that elementary knowledge, the importance of which to the future well being of this country is becoming every day more and more generally recognised.'[29]

As on so many other occasions the first positive action was the result of private initiative. In January of 1874 Mr James Samuelson wrote to the School Board expressing his desire to provide additional accommodation for the teaching of science to the 'working classes' and suggesting that for this purpose the Board might set aside a room in one of their central schools to enable a laboratory to be furnished. Such an offer was characteristic of the man, for he epitomised the Smilesian philosophy of self-help; lacking formal education he had pursued education and self-improvement with a passionate zeal, eventually becoming a leading citizen of Liverpool and head of a large seed-crushing firm. The Board, needless to say, accepted his offer and a laboratory was built at Queen's Road Board School, quickly followed by another at Chatsworth Street Board School. These were the first science laboratories to be erected in the public elementary schools of Liverpool.

Events were taken a stage further when at a meeting on 19 February 1877 the School Board resolved:

That the Government, having marked the sense of urgency of teaching elementary science in public elementary schools, by including in it the table of specific subjects and by providing that larger grants shall be obtainable by passes in such subjects, the Board shall arrange for systematic teaching of elementary science in the schools and that the

School Management Committee be authorised to select for appointment at a reasonably salary a gentleman whose scientific attainments qualify him for giving and superintending such instruction.[30]

Mr William Hewitt, BSc, was appointed as a science demonstrator to give instruction in science to public elementary school pupils in the scientific subjects of the new Code and also to pupil-teachers and qualified teachers. Hewitt was allowed to put in a request for apparatus and the clerk was directed to instruct the Board's architect to draw up specifications for cupboards and a handcart that would be required by Hewitt. He was provided with the services of a young lad and a room was put at his disposal at the North Corporation School. Because it was impossible to provide each school with suitable apparatus Hewitt's equipment was stored at the science centre at the school, the necessary apparatus for the lessons being packed in boxes. By means of a handcart and errand boy these boxes were distributed to the schools where they were used by the teacher or by Hewitt. At the end of the lesson the apparatus was again packed in the box and taken to the next school on the rota. In this way, and by arranging suitable times and places, one box of apparatus served for a lesson to eighteen different classes per week – two forty-minute periods each morning and afternoon session The Friday afternoon was reserved for checking the apparatus and packing boxes for the next week. On Saturday morning the teachers who took the lessons attended the Centre and tried out the experiments.

It was soon found necessary to appoint assistant peripatetic science demonstrators who gave their whole time to visiting the schools, giving as a rule two demonstrations in the morning and two in the afternoon. Besides the demonstration the demonstrator left a card of questions and the teacher was expected to take notes of the lesson, revise it, and get the children to answer the questions on paper.

Apparatus was provided for mechanics, physics, chemistry, physiography and physiology, and with time the scheme expanded, the staff having to be increased. The peripatetic system reached its height between 1890 and 1900, when the number of assistant demonstrators numbered nine.

From 1890 onwards an extensive system of theoretical and practical science classes was established in the evening continuation classes open to artisans, clerks, shopkeepers and others, in addition to special evening classes for the elementary school day pupils and for pupil-teachers serving their apprenticeships in the day schools.

By the closing years of the century a system of elementary education had been established in Liverpool, and indeed nationally, which corrected many of the weaknesses of the early years. Children by then were more literate and better able to embark on secondary and advanced education and the supply of qualified and suitably trained teachers had increased so as to cope with the rapid expansion of a system required to provide free elementary education for all. The curriculum had been liberalised, there being many options available for instruction in a broad range of science subjects. The scientific instruction in day schools and evening continuation schools helped to create new cadres of potential students for scientific and technical education.

If any sector of English education can be said to be in a healthy state by 1900 that sector was elementary education. Elsewhere, between 1870 and 1914 fundamental shortcomings persisted; other sectors of education compared very unfavourably with their counterparts in several continental countries.

Chapter 3

Science and
the secondary schools

The growth and development of secondary education

No field of English education was without major defects in the nineteenth century, but none was so badly uncoordinated as that of secondary education. Its origins are to be found in private initiative and benevolence, but progress was more stultified here in consequence of the reluctance of the state to interfere and allocate adequate resources. Government action was confined to the setting up of numerous commissions, few of whose recommendations were implemented, and a Charity Commission whose function it was to oversee the considerable number of endowments, many of which were grossly abused. The Royal Commission reports provided critical evidence in abundance, but little action followed. It was not until the end of the century that the state began to take constructive steps to remedy its neglect of secondary education.

The situation that had been created by the end of the century is neatly summed up in the Board of Education Report for 1905–06. 'The most conspicuous fact that emerges', it recorded, 'is of how much there is yet to be done in secondary education . . . the shortcomings are too often little less than disastrous.'[1] This is a fitting epitaph on the development of secondary education during the period 1840 to 1900. For the greater part of this period the exact meaning of the term 'secondary education' posed great difficulty.[2] What constituted secondary education and where did the boundaries between it and other forms of education lie? Answers to these questions did not emerge until after 1900.

The confusion over the meaning of 'secondary' education arose because of the way in which a variety of types of school under the auspices of different bodies had become established in the absence of state control. 'Secondary schools', said the Board of Education in its Report of 1905–06, 'are of many different kinds and there are few generalisations which can be made to apply to them all.' The Board made no attempt to conceal earlier mistakes and in its Report of 1909 summed up the situation in the following terms:

That the State has any concern with secondary education is a comparatively modern idea in England. . . . The history of State connection with it began with the Public School Commission of 1861–64 and the Schools Inquiry Commission of 1864–67. It was apparently in that decade that the term 'secondary' as applied to schools came into recognised use in England. It came from France, where it has been invented as part of a general classification of education throughout its stages, from the lowest to the highest, in the three successive grades of primary, secondary and tertiary. In this country the term 'tertiary' has never come into use at all, and the term 'primary' has been mostly replaced by the term 'elementary'. The Elementary Education Act of 1870 established this latter term in official usage. Hence the term 'secondary' has been left in the air, and this is a sort of symbol of the way in which secondary education itself was for long neglected after a national system of elementary education had been established on the one hand, and on the other University Education. This isolation and consequent neglect of secondary education over so long a period is at the root of the difficulties which have had to be faced in the last few years in all grades of education in England.[3]

The Board's views were not new. The Report did, however, add official weight to the incisive criticisms of observers during the previous half-century. Notable among these was Matthew Arnold who claimed that 'the idea of science is absent from the whole course and design of our education'.

Arnold's rather too sweeping statement was justified only in reference to the private schools and the universities of Oxford and Cambridge. His assessment is not applicable if a broader view of secondary education is taken. Such a view encompasses not only public schools and grammar schools but also mechanics' institutes and the science classes of the Department of Science and Art (a Department set up by the government in 1853 to distribute funds for the instruction of the industrial artisans). Furthermore, in the years following Arnold's publication higher grade board schools and 'organised science schools', whose activities fell within the area now recognised as secondary education, were established.

Arnold's censure coincided with the Report of the Schools Inquiry Commission (the Taunton Commission) in 1868. This Commission, under Baron Taunton, produced a comprehensive and constructive report (it ran to nine volumes) which advocated the placing of secondary education in the hands of specially constituted local authorities answerable to a central statutory body under a Minister of the Crown. Such a scheme was ultimately to form the basis of the organisation of secondary schools, but as the Board of Education Report pointed out in 1909: 'the formidable inertia of the nation reinforced by intense jealousy of state interference and dislike of public control held up much needed reforms'.[4]

The rationalisation of secondary education was repeatedly postponed and a cohesive pattern was not laid down until the turn of the century. State concern with secondary schools was first reflected in the appointment of the Commission under the chairmanship of the Earl of Clarendon 'to inquire into the Revenues and Management of Certain

Colleges and the Studies Pursued and the Instruction Given Therein'. The Clarendon Commission examined Charterhouse, Eton, Harrow, Merchant Taylors', Rugby, St Paul's, Shrewsbury, Westminster and Winchester. It was the first official body to draw attention to the absence of science in the curricula of the leading schools of the country. This was not unexpected, but what occasioned greater surprise was its extremely adverse criticisms of the standard of teaching of the classics in these schools which was found to be largely philological and inefficient while other studies were considered to be inferior.

The country barely had time to assimilate the Clarendon Commission Report before it was presented with the far more wide-reaching Report of the Taunton Commission, which had the task of studying schools 'not examined by previous commissions', namely, the Clarendon and Newcastle Commissions, which had investigated the education of the industrial classes. The Taunton Commission arranged the remaining schools in three distinct categories: endowed schools (schools maintained wholly or partly by means of a permanent charitable endowment); private schools (some 10,000 schools which were the property of the masters who conducted them); and proprietary schools (either the property of individuals or of companies or of corporations).

The scope of the Commission's survey was vast; it comprised 674 schools, of which no fewer than 152 were considered by the Commission to be offering elementary education. The pupils in attendance at the remaining schools amounted to 35,000 or, in other words, some 70 pupils per school. The survey embraced such schools as: Christ's Hospital (775 boys); City of London School (641); King Edward VI, Birmingham (514); Manchester Grammar School (315); Uppingham (303); Wellington (270); Dulwich College (216); Bedford School (205); and Leeds Grammar School (190), but the majority had very small numbers in attendance. For instance: St Albans had 33 pupils; Brighton 20; Chigwell 21; King's School, Ely 39; Giggleswick 39; Maidstone Grammar School 54; and Exeter Grammar School 55.

The tone of the Taunton Commission Report was highly critical, particularly with regard to the place of science teaching in the schools. One positive advance resulting from the Report was the setting up in 1869 of the Endowed Schools Commission to correct the uneven geographical spread of endowments with powers to develop schemes for the better government and management of endowed schools. The Commissioners also made other far-seeing recommendations, including that of a system of inspection. These were not implemented and the creation of the Endowed Schools Commission alone hardly did justice to the work of the Taunton Commission.

By the Endowed Schools Act of 1874 the Endowed Schools Commission was merged into the Board of Charity Commissioners but the deficiences remained. A Commission on technical instruction under Sir Bernhard Samuelson (the Samuelson Commission) in the 1880s reported that

The transfer of the functions of the Endowed Schools Commission has not had the effect of increasing the rate of progress in the reorganisation of our secondary schools – we learn that there are still endowments available for education amounting to upwards of £200,000 a year which have not been dealt with by the Commissioners – also the existing endowments are very unevenly distributed over the country.[5]

Another decade was to pass before a further Commission on secondary education under James Bryce (the Bryce Commission) produced a Report which provided the blue-print for a national and effective system of secondary schools.

Meanwhile other developments had taken place which were to have a significant influence on secondary education. The Department of Science and Art, which had been set up ostensibly with the object of enabling the industrial artisan to become more acquainted with the elements of science underlying his art, was, from 1859 onwards, distributing funds for the support of evening science schools. These classes, as well as attracting artisans, craftsmen and clerks, were also attended by teachers, pupil-teachers and pupils from the upper forms of the secondary schools. The classes to all intents and purposes were a form of secondary education, as for many of the students the instruction was 'remedial' secondary education in the sciences, work which they should rightly have done at school.

Another innovation of the Department was the creation of 'organised science schools' in 1872. These had to provide a three-year course of instruction in a group of related science subjects; several forms within a secondary school could be so arranged as to be 'recognised' by the Department as an organised science school. By the end of the century there were over a hundred of these throughout the country, providing a judicious blend not only of literacy and scientific instruction but also of manual and commercial instruction. Another development which became linked with the Department was the higher grade board schools. Several of the school boards created by the 1870 Education Act established higher classes in their elementary schools, such schools becoming known as 'higher grade' schools. Several of these were recognised by the Department of Science and Art as 'organised science schools' and as such became eligible for the Department's grants.

The debt that the country owed to the Department was readily acknowledged by the Bryce Commission in 1894. 'The Department of Science and Art', it said, 'had encouraged studies which our traditional methods of education had ignored, fostered institutions that without it could never have lived . . . and . . . created our interest and an attitude of mind which has been a real culture to multitudes'.[6] It can be claimed with some justification that 'the Department sowed the seeds of science education for the people, it spread the learning to an extent probably totally unanticipated, it provided indirectly almost the entire secondary education for the masses for thirty years'.[7]

The work of the Department received a great impetus from the passing of the Local Taxation Act in 1890, as a result of which certain revenues collected from taxes on spirits were earmarked for technical instruction. Local authorities set up 'technical instruction' committees to distribute their share of this money. Fortunately they adopted a very broad definition of technical instruction and the result was that grants were given not only for the Department's classes but also for the support of scientific instruction in secondary schools, including the endowed and proprietary schools.

Clearly by the time the Bryce Commission was appointed in 1894 there were numerous bodies participating in the provision and funding of secondary education: the Charity Commissioners (formerly the Endowed Schools Commission), the school boards, the Department of Science and Art and the technical instruction committees. This led to fragmentation and lack of cohesion. Bryce had been the Local Commissioner for the North-West for the Taunton Commission, and his report to that Commission revealed his grasp of the defects inherent in the secondary education system – the uneven distribution of endowments, the overall inadequacy of finance, the absence of inspection, the paucity of free places and the narrow curriculum. Bryce's close familiarity with the field may have had much to do with the early publication of the Commission's Report only seventeen months after the Commission had been appointed. In some respects the Bryce Commission merely reiterated, if in more sophisticated and detailed terms, the major findings of the Taunton Commission. But in other ways it broke new ground. It was the first national body to attempt a visionary definition of secondary education in which science found a rightful place, a definition which, had it been adopted in the 1860s, would have altered the face of English secondary education.

Unity and integration were the two goals the Bryce Commission set itself: 'The system which we desire to see introduced may rather be described as coherences, an organic relation between different authorities and different kinds of schools which will enable each to work with due regard to the work to be done by others.'[8]

The central problems facing secondary education were inadequate finance and a lack of organisation. There were several sources of finance at both national and local levels. At the national level the Charity Commission looked after the endowments of the grammar schools and the Department of Science and Art aided some 256 evening secondary schools and 28 organised science schools; the local level 'whisky money' was distributed via the local authorities who had been empowered to levy a penny rate following the 1891 Act; forty-eight county councils spent £316,969 on education, of which £17,169 went on secondary education, whereas sixty-one county boroughs, although devoting £160,084 of whisky money to education, spent very little on secondary education as such. The Bryce Commission estimated that the total amount of money available for the grammar schools was £170,000 from the Department of Science and Art and £560,000 under the Local Taxation Act, while a further £640,000 could be raised by applying a penny rate universally. Local authorities were loath to raise rates and very little money came from this last source. Taken as a whole it added up to an inadequate provision of secondary education in the country.

Money, however, was not the main problem: 'Large powers', the Bryce Commission stated, 'are already distributed among the various separate agencies which deal with particular parts of secondary education. It is not so much the extension of these powers as the harmonising of the agencies that exercise them that is urgently required.'[9] To overcome 'the usual results of dispersed and unconnected forces, needless competition between the different agencies and a frequent overlapping of effort'[10] the Bryce Commission proposed a single statutory body presided over by a Minister which would supervise action by local authorities in whom responsibility for secondary education was to be invested. The Report thus was the springboard which paved the way for the Board of Education Act of 1899 and the Education Act of 1902. It was a turning point between the old and the new, between disorder and lack of direction on the one hand, and order and systematic organisation on the other. With the Acts of 1899 and 1902 a 'system' of secondary education was beginning to emerge, for the Acts established the framework within which secondary education could flourish and expand and created an efficient administrative machine that was so notably lacking previously.

The particular service rendered by the Education Act of 1902 was that it made provision for an organised system of secondary education and at the same time made the local education authorities in the towns and cities responsible for the provision of all other grades of education (save university education), thus emphasising the essential unity of education.

The first Report of the new Board of Education pointed out that:

It will be clear that no comparable figures can be given for the past fifty years or even twenty-five years as regards the increased provision of secondary education or the increase in the number of pupils and teachers in secondary schools, for no figures are available as regards the great mass of secondary schools before they came under the administration of the Board.[11]

But it was now possible for the first time to measure progress. The finance available for the support of secondary education doubled between 1904 and 1908. In the period between 1902 and 1914 more progress was achieved than in any comparable period since 1840 and this is reflected in the statistics presented in the annual reports of the Board of Education. In 1902 the number of schools recognised by the Board was 272 in which some 32,000 pupils were taking approved courses; by 1914 there were 910 schools eligible for grant with 170,000 pupils.

The Acts of 1899 and 1902 enabled local authorities to proceed with the creation of secondary schools, schools which were considerably free of the classical tradition. The new Regulations for Secondary Schools were built around the old 'payment-by-results' provisions of the Science and Art Departments. Schools of science which had been providing a systematic course of instruction in science within a broader course of liberal education were now designated Division A Schools. Division B Schools could apply for grants on submission of a syllabus of general instruction which included a scheme for a three- to four-year course in science in which at least nine hours a week were devoted to mathematics and science. The major burden of financing the schools fell on local authorities. Although scholarship schemes were improved and extended fees still played an important part, for, as the Board Report of 1902 stated: 'Grants are intended to supplement and not to supersede local effort, 25 per cent of expenditure should be met by local contributions such as fees, subscriptions, endowments or grants from local authorities.'

Grants based on 'payment-by-result' were replaced by 'payment-by-inspection' grants in 1904, offered not only to local authority schools but also to the private and endowed schools, several of which now came under the Board scheme. They found the revised and improved grants of 1907, under which any school which offered 'free places' to 25 per cent of its scholars was eligible for grants, even more attractive. This step was responsible for a rapid increase in the number of 'free place' pupils in the country's secondary schools. No fewer than 60,000 (35 per cent) of pupils were on free places in 1914 compared to 5,500 receiving aid of varying degrees in 1900. Huxley's 'educational ladder' was becoming a reality.

The Regulations of 1904 made obligatory for those schools receiving grants a curriculum in which at least three hours a week was devoted to science. Many of the local authority municipal schools had previously been 'organised science schools', and as such gave considerable emphasis to the sciences. Critics saw the 1904 Regulations as being detrimental to science, claiming that the new Regulations forced the new municipal secondary schools to model themselves on the traditional curricula of the grammar schools and public schools. We are inclined to a more approving view, for while the municipal schools might have been adversely affected, other schools, which were by far the majority and which had displayed a long hostility and antipathy to science, were now forced to provide at least three hours of science instruction if they wished to earn grants. This marked the point at which science became an accepted study in all reputable schools.

The public, grammar and private schools

The Clarendon Commission was the first official indication that all was not as it should be with England's leading schools. The Commissioners in their Report of 1864 cannot be accused of pulling their punches; but while they had misgivings, they nevertheless affirmed their faith in the public school system:

Among the services which the schools have rendered is undoubtedly to be reckoned the maintenance of classical literature as the staple of English education, a service which far outweighs the error of having clung to these studies exclusively. . . . It is not easy to estimate the degree in which the English people are indebted to these schools for the qualities in which they pride themselves most . . . for their capacity to govern others and control themselves, their aptitude for combining freedom with order, their public spirit, their vigour and manliness of character, their strong but not slavish respect for public opinion, their love of healthy sports and exercises. . . . These schools have been the chief nurseries of our statesmen; in them, and in schools modelled after them, men of all the various classes that make up English society, destined for every profession and career, have been brought up on a footing of social equality . . . and they have had perhaps the largest share in moulding the character of the English gentleman.[12]

Here was a momentous statement which put the imprimatur of approval on classical education for a further thirty years.

To assert, as the Commissioners did, that boys leaving these schools were 'destined for every profession' revealed a serious ignorance of the world of science and technology, few of the leaders of which had received a public school education. Had the influence of the Clarendon Commissioners been confined to the nine schools the damage would have been limited in extent. But it did not stop there. Such was the prestige of these schools the implications were far-ranging, for many other schools sought to emulate them.

The reputation of the schools examined by the Clarendon and Taunton Commissions was at a low ebb in the 1840s, the numbers at Westminster, Charterhouse, Harrow and Shrewsbury had in each case dropped below a hundred but owing to the work of headmasters such as Butler of Shrewsbury (1798–1836), Arnold of Rugby (1828–42) and Vaughan of Harrow (1834–52) the moral tone of these schools was improved, men who had served under them were appointed to other leading schools and the influence of the reformers spread. Edward Thring of Uppingham was an outstanding example; by his efforts he rescued the school from obscurity and transformed it into one of the most progressive of public schools. These schools quickly became desirable, both intellectually and socially, and they were adopted as the model for others which sprang up everywhere after 1840 with the coming of the railways.

The curriculum of the nine schools examined by the Clarendon Commission was in 1840 almost exclusively classical. One of the few concessions had been the introduction of mathematics in the 1820s as an 'extra', students wishing to study the subject being charged additional fees. By 1864 mathematics was taught in all the nine schools, the time devoted to it ranging from three to ten hours a week. The staffs of the schools comprised eighty-four teachers of classics, twenty-six teachers of mathematics and eighteen teachers of modern languages but the latter two areas of study were eclipsed by the emphasis given to classics:

Mathematics and modern languages share the disadvantages of being subordinate to the principal study, which is that of the classical languages. The chief honours and distinctions of the schools are classical, the headmasters and where the tutorial system exists the tutors, are men distinguished chiefly as classical scholars and are attached more or less ardently to classical learning.[13]

Although the demands of classics took pride of place over every other consideration the Clarendon Commission surprisingly found that the level of classical knowledge among the young men finishing at the nine schools left much to be desired. The Commission's general conclusion was 'that the average of classical knowledge among young men leaving school for college is low'.[14] W. F. Bushell, himself a schoolmaster later in life, and a pupil at Charterhouse towards the end of the nineteenth century, has given a description of classics teaching in his memoirs:

Most of the time was spent translating Latin and Greek authors. . . . On the first afternoon we were told to translate a certain English poem into Latin verses. My prep school had neglected to teach me the process and . . . I did not understand. No attempt was made to explain anything! . . . I am quite sure that the time of most boys was elaborately wasted. I doubt if the grammar and composition did me any good. My imagination was starved. . . . We should have gained something if we had read classical authors in translation but we spent each evening in attempting to get up 20–30 lines of the classical author set for preparation. It was dismal intellectual food and few benefited from it.[15]

If such was the case with classics little could be expected in other areas of study: 'In arithmetic and mathematics, in general information, and in English, the average is lower still and in arithmetic and mathematics the public schools are especially defective and this observation is not to be confined to any particular class of boys.' The net result was 'that of the time spent at school by the generality of boys, much is absolutely thrown away as regards intellectual progress'.[16]

As to science the Commission was of the view that 'natural science, with slight exceptions, is practically excluded from the education of the higher classes in England'. Opinion among the headmasters was that classics was the most appropriate study for first class minds whereas 'modern studies' had some value for the less able. Science, in particular, was not considered to have high intellectual or educational value. Thring saw some value in teaching science for 'there the most backward in classical knowledge can take refuge. There they can find something to interest them.' Temple's objection to science at Rugby was based on his belief that science 'did not have any tendency to humanise. Such studies do not make a man more human but simply more intelligent.'[17] But the

Clarendon Commissioners took issue with the headmasters over the matter of science teaching, 'We are convinced', they declared, 'that the introduction of the elements of natural science into the regular courses of study is desirable, and we see no reason to doubt that it is practicable.' This is encouraging but the effect is partly nullified by what followed: 'We say the elements because the teaching must necessarily be *elementary* [authors' italics] . . . we do not desire that natural science should occupy a large space in general education . . . class teaching for an hour or two in the week will be found to produce substantial fruits.'[18] Exactly what these fruits were the Commissioners did not specify and it is difficult to envisage such recommendations leading to any radical or dramatic results, though they may have ruffled the feelings of the headmasters at the time, for the position of science in the nine schools fell below even the modest level advocated by the Commissioners.

At Rugby in the 1850s J. M. Wilson, a pioneer of science teaching, was appointed and science lecture rooms and laboratories were built at a cost of £1,000. Instruction in science was not compulsory, it was regarded rather as a substitute for modern languages and entailed an extra fee of 6*s* 6*d* (32½p) and five guineas (£5.25) for use of the laboratories. Wilson confessed to the Clarendon Commissioners that he was a mathematician with no experience of experimental study. He had been appointed as a mathematics teacher, but Dr Temple had supposed that he could 'get it up sufficiently for the purpose' by grafting physical science on to his mathematics.

The only other recognised teacher of science among the nine schools was D. M. Stewart of Charterhouse. As to the others, the Commissioners found no science as such being taught at Eton; during the winter terms one lecture a week was given and these embraced a miscellaneous range of topics. At Harrow there was a considerable number of masters 'who are interested in science' but there was no direct instruction in it. Lectures on miscellaneous topics were a feature at Winchester, but the Commissioners did not look for much improvement there for the Headmaster, Dr Moberley, had informed the Commissioners that 'science is worthless'.[19] Very little could be said of science at Westminster, Charterhouse, St Paul's, Merchant Taylors' or Shrewsbury. One famous product of Shrewsbury was Darwin; it could hardly be claimed, however, that the school played a vital role in setting him on his path to fame:

Nothing could have been worse for my mind than Dr Butler's school, as it was strictly classical, nothing else being taught, except a little history and geography. The school to me was simply a blank. . . . My brother worked hard at chemistry and I was allowed to aid him as a servant in most of his experiments. . . . The subject interested me greatly . . . but . . . I was once publicly rebuked by the Headmaster, Dr Butler, for thus wasting my time on such useless subjects.[20]

In the year immediately preceding the Clarendon Commission's investigation, schools other than the nine had been turning their thoughts to 'modern studies', several schools having created distinct departments for the promotion of such studies. While not against the idea of modern departments in principle, the Clarendon Commission did not consider such an arrangement a suitable one for the leading nine schools. In its view:

The public schools are, and we think they ought to be, essentially classical schools, and we do not think it advisable that they should propose to their scholars alternative courses of study, to each of which equal honours must be paid, the one in which a course of Greek and Latin should hold the principal place, and the other a course in which little account should be made of Latin and from which Greek should be excluded altogether.[21]

The failure of the Clarendon Commissioners to take a more progressive line on the respective educational merits of classics and science meant that less prestigious schools had to take on the mantle of pioneers and to try to break the stranglehold that classics had established over English secondary education.

The schools which came within the sphere of influence of the leading nine were dealt with in the massive survey carried out by the Taunton Commission.[22] They fell into three groups: endowed, proprietary and private. In two out of three towns in England there was no school above the level of an elementary school and in the remaining third the schools were often lacking in size and deficient in quality. The supply of schools was thus wholly inadequate to the needs of the country and to make matters worse educational endowments were unevenly distributed; these ranged from £42,000 in the case of Christ's Hospital to as little as £5 in many cases; the total net income for Cornwall was £400 whereas for Lancashire it exceeded £9,000. Yet in Lancashire there were no grammar schools in Liverpool, Salford, or St Helens, while the number of students in the grammar schools of other towns was often small; the school at Oldham for instance had 39 boys, at Rochdale 40, Wigan 48, Barnsley 50, Chorley 22, and Widnes 45. At Liverpool the Free Grammar School was forced to close down in 1803 and that at Bristol was closed during the period 1829 to 1848, while Sedburgh and Wakefield had twelve pupils apiece in 1838.

The endowed grammar schools (a school was considered to be a grammar school if its founder had intended that the school should teach Latin and Greek) were expected to provide at least a higher than rudimentary education, but the Commission found many of the schools to be shamefully neglected, governors grossly mismanaged their affairs and even misappropriated the endowments; and 'many masters enjoyed an unshakeable security while doing little work'. The schools were also expected to prepare able boys for the universities, that is for Oxford and Cambridge. Like the public schools the endowed schools rarely sent their more able pupils to one of the London University colleges, to the

Royal College of Chemistry or to Owens College Manchester. In the view of the Commissioners only some eighty to ninety of the schools could be considered to be 'university' schools and their final conclusion was that 'the instruction given in the endowed schools is far removed from what the country has a right to demand'.

Proprietary schools, the majority of which were less than fifty years old at the time of the Taunton investigation, had frequently arisen as the result of the dissatisfaction of the middle-class parent, particularly those from commercial and industrial regions, with the exclusive cultivation of the classics found in the grammar schools. Proprietary schools provided a good classical education but gave more scope also to mathematics and modern languages; examples of this type of school were Malvern, Haileybury, University College School, Liverpool Institute High School and Liverpool Collegiate School.

Private schools abounded everywhere; they varied from 'good' to 'very bad' and generally speaking were 'lamentably unsatisfactory'. They were often found in neighbourhoods which were so sparsely populated that they could be little more than elementary schools but even in 'the suburbs of Manchester and Liverpool they gave an education incomparably worse than in the average National or British School, yet charging twice as much for it'.[23]

The elite of the schools examined by the Taunton Commission included some of the better grammar schools and proprietary schools. The position of science in these was more satisfactory than it was in the nine (Clarendon) schools, though still in general being far from satisfactory. The reason for this was that science teaching was at the time a recent innovation; it had been introduced into a few schools only. The Commission found that: 'the place of science is an unsettled and unsatisfactory one. In very few schools does it form a part of the regular curriculum, there is often, therefore, a want of proper apparatus and material, and the boys who learn are set to do so at odd times or perhaps once or twice a week.'[24] The headmasters of these schools, like those of the public schools, were imbued with the virtues of the classics but with regard to science there was 'the greatest diversity of opinion as to its value . . . some hold the strongest conviction of the importance, others express hesitation and misgiving and doubt if it has a place of any real value as an educational instrument, and a few discredit its utility entirely'.[25]

There were many who were in favour of science but the majority regarded it as educationally inferior to both classics and modern languages and were of the opinion that it had no value as a form of training of the mind. Some saw it as an imparting of knowledge after the mind was trained, others thought that it might be advantageously substituted for part of the classics in the case of 'those boys *not* [authors' italics] going on to the universities'. The Commissioners concluded that the views of headmasters about science were related to their degree of acquaintance with it.

A defect of the Taunton Commission Report, so admirable in other respects, was its failure to make strong recommendations in favour of science teaching. The Report contained a hundred pages of recommendations, the two issues discussed at greatest length being the extent to which Latin and Greek should be taught in the secondary schools and the issue of religion. Science did not appear in these recommendations.

The cause of science might have suffered as much from indifferent teaching as from its absolute exclusion from the schools:

At present it not uncommonly happens that natural science, accepted as a necessity, is delegated to some master of no great mark, whose task it is to get up as much information about it as may be supposed sufficient. . . . This master, besides being wanting in all but the most superficial acquaintance with his subject, is often ill-supplied with apparatus, as well as deficient in skill in manipulation. . . . In other cases it is thought that all the demands of natural science may be met by engaging an occasional lecturer to deliver a few popular lectures. . . . We cannot wonder that when it is treated in this way it should be pronounced superficial and incapable of disciplining the mind.[26]

The Taunton Commission in its recommendations stated that due regard should be paid to the spirit of the founders' wills whose intention was to provide education and to give openings to poor boys of exceptional ability. The founders had wished to produce 'cultivated' men by providing a 'liberal education'. However, the course of instruction

is too narrow. . . . In grammar schools, instruction in Latin and Greek is very frequently ordered, and the courts have held that where it is not expressly ordered the word 'grammar' must be presumed to imply it. It was the best instruction of the time, the only instruction which could then be considered worth having for its own sake; and by ordering it the founders have plainly indicated what kind of education they meant to give. Their intention was to produce cultivated men . . . the purpose of a liberal education was to enlarge the range of ideas, to elevate the thoughts, to make men more truly human, better subjects and better Christians . . . [the founders] . . . cannot have intended to adhere to the means, if the result was to empty the schools and so to defeat the purpose itself. And this result has followed in a vast number of instances. The country is, in some places, thickly dotted with grammar schools, which have fallen into decay because they give undue prominence to what no parents within their reach desire their children to learn.[27]

It was increasing concern with the state of science generally in the country which led to the appointment of the Devonshire Commission shortly after the Taunton Commission reported. Its brief, considerably broader than that of the Clarendon and Taunton Commissions, included schools. Once again the spotlight fell on science teaching, earlier criticisms of the other Commissions being further reinforced.

Like that of the Taunton Commission this survey was comprehensive. The Devonshire Commission sat for six years meeting over eighty times and interviewing some 150 witnesses. Its results were published in eight reports and four volumes of evidence.

The Commission distributed a circular among 205 schools requesting information about science teaching; it received 128 returns indicating that science was taught in 63 schools which between them had 13 laboratories. There was an acute shortage of apparatus, 18 schools only having a limited supply available. These schools can be taken to include the most advanced schools in England in so far as provision of science is concerned, yet of 8,945 boys only 2,430 (25 per cent) were learning any science at all. There was a great disparity between schools such as Eton and Winchester on the one hand, which allocated two hours a week to the study of natural science, and Manchester Grammar School and Dulwich, which devoted four to eight hours to physics and chemistry, on the other. Two schools only could claim a substantial list of successes on the part of their pupils. These were the City of London School, which submitted a long list of successes in science (in 1864 four boys from the school went to the University of London to study science and nine to the Royal School of Mines), and University College School, which submitted a long list of successes in science. University College School claimed thirty-four honours degrees in natural science at Cambridge and forty at London.

Many of the schools which replied to the Devonshire Commission attempted to justify their neglect of science by pleading shortage of funds and difficulty in finding time for a new area of study in an already overcrowded curriculum. As with the Clarendon and Taunton Commissions an attempt was made to shift the blame on to the ancient universities. The Devonshire Commissioners were not impressed by these arguments and delivered the strongest note of censure yet delivered against the schools:

We regret to observe [it concluded] in many of the larger schools the number of science masters is totally inadequate. We fear that the fewness of the science masters in the great schools and the slowness with which their number is allowed to increase must, to a certain extent, be due to an inadequate appreciation, on the part of the authorities of those institutions, of the importance of the place which science ought to occupy in school education.[28]

There were, of course, exceptions to these censures: University College School and the City of London School made favourable returns to the Commission but several other schools had already developed modern sides and were to become notable for the way in which they gave emphasis to scientific studies. Such schools included Dulwich College, Cheltenham College, Rossall and Manchester Grammar School.

A fictional account of the changes introduced into traditional schools around the 1870s can be found in Somerset Maugham's *Of*

Human Bondage. His account of Philip Carey's stay at King's School, Tercanbury, is clearly based on his own schooldays at King's School, Canterbury. For centuries the school had trained men of the Church – bishops, deans, and canons, and above all country clergymen – and when young Carey first went to the school he found that the masters had no patience with modern ideas of education and hoped that the school would remain true to its old traditions. 'The dead languages were taught with such thoroughness that an old boy seldom thought of Homer or Virgil in after life without a qualm of boredom . . . and the general feeling was that mathematics was a less noble study than classics. Neither German nor chemistry was taught.' But Carey was not at the school long before the old headmaster retired and was replaced by the brilliant son of Perkins the draper. Young Perkins was full of progressive ideas and changes took place. 'Two ordained masters were taken on to teach mathematics and modern languages, science classes were instituted and army classes introduced. The older masters viewed these changes with distrust and said the character of the school was changing for the worse.'[29]

The schools mentioned above as being 'progressive' were not necessarily the best but they were representative of the new type of school which, usually established after 1840, offered the rising professional and commercial classes alternatives to the uniformity of the classics-oriented public schools and ancient universities. They quickly established themselves and gained rapid popularity, Cheltenham College, for instance, opened in 1841, by 1861 had 600 boys and was second only to Eton in size. Liverpool Institute High School, set up in 1838 as an offshoot of the Mechanics' Institution School (of which a new building, opened in 1837, contained a laboratory, together with classrooms for chemistry and mechanics), was as progressive as any in the country. Chemistry and natural philosophy were taught in the High School shortly after its inception and quickly proved to be very popular. But the enthusiasm for science was limited to a few members of staff in a few schools and was in any case true of the period after 1860 only. It would be simple enough to accept the contemporary arguments as to why science was not more popular and why it should not be more speedily introduced into the schools: classics was an established and proven discipline whereas the quality of science as a training for the mind was largely unproven; the schools were forced to gear their studies to Oxford and Cambridge; the lack of qualified science staff of high academic calibre made it difficult to provide science classes; above all the cost involved in providing equipment and laboratories was a considerable obstacle.

In defending themselves against the criticisms of the Royal Commissions the schools sought a scapegoat in the universities of Oxford and Cambridge. The usual procedure for the many boys in the public schools and grammar schools was to go on to Oxford or Cambridge. Such a move was not confined to the 'academic' boys for as the Devonshire Commission pointed out it was the fashion among the prosperous classes for their sons to add three or four years at Oxford or Cambridge to their schooling, not as a professional training but for social reasons.

As at the schools the fashionable studies at Oxford and Cambridge were classics and mathematics. There was a tendency for boys who were taught these subjects at the schools, and later studied them at the ancient universities, to return as masters, often to the same schools. Thus attitudes and values acquired at school were reinforced at university and the reinforced beliefs fed back into the school system. At Repton for instance during the second half of the century of 70 masters appointed 35 were from Cambridge and 34 from Oxford, no fewer than 63 of these were appointed in classics, but none were in science. At Dulwich College 67 appointments included 51 from Oxford and Cambridge; of these 21 were for classics and 11 for mathematics, the remainder taught music, writing and languages. Of the 67 two only were in science, the first being a German PhD. Of 63 new appointments at Uppingham between 1870 and 1914, 59 were Oxford and Cambridge men appointed to teach classics or mathematics.

Despite the reforms which had been pushed through at the ancient universities following the Royal Commission Reports in the early 1850s, it is clear that classics and mathematics still dominated the curriculum in the 1860s and 1870s. This is clearly brought out in Table 3.1.

Table 3.1 Fellowships at Oxford and Cambridge 1870

	Classics	Mathematics	Law and Modern History	Science
Oxford	145	28	25	4
Cambridge	67	102	2	3

The Chairman of the Endowed Schools Commission (set up in 1869) had no doubt that the fault lay principally with the universities. In a letter to the Vice-Chancellors of the universities he wrote:

The course of study insisted on by the universities governs the course adopted in schools, and hence the study of Greek and Latin becomes the highest aim of all great schools. . . . As long as Greek is made a sine qua non at the universities those schools of the new type which it is proposed to establish will labour under the serious disadvantage of being cut off from direct connection with the universities through a want of agreement in their course of studies with University requirements.[30]

The Devonshire Commissioners also considered that the ancient universities were a stumbling block to the introduction of scientific studies into the public schools:

Nothing, however, can have much effect on the grammar schools and middle class schools of the country, generally, until the universities which give the key to education in the country, allocate a fair proportion of their endowments to the reward of scientific studies. Till such knowledge 'pays' at the universities, the middle class schools which look more or less to them, cannot be expected to change their course of instruction.[31]

Scientific education was clearly inadequate at the universities as well as the schools. In the light of the special relationship between the schools and the ancient universities where did the root cause of the trouble lie? The universities blamed the schools for not sending them their brighter students to study science and the schools blamed the universities for not offering more scholarships and fellowships in the sciences. This was a constant theme running through the Clarendon Report as well as the later Taunton and Devonshire Reports. Sir John Lubbock, a member of the Devonshire Commission, expressed the circular argument in the following terms:

They do not prepare them [in science] at schools because there is not the same number of awards for it in the universities and the universities do not award them because science is not taught in the schools, and the schools do not teach them because they are not rewarded in the universities.[32]

In the early and middle parts of the century the Victorian middle classes pushed through many schemes of qualifying and competitive examinations for entry to professional bodies. Despite this they remained wedded to the outmoded liberal education of the public schools. W. J. Reader in his book *Professional Men* explains this in terms of the professional man's concern with social standing and his desire to get as near as possible to the pattern set by the landed gentry. The new found prestige and enhanced status of the public schools after mid-century were an irresistible attraction and, added to this, entry to Oxford and Cambridge was largely gained through the public schools and grammar schools. In England a public school education became a hallmark of the professional man. The exception to this was in science and engineering.

The nature of professional society changed radically during the final quarter of the century; the clergy declined in numbers whereas surgeons and physicians increased. But the most significant change was the emergence of engineers and scientists as professional classes; ommitted from the earlier Census reports they were cited as 9,400 and 1,200 in the Census of 1881.[33] They established new bodies to cater for their professional requirements; thus the Physical Society was set up in 1874 and the Institute of Chemistry in 1877. The Institution of Civil Engineers came into being as early as 1818, but towards the end of the century new technological bodies such as the Institute of Mining Engineers (1889) and the Institute of Mining and Metallurgy (1892) were formed.

These new professional classes by and large were not products of the public and grammar schools. Indeed the evidence of the Royal

Commissions and contemporary observers does not encourage one to have high expectations of the contribution of the established schools regarding the production of scientific manpower. Despite this adverse evidence, did the schools nevertheless succeed in producing a steady stream of boys who took up careers in science and engineering? In order to answer this, the registers and school rolls of a number of schools have been analysed. The period 1860 to 1890 was chosen as representing a transitional period in the history of the development of the English schools. The schools studied comprised Eton, Harrow, Marlborough, Rugby, Haileybury, Millhill, King's School, Canterbury, Repton College, Derby School, Uppingham and Dulwich College. The group encompasses the older, traditional schools (three of them were included in the Clarendon Commission survey) and some schools of the new type. The number of pupils analysed for each school was between 200 and 600, and altogether the careers of 3,076 boys were studied.

The number of boys taking up a scientific career amounted to 39 or 1 per cent of the total studied; Dulwich led the field with 6 per cent of its boys entering science and Millhill was second with 4 per cent. The same two schools also led the field in engineering, 11 per cent and 9 per cent of the boys respectively taking up careers in engineering; for the schools as a whole the figure was 4 per cent. In other words, only 115 boys out of over 3,000 became engineers; of the 115 boys, 73 were in civil engineering, 19 in mining engineering, 16 in electrical engineering and 7 only in mechanical engineering.

The other well-known characteristic of upper-class schools, namely, of being feeders for Oxford and Cambridge and for the traditional professions of law, medicine and the Church is illustrated by this study. Nineteen per cent of the boys went on to Oxford on leaving school; Dulwich and Millhill sent only 6 per cent and 5 per cent respectively but Eton sent 43 per cent and Rugby and Marlborough 24 per cent apiece. For Cambridge the picture was rather different, there being a greater degree of uniformity among the schools. With the exception of Eton (26 per cent) and Harrow (22 per cent) all the remaining schools sent about 12 per cent to Cambridge, the average for all the schools being 17 per cent. Between them Oxford and Cambridge took 36 per cent of the boys, that is, more than one in every three boys leaving these schools.

Turning to the professions one in five boys leaving school entered the army. Rugby with 30 per cent had the greatest number and Millhill with 8 per cent the smallest. Numbers entering the Church and law were considerably less. About 9 per cent entered the legal profession, ranging from 23 per cent at Rugby to 3 per cent at Dulwich. Eight per cent entered the Church, numbers varying from 15 per cent at King's School, Canterbury, to 5 per cent at Dulwich and Millhill.

Two facts serve to put the contribution of these schools in perspective. No fewer than 37 per cent of the products of the schools entered either the army or the profession of law or the Church; in contrast 5 per cent only took up careers in science and engineering. But it is misleading to view the schools as a single homogeneous group. There is a wide gulf between the well-established schools at Eton, Harrow, and Rugby on the one hand and Millhill and Dulwich on the other. It was considerably harder for schools of the former type to incorporate new studies into a long-established and acceptable curriculum than it was for the new schools. The majority of masters appointed in nearly all schools were classics masters[34] with some appointed in law or specifically for drawing, writing or arithmetic. As time went on a few were appointed to teach mathematics or modern languages but before 1880 one looks almost in vain for the master qualified to teach science. Dulwich is one exception. Between 1871 and 1885 six highly qualified scientists were appointed; these included three from Cambridge, a PhD from Jena and another from Heidelberg. Dulwich, along with City of London School, the Liverpool Institute High School and one or two other schools, can be taken as pioneers of scientific education.

Secondary education in an industrial area

In its Annual Report of 1905–06 the Board of Education commented that 'the most conspicuous fact that emerges [concerning secondary education] . . . is of how much there is yet to be done . . . the short-comings are too often little less than disastrous, (p. 49)'. Improvements were effected in the succeeding years but the Board was far from satisfied. It complained in the Report for the session 1910–11:

There is little doubt that the supply both of secondary schools and of scholarships is quite inadequate to meet the demand that exists, a demand that is very variable. . . . While in some areas the active demand for higher education is largely in excess of the existing supply . . . in others the effective demand has largely to be created by the supply, and a generation may have to pass before there is a sufficiently educated public to appreciate the need, and to cause the provision to be made, for the education of the next generation. . . . What is necessary is a full realisation among a wider public of the value of education economically, socially and intellectually (p.105).

No better region can be selected to highlight the weaknesses and deficiencies of English secondary education in the nineteenth century and also to illustrate the truth of the above observations than Lancashire, the home of the Industrial Revolution. A population of $3\frac{1}{2}$ million in 1880 was primarily involved in cotton goods manufacture and its ancillaries, bleaching, dyeing and soap boiling. But around Manchester heavy engineering and manufacture existed in great concentration and whereas Liverpool was predominantly a commercial centre its environs had experienced a long tradition of diverse crafts and industrial processes. Coal was mined in the area from early days and the spinning and weaving of linen, tanning and leather making were widespread. Watchmakers, springmakers and nailmakers demonstrated craft skills and such skills passed on by craftsmen trained to work in metal to a high degree of accuracy later played an important part in machine making and engine building. Pottery, sugar-baking and glass manufacture were other local industries and the growth of St Helens and Warrington is particularly associated with glass, copper and chemicals.

The ready availability of coal and salt drew Ludwig Mond[35] to Northwich in 1873 to set up as an alkali manufacturer, but before this James Muspratt[36] had ensured that first Liverpool and later Widnes were to become leading world centres for alkali manufacture. Across the Mersey from Widnes William Lever's soapworks created the new town of Ellesmere Port. Shipbuilding was another traditional industry in Liverpool and in the nineteenth century competition came from the town of Birkenhead which grew up around William Laird's shipyards. The whole region then, from Liverpool across to Manchester in the east, to Preston in the north and Northwich in the south was teeming with a proliferation of richly diverse industrial, manufacturing and commercial activities. Traditional skills and crafts passed on from father to son or master to apprentice played a notable role and in Liverpool itself a commercial education based on mathematics and bookkeeping was the primary requirement which the middle-class schools of the Institute and Collegiate set themselves to provide.

But new industries, especially the new chemical industries, created different needs; and so did the traditional processes as they became increasingly complex, less empirically and more technologically based. While the pool of practical expertise was considerable, the 'second' industrial revolution of the second half of the nineteenth century demanded a greater emphasis on theoretical instruction. On the whole the conventional secondary schools failed to make this available. Liverpool and Manchester relied on a handful of excellent schools, while outside these cities the new schools of Rossall and Stonyhurst were added to the traditional grammar schools at Preston, Bury, Warrington, Wigan, Bolton, Burnley, Blackburn, Rochdale, Oldham, Farnworth, Leigh, Newchurch, Chorley, Colne, Middleton and Crosby. James Bryce, Assistant Commissioner for the North-West to the Taunton Commission, found in 1868 that Stonyhurst and Crosby were essentially classical schools and at Rossall science was only taught on the modern side. The grammar schools, he said, suffered from 'deep rooted theological and political jealousies', and nonconformists tended to look on them with aversion. In a stronghold of nonconformity this may have accounted for the fact that ten of them had a school population amounting to only 669 pupils. These served a total population of 464,541; in other words only 1.5 per 1,000 of the population was in a local grammar school. The schools were adversely affected, too, by the tendency of the richest classes in Manchester, Liverpool and throughout Lancashire to send their children away to school to be educated.

At Liverpool one of the first tasks the Education Committee created by the 1902 Act set itself was to determine the extent and quality of secondary education in the City. It was fortunate to obtain the services of Michael Sadler to carry out a survey. He reported in due course that he found it difficult if not impossible to arrive at the number of children who ought to be attending the City's secondary schools. As far as he could ascertain the attendance figure was 1.9 per 1,000 of the population (the Schools Inquiry Commission of 1868 had adopted 12.2 as a reasonable yardstick). Sadler pointed out that the comparable figure for Prussia in 1902 was 5.4, and for the City of Cologne it was 8.7 per 1,000.

After the closure of its Free Grammar School in 1803 Liverpool, the largest town in the North-West, had no grammar school for some time. The first school for boys was founded in 1817 by a group of merchant bankers and brokers. This was a small select classical school, the first schools of repute being founded some twenty years later, the first by the Directors of the Mechanics' Institution and the second by the Church of England. All three were fee-paying schools to which there were few free place scholarships until the last quarter of the century. Of the three it was the Liverpool Institute High School that was most worthy of note; its fees were kept low, for it was intended to serve the sons of those whose means were too limited to provide their children with a good classical education. The school, which provided a broad curriculum including the sciences, was the first school in the country to erect science laboratories.

By the end of the century many more secondary schools had been founded, several by the local authority. Even so in 1902 the *Liverpool Courier* claimed that secondary education was going backward in the City for it had been 'left to the haphazard of private enterprise'. This view was echoed by a Special Sub-Committee set up by the Liverpool Technical Instruction Committee which reported: 'The position of secondary education in Liverpool is altogether unworthy of the City. . . . Secondary education in the last twenty years has made comparatively little progress, in some respects it has gone backward and today is altogether inadequate to the wants of the City.'[37] The Sub-Committee emphasised that the Board of Education had repeatedly drawn attention to the factors responsible. These were mainly insufficient provision of schools, lack of endowments which caused the schools to charge excessive fees in order to pay their way but which also excluded large sectors of the population, and the complete dearth of scholarships – only three out of every thousand elementary school children proceeded to the secondary schools in 1902 and few of these were on 'free place' scholarships. The principal weakness according to Sadler was the lack of endowments; in Birmingham the annual value of educational endowments was over £37,000 or £79 per 1,000 of the population, in Bristol £20,000 or £89 per 1,000 whereas the corresponding figures for Liverpool were £350 and 14s (70p) per 1,000. Sadler's explanation for the lack of endowments was that the commercial success of Liverpool as a great port had bred apathy in the City.

Both Bryce in 1868 and Sadler in 1902 discovered that the short-term interests of the commercial sector of merchants and brokers were inimical to academic education; a university training or prolonged stay at school was considered to unfit a merchant's son for a business career. The argument presented to Sadler ran on the following lines:

Out of the estimated ship's tonnage of the world, more than a quarter belongs to Liverpool. Why should things not go on as they are? Is not the prosperity of Liverpool due to her geographical position? . . . Her port not her education it might be argued is the cause of her wealth. Why do more than is already done for the upkeep of the secondary schools? Why educate commercial recruits at public expense?[38]

It was ironical that such a view had any credence at this stage for while Liverpool's prosperity had been assured at one time the danger signals were now there for all to see.

Earlier, in 1896, the *Liverpool Daily Post* had attempted to assess the fortunes of the port in a series of six articles entitled 'Liverpool and its trade'. These pointed out that trade was being diverted to Manchester (due to the opening of the Ship Canal) and to Southampton. An ominous sign for the future was that the total tonnage of vessels entered and cleared at Liverpool in 1895 was 10.5 million whereas the corresponding total for Hamburg was 12.5 million.

It is against this background that Sadler's final judgement regarding secondary education must be viewed:

Secondary education [he stated] means at present far less to Liverpool than to Hamburg or New York. . . . Liverpool has allowed its secondary schools to receive less than their proper share of public help, of public interest and public attention. No one . . . can fail to be struck by the backwardness of her resources in respect of secondary education. . . . When every allowance has been made, the final outcome is unsatisfactory.[39]

Manchester, unlike Liverpool, was fortunate in having an endowed grammar school, the Manchester Grammar School. Not untypically of this type of school it was found by the Taunton Commission to have some weaknesses. In a number of respects, however, it was the foremost among the great day schools of England. There were several other excellent schools, too, the Hulme Grammar School, Pembleton High School and North Manchester High School. In addition Manchester led the way in establishing higher grade board schools. These were well attended for 'the class of parents who are prepared to pay four guineas a year for their sons' education and no more, have not found schools in Manchester at that price, and have sent their sons to higher grade schools'.[40] On paper it would appear that the area was adequately equipped but in the opinion of F. E. Kitchener, Assistant Commissioner for the North-West to the Bryce Commission, 'the provision in Manchester is considerably less than in Liverpool'.[41] Thus despite Sadler's strictures of Liverpool secondary school provision this was not only better than Manchester but also of Lancashire in general. Both Bryce in 1868 and Sadler in 1902 found that boys streamed into the Liverpool schools from the surrounding area, and Kitchener was of the opinion that Liverpool was better provided for than any town in the North-West.

The first Director of Education for Lancashire, H. Lloyd Snape, on taking office discovered that no official list of secondary schools was available. Consequently a circular letter was distributed to town clerks seeking information. The returns gave a figure of 232 schools: 31 included the term 'grammar school' in their title; 26 were termed 'high school'; the others included schools of science, intermediate secondary schools, schools of science and art, and higher grade board schools.[42] The uneven distribution of schools, unrelated to population and needs, is revealed in a study of these schools. Formby, a small village of a few thousand, had four schools and Southport 28, whereas there was no grammar school at Widnes, centre of the chemical industry, nor at Oldham, while at St Helens there was no provision for secondary education before 1870. The endowed grammar schools were generally small and in rural areas; 26 of them had an average of less than 58 boys in each and three only exceeded 100 boys. The 'schools of science' in contrast tended to be in industrial towns such as Accrington, Nelson and Darwen.

A few years earlier Kitchener, following his travels round Lancashire, had concluded that:

the secondary education of the country is not sufficiently provided in the local secondary schools in the existing endowed schools and reliance on private enterprise means pleasant and attractive places such as Southport and Cheshire become happy hunting grounds for private schoolmasters whereas smoke and machinery drive them away, the result being that generations are left unprovided for.[43]

The Director's survey revealed that out of 232 schools only 12 had laboratories and provided practical instruction. This was a surprisingly low figure for there had been great emphasis on science in schools since the 1870s. Bryce in his report to the Taunton Commissioners in 1868 had commented: 'It is quite recently that science has been introduced in Lancashire and its place at present is an unsettled and unsatisfactory one. In very few schools does it form part of the curriculum.'

In Bryce's day Warrington grammar school had no laboratory provision nor proper accommodation for science teaching; neither did Wigan nor Farnworth Grammar Schools. St Helens was in a worse state for no grammar school existed until the Cowley endowments of 1882. The lead in this direction was given by the new schools of science to be found at Accrington, Colne, Darwen, Nelson, Moss Side and Widnes.

The best of these was that at Widnes, which had laboratories in physics and chemistry and a well-qualified science staff. There were 218 boys and girls in the school (129 of them as 'free scholars'), pupils being drawn from the industrial areas of Widnes, Warrington, Sankey and Bold. It was a fitting example of what an enterprising local authority could do in the way of science provision.

It is clear that secondary education in the heavily industrialised hinterland of Liverpool and in Lancashire generally was even inferior to that provided in the City itself, inadequate though that was. Earlier it was seen that the commercial interests of Liverpool and Manchester impeded the quality of work in those two cities; it is only fair to point out that the same criticism cannot be made of Lancashire industrialists. The chemical firm Crosfields at Warrington, for instance, was a keen supporter of all forms of education, David Gamble at St Helens promoted the Cowley secondary schools for boys and girls, and Frederick Gossage, a Widnes industrialist, was instrumental in rebuilding Farnworth Grammar School. But these initiatives stand out against a background of neglect of secondary education, a neglect that was inimical to the progress of science.

The new century

Despite the considerable progress that was made following the 1902 Act the coming of war quickly revealed deficiencies in science. A Committee was appointed in 1916 under the chairmanship of Sir J. J. Thomson to investigate and report on the 'Position of natural science in the educational system of Great Britain'. This Committee began its report in 1918 with the phrase 'Not for the first time educational conscience has been stung by the thought that as a nation we are neglecting science'.[44] A half-century had elapsed since the Clarendon Commission first drew attention to this omission and yet after several Commissions the familiar theme of the neglect of science was central to this latest report.

For the greater part of this period the claims of science had been met with resistance, if not with hostility. But the war changed all that – if only temporarily. 'Just now everyone is prepared to receive science with open arms, to treat it as an honoured guest in our educational system.'[45] It was those schools which formerly were organised science schools under the Department of Science and Art, and those established since the 1902 Act, which pleased the Committee most, for in these science had been included on an equal footing. But many such schools were populated by social classes which formerly had been denied secondary education and pupils came from a background in which it was the accepted custom to begin work at an early age. Among their parents there was no appreciation of the value of secondary education and a greater reluctance to forgo wages of fourteen-year-olds. This was a serious defect of these schools and led to a dearth of pupils willing or able to remain at school for advanced study.

The Committee found that the majority of the larger public and preparatory schools by this time had been organised into separate classical and modern sides. However things were not as satisfactory as one would have supposed. On the modern sides the time given to science was as a rule adequate, but science had received scant attention on the classical sides of the schools. Furthermore, the classical sides included a larger proportion of the abler boys: 'In our view', said the Thomson Committee, 'it is a very real defect in the public school organisation that boys should in many schools have to make their choice between a classical side in which science is almost wholly neglected and a modern side in which the general educational conditions are in many ways unfavourable.'[46] This policy also affected university entrance. In the period 1906 to 1915 scholarships and exhibitions held by university entrants in science accounted for 10.6 per cent of all awards whereas classics in contrast took a 60 per cent share. The significant finding was that no fewer than 80 per cent of the classical scholarships were gained by boys who had been awarded entrance scholarships to their respective schools and had subsequently been directed towards classical study.

Private schools played a much larger part in the educational provision for girls than it did for boys and the scientific education of girls had progressed to a considerably less extent than it had for boys. Elementary physics, chemistry and botany were taught in many schools, but botany was the favoured subject of instruction after the age of fourteen, the number of schools in which there was any serious teaching of physics was 'quite insignificant'. In short, science teaching in girls' schools was 'less favourable' than that in boys despite the progress made after the turn of the century.

The supply of good teachers of science had always been a problem and there had been 'a great shortage of science teachers for some years before the war'. The war accentuated the gravity of the situation; industry was already competing for the services of those who in ordinary times would have looked forward to science teaching as a profession. In the future competition was likely to grow even more severe. In one respect things had not moved forward since the Taunton Commission's findings, for the Thomson Committee confessed:

We cannot regard it as anything but unsatisfactory that it should be impossible to form even a rough estimate of the number of children receiving secondary education in this country or of the value of that education. It is disconcerting to find that the total number of children receiving secondary education in Great Britain at the present time is quite unknown.

Across half a century one finds an echo of Matthew Arnold's words of 1868 for the Commission appealed for 'the neglect of science' to be remedied 'in the national interest'.[47]

Chapter 4

Technical education

The mechanics' institute movement

The main agents of technical education throughout the greater part of the nineteenth century were the mechanics' institutes. Government intervention was limited initially to the disbursement of funds through its Department of Science and Art, under whose auspices science classes became widespread throughout the country. Further funds were made available as a result of the Technical Instruction Act of 1889 and the Local Taxation Act of 1890. Developments were piecemeal and relied greatly on voluntary initiative and effort. Until the end of the century there were no defined lines of demarcation between the various sectors of education. Technical education ranged over everything from higher elementary education at one end to advanced technological instruction, trade education and technical processes at the other. The advance of technical education was not helped by the uncertainty and vagueness on the part of its foremost proponents. In Cardwell's words: 'It seems in short to have been the case that many enthusiastic advocates reduced themselves to the position of proclaiming "we cannot say what technical education is, but we must have it".'[1]

As Britain moved swiftly from a primarily agricultural economy to an industrialised state at the beginning of the nineteenth century the view prevailed widely that the Industrial Revolution with its specialisation of processes and technological innovations demanded workmen with higher literacy levels than their predecessors. This concern with literacy was matched by a firm belief that in the rapidly changing conditions the skilled workman would require at least a basic knowledge of the elements of science. The artisan was seen as the cornerstone of technical education and it was the perception of his needs by the leaders of society which underpinned thinking about technical education throughout the greater part of the century; this was a major factor responsible for the low status of technical education in nineteenth-century England.

Until late in the century, however, the skilled worker often lacked the basic educational skills to enable him to benefit from such educational provision as was especially created for his purpose. Courses intended for the artisan did not attract the anticipated numbers; instead they were attended by clerks, shopkeepers and school teachers. The problems posed by the lack of preparedness of the artisan were quickly appreciated by the founders of the first mechanics' institute, the Edinburgh School of Arts, established in 1821. After only three years of existence the Directors came to the conclusion that

> to convey any solid instruction in these branches [mechanical philosophy and chemistry] such as the workman may turn to practical account requires all the time he has to bestow. . . . We have found that, to teach the elements of chemistry requires at least thirty lectures. . . . The same number of lectures have been found scarcely sufficient for a very limited course of instruction in the principles of mechanical philosophy.[2]

The sponsors of artisan education were up against the formidable problem of the inadequate education of their intended students. This could not adequately be overcome given that the prevailing view was that the education of artisans should be confined to evening classes. The third report of the School of Art indicates the hardship evening instruction imposed on the working man:

> He, the artisan, must be in his workshop from six in the morning to seven o'clock in the evening. As he must go home to take some refreshment after work and . . . will generally put off his working dress, he cannot conveniently reach the lecture room sooner than half-past eight o'clock. . . . No lecture can be less than an hour long so that it will be nearly ten o'clock before he can reach home; and he will then be fully prepared for rest. Thus it is evident, that supposing a workman to devote the whole of his leisure time to this object, an hour and a half in the day is the utmost he has at his disposal.[3]

During the first quarter of a century a ferment of activity favourable to science led to the formation of local societies throughout the country. Although intended primarily for the study of science in a general cultural context they had, too, a bearing on technical education. In London, bodies such as the London Institution (1805), the Philomathic Institution (1807) and the Russell Institution (1808) showed a catholic interest in science and the arts while in provincial towns the pattern was set by the literary and philosophical societies. Societies of this name (or occasionally philosophic and literary society) were established in Manchester and Newcastle before 1800 and then at Liverpool (1812), Leeds (1820) and Sheffield and Hull (1822). Generally these were to promote science and literature by the reading of papers, and by lectures, formation of museums and libraries, and the establishment of laboratories with apparatus.

A body of a different character, however, was the Royal Institution of London founded in 1799,

> for diffusing the knowledge and facilitating the general and speedy introduction of new and useful mechanical inventions and improvements, and also for teaching, by regular courses of philosophical lectures and experiments, the application of these discoveries in science to the improvement of arts and manufactures, and in facilitating the means of procuring the comforts and conveniences of life.[4]

As it happened the Royal Institution did not develop on technical lines. It achieved instead an international reputation as a centre of chemical research.

The Royal Institution of Liverpool was in part inspired by the London body but was more cultural in character, so was the Royal Manchester Institution (1823). The interest in applied science was reflected, however, in the Scottish Society of Arts (1821), and the Royal Cornwall Polytechnic Society (1833).

The literary and philosophical societies and the polytechnic societies are examples of middle-class initiatives to develop and popularise applied science. The Liverpool Literary and Philosophical Society founded in 1812 saw itself as 'a body seeking to foster original inquiry and learned research'; its main activity was the provision of a lecture programme which after 1840 appeared in printed form in its *Proceedings*. These lecture programmes embraced a diversity of subject areas but often dominant was applied science, with particular emphasis on local conditions.

The widespread concern felt about the general education of the artisan and, in particular, his lack of basic instruction in science, gave rise in the second quarter of the century to the mechanics' institute movement. It was naïvely assumed that this form of institution relying on the principle of voluntaryism would solve the problem of the scientific training of the artisan. The stated objectives of the London Mechanics' Institution, established in London in 1823, was fairly typical of the aims of the major mechanics' institutes. This was 'the instruction of the members in the principles of the arts they practice or in the various branches of science and useful knowledge connected therewith', to be accomplished by the provision of a library, a museum of machines and models, public lectures, elementary classes in arithmetic, geometry, navigation and commercial subjects, a workship and a laboratory for experimental philosophy.

The origins of the movement can be traced to Dr George Birkbeck, a medical graduate of Edinburgh University. In 1799 he was appointed Professor of Natural Philosophy at Anderson's Institution, Glasgow. John Anderson, who had held a chair at Glasgow University from 1757 until his death in 1796, had bequeathed his estate for the establishment of a rival university, but his trustees founded instead a body known as Anderson's Institution (1796). Birkbeck quickly offered a special course of lectures, free of charge, on 'the mechanical properties of solid and fluid bodies' and was soon attracting 500 artisans to the lectures. They continued until in 1804 he left for London, where he became a prime mover in the formation of the London Mechanics' Institution, which was later to bear his name as Birkbeck College. The mechanics' class at Anderson's Institution decided, in July 1823, to break away and form an independent body known as the Glasgow Mechanics' Institution. Two years earlier the Edinburgh School of Arts had been set up, which, despite its name, was the first genuine mechanics' institute.

The movement spread quickly after the formation of the mechanics' institutes in Edinburgh, Glasgow and London in the early 1820s. At least thirteen new institutes came into existence in 1824, and about seventy in 1825. By 1826 there were over a hundred.

But whilst the principal aim of the London Mechanics' Institution and that of many other institutes reflected the vocational needs of the artisan, the motives that inspired the founders were diverse; employers sought better educated and industrious workmen, politicians hoped the institutes would provide training in self-government, others hoped that they would help to alleviate the misery of the working classes. Birkbeck himself saw them as agents of cultural education for liberating the mind and enriching understanding.[5] Such a diversity of objectives was not easily attainable within a single institute. Given the confusion as to objectives, which way were the mechanics' institutes to go? Conflict arose between the desires of the mainly middle-class founders and the aspirations of the working-class members. Contemporary observers claimed that the working classes drifted away because they often did not find at the mechanics' institutes the opportunities they required, although the evidence suggests that the skilled worker continued to attend in addition to 'manufacturers' clerks, warehousemen and shopkeepers'.[6]

To the modern reader the term mechanic has a fairly precise meaning but the assessment of the success of the mechanics' institutes has been somewhat confused due to the different interpretations given to the term. For whom were the mechanics' institutes intended? Clear guidance on this point has been provided by Professor Kelly:

It is, however, a mistake to link the movement, as is often done, specifically with the development of the factory system. Almost inevitably, we tend to associate 'mechanic' with 'machinery' but in the 1820s, when the first mechanics' institutes were founded, the power driven factory was not at all extensively developed outside the textile areas, and the name 'mechanic' did not mean primarily a machine operative. In so far as it had a precise meaning, it meant, on the contrary, a craftsman, a 'tradesman' in the northern sense; but its meaning was often extended to cover all manual workers, or, more vaguely still, all who belonged to the 'working class'. In fact it was the skilled craftsman rather than the machine operative who at this period needed to keep abreast of new inventions, new processes, and new materials, and it was to this group that the first efforts in the education of mechanics were directed.[7]

Whatever the actual composition of their support, it is certainly true that the movement had a popular mass appeal; in 1826 there were 100 mechanics' institutes, by 1850 there were some 700.[8] Nearly everywhere the management of the mechanics' institutes was based on democratic lines; it involved workers, manufacturers, tradesmen, merchants, engineers, doctors and other professional groups. Some mechanics' institutes succeeded in becoming established almost entirely on the basis of working-class support, examples being Keighley, Halifax and Huddersfield. The economic depression of 1826 brought to an end the first phase of the mechanics' institute movement; between 1827 and 1831 many were forced to close down. The decade 1832–42 witnessed a new phase, an even more vigorous one than the first. While the first phase of activity had been confined largely to London, Scotland and the industrial North, in the second period the institutes spread into rural areas and every little market town had its mechanics' institute. In the larger cities several were to be found in close proximity.

Clearly not enough thought was given in many cases to priorities in objectives, nor to viability. After 1850 many institutes were forced to close down and several of those that survived led a hand-to-mouth existence. The most successful were those that stuck closely to a defined role based on serious and systematic scientific and technical instruction for those who desired it or could profit by it. There is little doubt that the potential audience was very considerable.

Those mechanics' institutes which gave prominence to scientific instruction were helped by the examination schemes arranged by the Society of Arts, the City and Guilds of London Institute, the Yorkshire Union of Mechanics' Institutes and the Lancashire and Cheshire Union of Mechanics' Institutes. Of special significance were the examinations and aid provided by the Department of Science and Art. Several mechanics' institutes, too, were linked to particular industries or firms such as railways, collieries and ironworks.

The instruction of the mechanic in the scientific principles underlying his trade was to be attained by two means: by public courses of lectures and by class instruction. The provision of public lectures was the principal activity of every nineteenth-century cultural society and institution. With regard to the mechanic it was probably the most wasteful and ineffective method of instruction. The London Mechanics' Institution began with lecture courses in chemistry, metallurgy and mechanical philosophy. With time there was a tendency to drift away from long and systematic courses on science, courses became shorter and a wide variety of subjects was introduced into the London lecture programme. The same was true at the Liverpool Mechanics' Institution where, in 1834, the programme included short lecture courses on: *Hamlet*, The Microscope, Stenography, Milton, Mechanics, Combustion, Music of Ireland, Production and Use of Silk, The Middle Ages, Oratory, Perspective, Phrenology, Early and Home Training of Children, Sanitary Regulations and German Customs.

The public lecture went through many changes of fashion during the nineteenth century, but certainly as far as, for example, Liverpool is concerned it had reached its heyday by mid-century. The evidence available suggests that the same was true elsewhere. Thus serious and lengthy lecture courses had given way to short popular lectures. An element of entertainment and relaxation crept in in other ways through concerts and soirées. According to Hudson in 1851 lectures

have met with a premature decay. From complete courses of ninety and sixty lectures upon one branch of physical science, lectures have dwindled to an average of three in each course, and a general practice of having one lecture for each branch of science. In the choice of subjects the change has been equally unfavourable; the plain and easily understood discourses on the elements of the sciences, and their application to the useful arts, illustrated by numerous experiments have been abandoned; and the preference shown for light literature, criticism, music, and the drama, has given just occasion for the statement, that even the elder Metropolitan Mechanics' Institution, since its establishment, has given more attention to the Drama than to the entire range of physical science.[9]

In the conditions prevailing during the period 1825–40, erudite lecture courses in science were of little value to often illiterate workmen. Fortunately there were those among the founders of mechanics' institutes who had hit on the right answer when they provided elementary class instruction in reading, writing, arithmetic, geometry and commercial subjects. 'Mutual instruction' classes were also formed in mechanics, chemistry and other scientific subjects, albeit at a fairly elementary level. At Liverpool Mechanics' Institution elementary classes were provided at an earlier date than lecture courses and eight years after their formation there were no fewer than thirty-three classes – adequate testimony of the need for them and their popularity among an educationally deprived section of the population. Class instruction in basic subjects such as English, arithmetic and geometry was the form of activity that was most highly commended by Hudson:

The most important feature in the Mechanics' Institution has ever been the evening classes. The formation of this department was an immense improvement upon the old 'night schools', which were generally conducted by one master, who was surrounded by his pupils, engaged in dissimilar tasks at the same time – thus one would be writing, another learning grammar, a third geography, and a fourth at arithmetic. The regulations of a Mechanics' Institution, on the other hand, are definite. The studies are under-taken at fixed periods, and one subject alone entertained at a time.[10]

But if the class of persons who took advantage of this privilege were ill-equipped in terms of basic education, it is equally true to say that in many areas the children of middle-class parents were deprived of a suitable education at a secondary level. Liverpool was one such area, as no grammar school existed in the city and the Directors of the Mechanics' Institute unwittingly met this need when they opened a day school for boys 'unwittingly', for their intended object was to 'fit the pupils to understand and appreciate the evening science lectures'. The London and Manchester Mechanics' Institutes also attempted to create day schools but neither succeeded in establishing a school on a permanent footing.

The establishment of schools and the provision of systematic class instruction were two useful roles for the mechanics' institutes. Of course the latter served a 'remedial function', but after mid-century it became rather less necessary to provide elementary instruction in basic subjects. A new avenue, however, had been opened up by the establishment of the examinations' scheme of the Department of Science and Art, and many mechanics' institutes were astute enough to grasp this new opportunity by organising classes approved by the Department. By 1880 the Department estimated that there were 4,000 students attending science classes at mechanics' institutes who were eligible for 'payment by results'. The aid was, of course, given to the teachers engaged in the classes. Of significance was the fact that out of 4,000 students some 1,000 were in attendance during the day and it requires little imagination to realise that in an era without 'day-release' few of these were mechanics. The insistence on 'evening classes' was the undoing of English education in the nineteenth century; a visiting American Professor from the Massachusetts Institute of Technology observed while on a visit to England in 1900: 'These night-schools are so common that they have undermined the influence of the day-schools.'[11] It cannot be denied that to begin with mechanics' institutes had a spectacular success and with the waning popularity of public lectures, and the transfer of their role as pioneers of libraries and museums to local authorities, many of them adapted by creating schools and forming science classes with outside bodies, while others which did not were forced to close. Eventually these roles, too, were absorbed by the local authorities, but some institutes survived, often under other names such as technical institutes and colleges. Thus the mechanics' institutes at Manchester, Glasgow and Edinburgh have survived as technological universities and that at Liverpool maintained a tradition of providing good secondary school education for bright working-class boys and girls.

Were mechanics' institutes what was really wanted by the working classes? They certainly met many of the needs. The principal aim was the 'instruction of the members in the principles of the arts they practise and in the various branches of science' with a view to stimulating invention and making workmen more efficient. Ironically the British workman was admired for his skills throughout the nineteenth century and was considered to be superior to his continental counterpart. This, however, had little to do with theoretical training or knowledge of science, for in this respect several of the continental countries were superior.

Viewed strictly in economic terms what England needed was trained manpower. Although mechanics' institutes with their science classes contributed some small measure to this they were not part of a cohesive scheme based on clearly defined aims and objectives. Perhaps the fault for this cannot be placed on the shoulders of the founders of the institutes. It was said of Birkbeck that he was sincerely devoted to the cause of working-class education, as no doubt many other founders were. Possibly their energies and drive would have been more usefully employed had they been channelled into creating pressure groups to demand suitable and appropriate government sponsored education for the working classes. It is to be wondered what it was about mechanics' institutes that appealed so greatly to the manufacturing and commercial middle classes who founded and supported them with such beneficence. The income of the Liverpool Mechanics' Institution in 1839 was £4,000, and large donations were given by several individuals; the Liverpool School of Science, thirty years later, stumbled on from one financial crisis to another, receiving paltry support from merchants and industrialists. Technical education later in the century never attained the grip on the popular imagination that mechanics' institutes had in the earlier part of the century. The very success and popularity of the mechanics' institute movement tended to divert attention from the shortcomings of English technical education.

State action: the Department of Science and Art

State action was indicated in the Queen's Speech from the Throne on 11 November 1852, in which a comprehensive scheme for art and science was promised. A Division of Science was added to the already existing Department of Practical Art to form a new Department of Science and Art. The principal object of the Science and Art Department was to encourage the teaching of the applied sciences by means of museums, science schools, public examinations, payment of grants according to results and the preparation of scientific examples. In the opinion of Henry Cole, first Secretary of the Department of Art (after 1858 sole Secretary of the Department of Science and Art), 'the work thus done is mainly done by the public itself on a self-supporting basis as far as possible, whilst the state avoids the error of continental systems, of taking the principal and dominant part in education'.[12]

The Science Division of the Department began by 'recognising' certain existing 'schools of science or trade' which were already endowed by a patron or a charitable trust, and granted aid to them. Such institutions consisted of a handful of navigation schools and trade schools and this first attempt at funding scientific instruction was not particularly successful. By 1859, apart from the navigation schools, classes aided by the Department were to be found only at Aberdeen, Bath, Bristol, and Wigan. In that year the Department altered its tactics and in a Minute proposed that: 'Any school or science classes existing or about to be established and approved by the Department may apply through its managers for a certified teacher in the following branches of science: I Practical and descriptive geometry; II Physics; III Chemistry; IV Geology and mineralogy; V Natural History.' Additional subjects were added from time to time and eventually they numbered twenty-five. 'Managers' could be a School Board (after 1870), the governing body of an endowed school, or an *ad hoc* committee formed for the specific purpose of superintending and managing a school or class to be aided by grants from the Department of Science and Art. The managers were obliged to appoint a secretary and provide suitable premises and apparatus, though the Department contributed 50 per cent of the cost of apparatus. The aid took the form of payment by results to teachers: 'The bonuses offered for giving science instruction shall not be paid until the results have been demonstrated.' Persons suitably qualified to teach the Department's science subjects were at a premium, and to create the necessary teaching body the Department held its own examination for those intending to teach in its classes. A year later the Department agreed to grant teaching certificates to students without their having to sit qualifying examinations, instead a pass in the Advanced or Honours Stage in their examinations being sufficient to qualify them to become a teacher. This meant that an individual could be a student one year and a teacher of the same subject in the following year.

The essence of the Department's scheme was that it enabled the formation of the local management committees (of no less than five responsible persons) under a chairman and secretary to arrange premises for the conducting of science classes. The cost of providing suitable premises and of the heating, lighting and cleaning of such premises, was borne partly by student fees, but mainly by the managers themselves. The local committees were also responsible for the books and apparatus and for conducting the examinations on the results of which the payments to teachers were to be made. The new scheme was intended to create 'a system of spreading science from below upwards'.[13] The central philosophy behind it was revealed in the Minute of 1859 which stated that: 'It is to be hoped that a system of science instruction will grow up among the industrial classes which shall entail the least possible cost and interference on the part of the State.' The scheme was to be mainly for the benefit of the artisan, who was entitled to attend the classes without payment of fees. It entailed minimal cost for the central government which wanted to be involved as little as possible, the emphasis being on local initiative.

The Department of Science and Art owed its origins to the growing awareness of the possible danger of England losing its industrial supremacy, and to the consequent belief that this might be brought about by the absence of any effective system of technical education for the industrial artisan. To what extent did the Department meet the need of the artisan? The definition of artisan was laid down in the annual reports of the Department. In 1865, for example, artisans included 'those in receipt of weekly wages or who support themselves by manual labour or their children; those paid at longer intervals than a week but also support themselves by manual labour; small shopkeepers, small tradesmen, village carpenters and policemen; and clerks and shopmen who cannot afford the fee of a middle-class parent'. If, however, a student fell into any of the above classes yet earned £200 a year then the teacher was not eligible for payment on account of that student. This financial limit was raised progressively as the century wore on, and by 1899 the position at the Liverpool School of Science was that nearly two-thirds of the students were in the artisan or 'government student' category; the remainder, which included clerks and shopkeepers, were mainly teachers or pupil teachers.

In the difficult times that mechanics' institutes faced at mid-century in seeking a new role, the emergence of the Department of Science and Art seemed a happy augury of better times for after 1859 the way was open for mechanics' institutes to cooperate effectively with the Department. The years of patient groundwork with elementary classes in science could now bear fruit, for it became advantageous for mechanics' institutes to organise classes in collaboration with the Department.

By 1865 of ninety-four centres running the Department's classes no fewer than forty per cent were mechanics' institutes and over sixty per cent of the pupils under instruction were attending institutes (see table 4.1). The number of mechanics' institutes working with the Department reached a peak around 1885, thereafter declining. Many of them ceased to exist, while others changed their titles and functions and could no longer be considered as mechanics' institutes. Not all the institutes which joined at an early date are found in later annual returns of the Department; either they no longer participated or they had closed. Many of the institutes which were generally recognised to be among the foremost in the country were found to have large numbers under instruction in the Department's classes and continued to have throughout the period; these included Burnley, Crewe, Huddersfield, Leeds, Liverpool, Manchester, Newcastle upon Tyne and Stalybridge. During the period to the end of the century no fewer than 180 institutes cooperated at one time or another. Considering the very rapid rate at which mechanics' institutes went out of existence in the second half of the century a substantial proportion of institutes therefore collaborated with the Department.

In 1879 there were seventy mechanics' institutes which ran classes in conjunction with the Department of Science and Art. The most popular subjects studied were mathematics and chemistry, enrolments being 1,498 and 1,425 respectively. Enrolments for magnetism and electricity (1,275) and machine construction and drawing (1,128) were almost equally high. Those for applied mechanics, steam and mining, on the other hand, were disappointingly low – 665, 634 and 92 respectively. The demand it seems was in the pure sciences, applied sciences not having nearly as great a support. One can merely speculate as to whether these enrolment figures, favourable to the pure sciences, reflect the significant proportion of teachers and pupil-teachers in attendance at the classes.

Table 4.1 Collaboration between mechanics' institutes and the Department of Science and Art

Year	No. of Department centres in existence	No. of Department centres which were mechanics' institutes	%	No. of pupils under instruction at Dept. centres	No. of pupils under instruction at mechanics' institutes centres	%
1864	94	35	40	1,500	1,140	6
1875	1,336	90	7	48,546	3,327	6
1880	1,299	69	5	59,519	5,232	8
1885	1,268	101	7	56,777	6,017	11
1890	2,063	72	3	133,821	5,951	5
1899	2,027	40	2	138,370	2,992	2

Table 4.2 Class centres aided by the Department of Science and Art 1880 (England and Wales)

Schools		Adult/Artisan centres	
Board schools	152	Mechanics' institutes	70
Schools (various)	140	Schools of science/ Schools of science and art	60
Church of England/ Roman Catholic	86	Institutes (other)	35
National schools	80	Works' schools	20
British schools	49	Working men's club/ institute/hall/college	18
Wesleyan	41	Schools of art	14
Grammar schools	37	Cooperative rooms/hall	13
Colleges or collegiate schools	27	Literary institutes	10
Other middle class schools	19	Town halls	8
Congregational	8	Free libraries	8
Baptist schools	7	Museums	6
Methodist schools	5	Atheneums	5
Orphan schools	4	Miners' institutes	4
Sunday schools	3	Schools of science and art and literary institutes	3
Presbyterian schools	3	Literary and scientific institutes	3
		Royal Institutions	3
		Equitable pioneer rooms	3
		Temperance halls	3
		Science schools	3
		Science and art institutes	2
		Technical schools	2
		Mutual improvement societies	2
		Railway and literary institutes	1
		Polytechnic institute	1
		Trade and mining school	1
		Agricultural school	1
		Other	124
Total	661		423

Table 4.3 Distribution of Department of Science and Art students and centres among counties 1880

County	Number of students	Students per 10,000 population	Number of centres	Centres per 100,000 population
Warwickshire	2,360	31.9	39	5.3
Lancashire	9,706	28.1	186	5.5
Northumberland	894	27.7	21	4.9
Devon	1,518	25.3	52	8.6
Leicestershire	703	21.9	10	3.1
Yorkshire	5,574	19.3	165	5.7
Cornwall	614	18.6	36	10.1
Dorset	308	16.2	10	5.5
Durham	1,387	16.0	50	5.8
Nottinghamshire	626	15.9	16	4.1
Cheshire	893	14.0	25	3.9
Worcestershire	490	12.9	24	6.3
Gloucestershire	847	12.9	23	4.0
Westmorland	80	12.5	1	1.6
Derbyshire	545	11.1	21	4.5
Hertfordshire	210	10.5	6	3.0
Northants	271	10.0	9	3.3
Wiltshire	241	9.3	10	3.8
Bedfordshire	117	9.0	4	2.6
Kent	826	8.4	21	2.1
Hampshire	482	8.2	13	2.2
Staffordshire	738	7.5	29	3.0
Oxfordshire	133	7.4	6	3.3
Berkshire	149	6.7	7	3.2
Cambridge	72	6.5	3	1.6
Norfolk	274	6.2	8	1.8
Buckinghamshire	149	6.0	4	2.2
Sussex	249	5.1	5	1.0
Huntingdonshire	30	5.0	4	6.6
Essex	286	5.0	9	1.5
Monmouthshire	94	4.5	6	2.9
Somerset	211	4.5	10	2.2
Lincolnshire	204	4.3	8	1.6
Surrey	520	3.6	16	1.1
Suffolk	128	3.5	5	1.4
Shropshire	82	3.3	6	2.4
Cumberland	123	3.0	3	1.2
Herefordshire	25	2.1	1	1.0
Middlesex	357	1.2	12	0.5
London	8,807	23.0	150	4.2
Scotland	6,128	16.2	137	4.0
Wales	1,520	11.2	59	4.2

The figures for centres other than mechanics' institutes illustrate a similar pattern. In twenty London centres the respective figures were: mathematics 650; heat, light and sound 350; chemistry 350; applied mechanics 90, and steam 700. Those for botany, animal physiology and physiography were disproportionately high. In seventeen centres in the heart of the industrial area of County Durham the total of enrolments for the applied sciences was 270 as compared to 467 in the pure sciences. In practical terms, therefore, much of the investment of the Department was directed not at technical education but at correcting the deficiencies in basic scientific education in the secondary schools.

After a slow beginning the Department's scheme met with considerable success as local bodies of one kind or another joined in the programme. In the decade after 1865 there was a remarkable jump in the number of centres at which classes were held—from 94 to 1,336. Classes were held in schools of every description, in training colleges, lyceums and atheneums, literary and scientific institutes, and 'schools of science'. A measure of the success of the Department is revealed in the statistics presented in its annual reports. Tables 4.2 and 4.3 represent an analysis of the year 1880.

Science classes aided by the Department were held in a wide variety of centres and Table 4.2 indicates that in 1880 some three-fifths of these were schools of one kind or another. Although many of the students attending school centres would have been artisans it is likely that such centres would have mainly attracted a different type of student, in particular teachers or pupil-teachers. Although the numbers given in Table 4.2 for 'school' centres and 'adult or artisan' centres cannot be taken to strictly represent the proportion of middle class and artisan students they do, nevertheless, suggest the possibility that artisans may have represented a much smaller proportion of the student population than was generally assumed.

Many industrial works took the initiative in forming their own evening schools. At Luton, for example, one engineering works ran its own school and other examples of these were: Staveley 'Works Boys School' at Barrow Hill, Derbyshire; 'Colliery School' at Tibshelf, Derbyshire; Tudhoe 'Colliery School', Co. Durham; 'Telegraphists' School, GPO, Aldersgate, London; Messrs Maudslay, Sons and Field's School Room; 'Copper Works School', Burry Port; Llynvi Ironworks School, Maesteg; Hendy Tinplate Works School, Swansea. In Northumberland 'works schools' were especially common, there being seven in all. There were mechanics' institutes and literary institutes whose members were exclusively railway employees; for example, there was a Great Western Mechanics' Institute at Stratford. The Royal Arsenal at Woolwich, too, had its own mechanics' institute.

The philosophy underlying the formation of the Department of Science and Art was that of local initiative based on the belief that the government should not do for the people what the people ought to do for themselves. The consequences of this policy are revealed in Table 4.3 which gives the distribution of students and centres among the counties in 1880. The table illustrates inequalities in provision between one part of the country and another. A student in Warwickshire was three times as likely to be in a science class as one in the nearby county of Derbyshire and ten times as likely as a student in Surrey. This cannot be entirely attributable to a disparity in the number of centres for Warwickshire and Derbyshire, for in relation to population they had a similar provision of centres. The reasons might have been related rather to the nature of the centres provided, or perhaps to the efforts made by the sponsors to attract students. Whatever the causes it cannot be denied that there were wide discrepancies in student enrolment from one area to another. Column 4 in Table 4.3 also indicates the paucity of provision.

The Department's Annual Report for 1880 indicates that in that year there were 59,519 students under instruction; the total amount paid to teachers 'on results' was £38,045 or 12s 10d per student. The annual expenditure of the Department was £318,125 but this included the financing of museums of the Geological Survey, and grants to the Royal Zoological Society. Of the amount spent directly on science instruction, £41,177 was spent on aid to schools of science and art, £34,083 on public elementary schools and £20,521 on artisans attending night classes, giving a total of £95,781. Even assuming, therefore, that all the science classes of the Department were concerned with technical education, which was far from being the case, the total national expenditure by the central government on technical education was £95,781 or 0.0095 per cent of the national income in that year. According to Hipwell the Department earned the epitaph appropriate for all educational institutions in the nineteenth century, namely, that it 'did great work in the face of great odds'. It 'had to spread the study of science among a people, a vast number of whom were illiterates, with limited financial resources'. It also 'sowed the seeds of scientific education for the people' and 'provided indirectly almost the entire secondary education for the masses for thirty years'.[14]

Private and local initiatives in technical education

The government made its first intervention in technical education with the setting up of the Department of Science and Art. Nearly forty years elapsed before further significant action was taken. Meanwhile, through-out the country numerous individuals, either separately or collectively, were making very considerable contributions to the advance of technical instruction. Three examples have been chosen to illustrate this: the City and Guilds of London Institute, the Whitworth Scholarships, and private technical schools in Liverpool.

In London feeling was growing during the 1870s that the wealth of the ancient guilds was not being put to effective use. One of the original purposes of these foundations had been the instruction of the apprentice in his craft and the view was that the ample funds of the guilds could effect substantial improvements in technical education. On 21 July 1873 the Prince of Wales conferred with the representatives on the best ways in which the City Companies could aid technical education. In the same year J. F. D. Donnelly, an Inspector of the Department of Science and Art, advised the Lord Mayor that the best help the companies could give would be to endow scholarships and bursaries at provincial colleges and to assist in the establishment of chairs and laboratories. While this recommendation was put into effect a sum of £10,000 was also set aside for a new technical college in the City itself. A working party of the guilds under the chairmanship of Lord Selborne suggested in 1874 that a sum of £20,000 be spent on technical education; at the same time it drew up a constitution for a proposed City and Guilds of London Institute.

At a meeting of the City of London Livery Companies at the Mansion House in 1876, it was resolved 'that it is desirable that the attention of the Livery Companies be directed to the promotion of education not only in the Metropolis but throughout the country, and especially to technical education, with the view of educating young artisans and others in the scientific and artistic branches of their trades'.[15] The City and Guilds of London Institute for the Advancement of Technical Education was formally inaugurated on 11 November 1878, with the Prince of Wales as President.

The City and Guilds began by taking over in 1879 the technological examinations of the Society of Arts and introducing a system of payment-by-results along the same lines as the Department of Science and Art. The Guilds' classes were for persons engaged in industrial operations: artisans, apprentices, foremen, managers and manufacturers. Students were awarded certificates and prizes on the results of examinations conducted by the City and Guilds. These were regarded as diplomas of proficiency which enabled operatives to obtain better employment and higher remuneration. Subjects initially were limited to cotton manufacture, iron and steel manufacture, and carriage building, but by 1885 the subjects included agriculture, hygiene, phonography, drawing and carpentry, alkali manufacture and the science of business. Clearly there were parallels between the Department's classes and those of the Guilds, but it was claimed that there was no overlap, for the Department's classes dealt with the scientific principles of a subject whereas the Guilds' classes dealt with technical aspects. For instance, the Department's payment-by-results scheme included inorganic chemistry whereas the Guilds' classes included alkali manufacture; likewise, the Department's classes on organic chemistry were matched by the Guilds' classes on coal tar products, oils, fats and varnishes.

The previous lack of success of the Society of Arts examinations was partly due to the fact that students had first to pass in four science subjects in the examinations of the Department of Science and Art. The City and Guilds reduced this requirement to one pass. This change, together with the introduction of payment-by-results, led to a very considerable growth in these examinations: in 1880 816 candidates offered themselves in 24 subjects, the respective figures in 1900 being 4,105 and 64, local centres increasing fourfold meanwhile. A weakness which was paralleled in the Department of Science and Art's scheme was that grants were contingent on examinations rather than on the quality of teaching and equipment. Teachers, too, were inadequately prepared, receiving little in the way of scientific instruction.

The City and Guilds did not confine itself to aiding technical classes in local centres. It had been the intention of the Livery Companies to foster a trade school at Finsbury allied to an advanced institution to be established elsewhere in London. The nucleus of a trade school already existed in the City in the form of classes in applied physics and applied chemistry. In 1881 the foundation stone of the City college – the first technical college in the country – was laid at Finsbury. This was to cater for artisans and act as a feeder for the corresponding advanced college of applied science. Day and evening schools were established at Finsbury, in workshop practice, pure and applied science, and technical subjects; evening classes were also provided in carpentry, joinery and bricklaying. The College thus broke with tradition in providing day classes which were made systematic, entry being conditional on passing an entrance examination. Many of those entering the day department were middle-class pupils on exhibitions who were preparing for advanced scientific instruction.

The site chosen for the advanced college of university status was at Exhibition Road, South Kensington. Opened in 1884, the City and Guilds contributed over 75 per cent of the cost of the Central Institution, which later became part of the Imperial College of Science and Technology. A three-year course was designed: the first year was devoted to general science, the second and third years to engineering, physics and chemistry. The curriculum was impressive; it included hydraulics, strength of materials, practical physics, electro-technology, fermentation, crystallography, oil chemistry and dye chemistry. The main purpose of the College was to produce teachers of technical subjects, but it was also intended to be of appeal to wouldbe architects, those set on a career in engineering or manufacturing and those who having already had industrial experience wished to study the sciences.

The work of the City and Guilds represented corporate and collective initiatives. Technical education in the nineteenth century was also characterised by the impressive contributions of single individuals, notable among whom was Joseph Whitworth.

In March 1868 Whitworth, a machine tool manufacturer of Manchester, wrote to the Department of Science and Art offering to endow thirty scholarships at £100 per annum for three years. His offer was accepted and he followed it up with a further endowment of sixty preliminary exhibitions at £25 per annum. Whitworth, who was born at Stockport, was apprenticed as a mechanic at an early age and later served at the Westminster workshops of Henry Maudslay (the originator of the first screw cutting machine). In 1833 Whitworth set up in Manchester as a toolmaker and by the 1860s he had become the leading machine toolmaker, being famous for his work on fine measuring and standardisation of screw threads.

The Whitworth scholarships and exhibitions were intended for the further education of young men 'in the theory and practice of mechanics and its cognate sciences, with a view to the promotion of engineering and mechanical industry in this country'. The impact and influence of this scheme were far-reaching. A study of the former pupils of the Liverpool School of Science illustrates this point. The first Whitworth scholarship to be awarded to a pupil at the School was in 1874; between then and 1883 the School gained thirteen scholarships and exhibitions. The Register of Whitworth scholars includes the names of forty Liverpool men. Among them were: H. W. McCann (1870) a pupil at the Liverpool Institute High School for Boys and later Senior Wrangler at Cambridge; J. A. Brodie (1879), an apprentice at the Mersey Docks, later the City Engineer and Associate Professor of Municipal Engineering at Liverpool University; Robert Holt (1886), later Professor of Engineering at Finsbury Technical College; John Wemyss Anderson (1891), an apprentice and later Professor of Engineering at Liverpool University; and William Thornton (1894), an apprentice and later Professor of Engineering at King's College, London.

Two other distinguished Whitworth Scholars had a significant influence on the academic and scientific life of Liverpool University. W. H. Watkinson, Professor of Engineering, had begun his career by gaining a scholarship whilst an apprentice in Glasgow workshops. Professor Hele-Shaw, the first Professor of Engineering at University College, Liverpool, had gained his scholarship as an apprentice at a Bristol shipbuilding works; this enabled him to study at the College of the West of England where he distinguished himself academically before going on to Liverpool. Such examples as these could be found throughout the country. For instance, in 1880 the chairs of engineering and of mathematics at Firth College, Newcastle College of Science, Mason College of Science and the Royal Artillery Institute were all occupied by former Whitworth scholars. Whitworth was taking on singlehanded a task which should have been appropriately undertaken by the government, namely, the provision of a national scholarship scheme.

The third example chosen illustrates that another area of urgent need was that of instruction in chemistry, particularly in view of the rapid growth of the chemical industry in the nineteenth century. Until well into the nineteenth century the value of chemistry was seen in terms of its applicability to medicine, drugs and agriculture. The pursuit of chemistry did not lead to any professional status or social acceptance and its recognition as an academic discipline was also slow to be established, despite the fact that it was taught at both Oxford and Cambridge in the eighteenth century. Opportunities for a limited amount of instruction were available; there were lectures at the Royal Institutions in London and Liverpool and in the eighteenth century there were courses at several dissenting academies in addition to the activities of numerous itinerant lecturers. Nevertheless, before the emergence of the two London colleges, King's and University, in the 1820s a formal chemical training in Britain had to be undertaken at one of the Scottish universities. Chemical knowledge was customarily attained through a medical education or apprenticeship to apothecary or druggist.

If opportunities for chemical training were hard to come by in the country as a whole, in Liverpool they were scant indeed at mid-century. Paradoxically, Liverpool had by this time become the leading centre of the 'heavy' chemical industry. Two remarkable initiatives by single individuals demonstrate the need that existed. The first of these was the formation of the College of Chemistry by Dr Sheridan Muspratt. Sheridan, the son of James Muspratt, was educated at a private school at Bootle and later went to the Andersonian Institution at Glasgow for nine months.[16] After losing £8,000 of his father's money in an ammonia soda plant he embarked on an equally disastrous visit to America attempting to sell soda ash and soda crystals, returning to England in 1842. Meanwhile, his father had met and befriended Justus von Liebig, the originator of the first organic chemistry laboratories. It was to these laboratories at Giessen University that James now sent his son to study. On gaining his PhD Sheridan returned to England to study further under Wilhelm von Hofmann at the Royal College of Chemistry in London. Sheridan, unlike his father and brothers, was a palpable failure as an industrialist but proved to have considerable teaching abilities. His experience of Liebig's and Hofmann's teaching methods no doubt influenced him in his decision to open the Liverpool College of Chemistry in a stable at the back of his house in Canning Street.

The term at the college consisted of two sessions of eighteen weeks each. Students brought their own small apparatus, reagents and gas being supplied. A good library of German and English works was provided. The fees ranged from 8 guineas (£8.40) per term for two days attendance each week to 12 guineas (£12.60) per term for six days attendance during the week. Sheridan Muspratt died in 1871 but his work was continued by others. From 1880 the college's classes qualified for grant from the Department of Science and Art and between 1880 and 1896 some seventy-five students were being taught there each year.

It was one of Sheridan's alumni, clearly impressed with the facilities offered at the College of Chemistry, who took it upon himself to invest in a similar venture. Norman Tate, the son of a clergyman, was born in Wells, Somerset, and educated there at the Chapter Grammar School. After a few years in pharmacy he came to Liverpool where he entered Muspratt's laboratory. He devoted himself to practical analysis and general chemistry, reading several papers before the Chemical Society of London and the Royal Society of Dublin.[17] He left Muspratt's College in order to join the firm of John Hutchinson, an alkali manufacturer of Widnes, where he was given charge of the various manufacturing processes and the construction and working of the chemical plant. Tate later became an independent analytical and consulting chemist acting as a middleman between merchant and buyer. The analyst crushed a sample of nut or palm kernels and granted certificates to the supplier indicating the percentage quantity of oil in the samples. Tate made his reputation as an analyst at the time of the West African trade, his speciality being oils, fats and waxes. He later gained a world monopoly on glycerine analysis for Unilever.

In 1870 Tate moved to Irwell Chambers in Old Hall Street, which he converted into a School of Technical Chemistry. Three years later he moved his school and his analytical laboratories to Hackins Hey, a typically narrow Dickensian street. Classes were held in a basement hall which survives today, between 9.30 a.m. and 5 p.m. on weekdays and 9.30 a.m. and 1 p.m. on Saturdays, lectures and laboratory facilities being also available on two evenings a week. Each student was provided with a separate bench and was supplied with chemicals, the student himself having to provide test-tubes, beakers and other apparatus. Tate's classes received recognition by the Department of Science and Art for payment-by-results, from 1870 the annual payments to Tate ranging from £18 to £73. Between 1880 and 1892 Tate received grants for a total of 1,100 students.

As in the case of Muspratt's college no records survive of the students who passed through the hands of Norman Tate and it is impossible to make an accurate assessment of the value of these institutions nor of the standards of work attained by them. It is probably not far from the truth to state that their contribution to the training of chemists on Merseyside was greater than that of any other single institution.

The emergence of a system of technical education in the final quarter of the century

The 1890s was a decade in which serious attempts were made to grapple with the problem of formalising technical education and creating for it a secure financial footing. This process really began with the setting up of the Royal Commission on Technical Instruction in 1881 under the Chairmanship of Bernhard Samuelson (later Sir) to inquire into the 'Instruction of the industrial classes of certain foreign countries in technical and other subjects, for the purpose of comparison with that of the corresponding classes in this country'. Samuelson was a Cleveland ironmaster and a Member of Parliament; the other members included Henry Roscoe, Professor of Chemistry at Owens College, Manchester, a former student under Bunsen at Heidelberg; Philip Magnus (later Sir), Director and Secretary of the City and Guilds Institute; Swire Smith, a woollen manufacturer; John Slagg, a cotton magnate and Member of Parliament, and William Woodall, a potter and Member of Parliament.

In its Report[18] the Commission reiterated many of the recommendations of the earlier Taunton and Devonshire Commissions with regard to the schools. Science instruction, it stated, should be greatly increased in the endowed secondary schools and the teacher training colleges. Its recommendations on the whole were not very radical and the Report tended to be over-complimentary to the British system though *The Times* was of the view that 'a serious commencement has been made of a national edifice of technical education'. While it conceded that most of the cost of higher technical education abroad was borne by the state, it adopted a negative attitude to state intervention: 'It will be necessary to look, in the main, to local resources for any large addition to the funds required for the further development of technical instruction in this country.'[19] One positive outcome of the Samuelson Commission was the creation in 1887 of the National Association for the Promotion of Technical Education (it later added 'secondary' to its title). This was a timely pressure group which had prestigious secretaries in Roscoe and Arthur Acland MP.

The creation of new county councils in 1888 made possible the Technical Instruction Act of 1889 (and its amending Act of 1891), by which local authorities were enabled to raise a penny rate in support of technical instruction.[20] This Act was followed in 1890 by the Local Taxation (Customs and Excise) Act, by which certain sums of money out of customs and excise duties were allocated to local authorities either to relieve the rates, or, following Acland's suggestion in the House, to subsidise technical education. Most authorities chose originally the former but gradually the amount spent on technical instruction increased until by 1898 out of this 'whisky money' (as it was called), which totalled £807,000, no less than £740,000 was being spent on education.[21]

Following the 1891 Act local technical instruction committees were made responsible for the distribution of the money raised under the Technical Instruction Act and for the 'whisky money'. Technical education was now being sponsored by more than one local agency, as the school boards set up by the 1870 Education Act, though constitutionally responsible for elementary education only, had moved into the secondary and technical fields. The school boards acted under the guidance of the central Education Department whereas the technical instruction committees, which frequently regarded themselves as guardians of both technical and secondary education, worked under the aegis of the Department of Science and Art at South Kensington. The activities of these two bodies inevitably overlapped and the confusion created was not resolved until the passing of the Education Act of 1902. This Act abolished the school boards and the technical instruction committees and put all forms of national education in the hands of the county councils and county borough councils. The new LEAs thus created appointed their own sub-committees to be responsible for the various sectors of education – elementary, secondary and technical.

According to the Act of 1889 'technical instruction' was defined as: 'instruction in the principles of science and art as applied to industries or employment ... but not to teaching the practice of any Trade or Industry or Employment'. And the chief aim of the Act was to 'especially benefit artisans, or in other words all who have left the Day Schools ...

for the local rate shall apply to persons who are not receiving instruction in the Obligatory or Standard subjects at an elementary school'.

Local authorities were reluctant to use the new powers given to them by the Act in order to raise the rates; they relied instead on the funds made available by the Local Taxation Act. For instance, between 1890 and 1896 in Liverpool £95,386 of the whisky money was spent on technical education, whereas only £10,361 was spent from the rates. In the same period Bootle spent £10,272 of the whisky money on technical education, but did not levy the penny rate. St Helens likewise did not impose the increased rate but spent £6,593 on technical education. An analysis of the returns furnished to the Department of Science and Art in 1894 reveals that of some 108 county councils and county boroughs less than a dozen were raising money under the terms of the Technical Instruction Act for spending on technical and manual instruction; the total income raised from this source was a mere £20,000.[22]

The task facing any newly appointed technical instruction committee was not easy. It was a formidable problem being responsible for financing technical education in relation to the confused picture of technical education then prevailing. A quarter of a century later a special sub-committee of the Liverpool Education Committee appointed in 1915 continued to find the matter of technical education 'a peculiarly complex and difficult one to deal with'. The reason for this in its view was

largely due to the fact that technical education stands aloof and insulated, in a singular way, from other branches of education. . . . It occurred to the Committee that its separated position may not be unconnected with the haphazard manner in which it commenced to take formal shape. Broadly, it may be said that, until the Technical Instruction Act of 1889 came into existence, the subject of technical education was being more or less experimented with. A division in Parliament set free from its designed purpose a certain sum of money and produced something of a quandary as to how the money should be used. As though by a happy thought, it was decided that the money thus unexpectedly available should be devoted to the development of technical education. The casual nature of its genesis, in its later form, seems to have marked and characterised technical education from that time on.[23]

At the time of the Technical Instruction Act the Department of Science and Art was made the final court of appeal as to what constituted technical instruction, and it had the right to decide whether any particular form of instruction came within the scope of the Act. All the twenty-five subjects appearing in the Department's regulations as being eligible for payment-by-results awards came within the meaning of the term. But the Liverpool Technical Instruction Committee in 1891 took upon itself a much broader definition of technical education. It drew up a seven-point scheme which included teacher training and instruction in manual subjects, art, cookery and domestic science. The creation of an 'educational ladder', too, that would enable pupils to pass from the elementary school through to the upper levels of education received high priority. The Committee immediately cleared with the Department its right to finance subjects not included in the Directory of the Department. Permission was given by the Department for the Committee to award grants for an extended list of subjects which ranged from commercial arithmetic and woodwork to fuel technology; the list also included the science and art of teaching, political economy, sanitary science, ship's carpentry and joinery, soap manufacture, telegraphy, electro-metallurgy and the science of oils and fats.

As soon as the Liverpool Technical Instruction Committee was constituted requests for aid came in from all quarters: the Industrial School, the Academy of Arts, the Orphan Boys' Asylum, the Navigation School, the Deaf and Dumb School, the Sanitary School, the Training School of Cookery. For the session 1892–93 the Committee was responsible for the disbursement of £18,495 granted to it by the City Council for the support of technical education. In distributing this money the Committee had a very liberal view of 'technical' education: the *major* portion, £4,275, was given to the Museums and Libraries Sub-committee of the City Council; the University College benefited to the extent of £1,750, mainly for physics, chemistry and engineering; the secondary schools of the City received £1,940 for science instruction; the Nautical College was given £1,535, School of Art £250 and the 'organised' science schools £300; classes for women and girls were supported to the extent of £385, teacher training by £85 and commercial classes by £173, a sum of £700 was set aside for evening continuation classes and £181 for a scholarship scheme. Most of the activities covered by the above organisations and recipients were within the fields of secondary or commercial or even higher education. The only sum which could be said to be devoted to activities falling within a stricter definition of technical education was £2,100 for 'technical instruction centres for workmen'.

The diversity of the requests from institutions appealing for support from the Technical Instruction Committee illustrates the complexity of the task facing it. There were no clear boundaries between technical education, commercial and higher education, thus the burden of helping to maintain the variety of organisations in these fields now fell on the shoulders of the Committee. Few requests for support were turned down and its liberal interpretation of technical education inevitably laid it open to criticism. One of its critics was Sir Arthur Forwood, MP, a former Mayor of Liverpool. Forwood had claimed in the House of Commons that money allocated to technical instruction committees was being wasted. When challenged later by Edward Willink, Chairman of the Liverpool Committee, Forwood replied that it was not only Liverpool that he was referring to. He wrote to Edward Willink from the House of Commons on 24 April 1896:

When I quoted an example of the frittering away of sums available for technical education our Liverpool Council was undoubtedly in my mind, although they are by no means alone in their policy of devoting money to purposes for which it was never intended.

. . . your Committee have been allocating the funds at their disposal to what may be termed secondary education rather than to technical instruction. I believe the intention of the legislature was to seek to develop the intelligence and skill of the handicraftsmen of the nation, so that in our manufactures and industries we should be able to compete in a more satisfactory manner with Continental countries, where, for years past, much training has been provided.

I do not think that for the present at any rate the country need be called upon to provide instruction in vocal or instrumental music, whilst algebra and higher mathematics, French and German are what is most needed with a view to increasing the quality of production of the engineer or the worker in textile fabrics to enable them better to withstand the keen and daily increasing competition in other countries.

Generally, I would add that those intended to be benefited by the technical instruction grants were the children of working men, or of those earning weekly wages.[24]

In view of the imprecise definition of 'technical education' it was inevitable that money would be allocated for purposes other than originally intended. It was characteristic of the way in which things were allowed to drift; all too often in the nineteenth century it was felt that problems would be solved by allocation of sums of money, often derisory sums, by central government and municipal authorities. Having said this there is no denying that the injection of whisky money was timely and life-saving for a number of institutions later to become technical colleges. Nowhere is this more vividly demonstrated than in the fortunes of the Liverpool School of Science. The early years of the School's existence, indeed, until the Technical Instruction Act, were financially precarious. It consequently turned with great relief to the Technical Instruction Committee for support. Grants were forthcoming from that body, but more importantly it underwrote the annual deficits of the School. This measure of financial support led to a greater stability and healthy outlook in the School.

The trials and tribulations of the Liverpool School of Science provides an excellent illustration of the difficulties encountered by early technical colleges. Founded with high hopes by a group of prominent citizens in 1861 to provide scientific and technical instruction for all classes but 'particularly the artisan class', it was constantly beset by acute problems of inadequate finance and accommodation. The main sources of income were annual subscriptions and donations by individuals. At its opening in 1861 over £3,000 had been raised, but after the purchase of fittings and apparatus what was left provided an annual income of a mere £137 a year. Few individuals contributed donations which during the period 1861–99 averaged some £40 a year; they fluctuated from year to year and could not be relied on as a source of steady income. Consequently the School was constantly in debt, coming near to closing on several occasions.

Early enthusiasm for the School soon waned, the numbers of students quickly fell off and debts accumulated, added to which in 1867 the sole teacher died. The prospects were not promising:

The future career of the School was not encouraging and as time lent distance to the first impulses, the public interest brought with it a statement of falling off of students whilst the debt of the School was steadily increasing. It was in 1866, when there were only 28 students and a considerable debt, that it was feared that the School would have to close – but after several committee meetings it was decided to make a further effort – and by careful managements and securing the hearty cooperation of both teachers and students the School had not looked back though always in debt, and greatly in need of means for further development, in addition to the payment of existing liabilities.[25]

The financial difficulties faced by the School were experienced by similar institutions which were forced to be self-supporting. Sir Philip Magnus, speaking at the School Prize Day in 1890, emphasised the fact that abroad such classes were supported by government, or by societies, chambers of commerce and municipalities, whereas in England they

depended on private benevolence, supplemented by the aid received as 'payment on results' from the Department of Science and Art and from the City and Guilds. Now it often happens that, although private benevolence is capable of initiating and launching an educational institution the interest flags after a time, some other body calls for public benevolence and the institution languishes. This, I fear, is the case with many of the provincial classes, which carry on from year to year a hand-to-mouth existence, not knowing where they are to provide the funds to pay their teachers' salaries and expenses.[26]

The title of 'School' adopted by the Committee was something of a misnomer, for after a time the classes were not confined to a single building or even a related group of buildings. The School owed its existence to the gift of a Free Library and Museum in 1857. This donation by Sir William Brown prompted a group of leading citizens to have a School of Science attached to the building. While the first classes were held in the Free Library others were quickly started elsewhere, and eventually classes were held in numerous centres scattered throughout the City; these included such unsuitable premises as the YMCA and the Sailors' Home. A total lack of laboratory facilities added to the problem of insufficient and inappropriate accommodation.

The arrangement of scattered classes considerably hampered the development of the work of the School; it was constantly alluded to in the reports of the Inspectors of the Department of Science and Art.

Without aid from the Corporation or from the government, however, the erection of a large single building would have been a great burden on the few public-spirited citizens who were responsible for its support. It is not surprising that centrally situated, purpose-built premises were not established until 1901.

Accommodation problems frequently led to the suspension or closure of classes. Both teachers and students were further hampered by the acute shortage of the most elementary kinds of apparatus and equipment, teachers constantly requesting such simple objects as magnets, glass tubes, sealing wax and files in their annual reports. The poor standard of the student entrants did not help either. Until the end of the century the elementary and secondary schools failed to fit students for any advanced instruction in scientific and technical work with the result that the School had to concentrate its efforts on elementary work; even as late as 1904 only 155 class entries out of 1,005 were above the elementary standard of the Department of Science and Art. Student unpreparedness applied particularly to the artisans for whom attendance imposed great strain, classes normally being held in the evenings and often not starting until 8.00 or 8.30 p.m.; they frequently fell asleep at their desks after long hours at work.

Uncertainty regarding the aim and purpose of technical education led to a lack of cohesiveness in the programme of courses. Inspectors remarked on the 'haphazard' unconnected nature of the classes and in 1909 described the School's provision as a 'heterogeneous swarm of more or less independent classes'. Earlier, in 1902, a Special Sub-committee set up by the Education Committee of the local authority seriously questioned the work being done; 'it appears doubtful' it reported 'whether some of the subjects taught are really within the scope of what the Education Committee understand as technical education'.

Such was the School of Science that catered for a diversity of students: foremen, analysts at chemical works, artificers at local foundries, draughtsmen, joiners, plumbers, gas engineers, lithographers, board school teachers, pupil teachers, ship-wrights, telegraphists, water engineers. It was by no means worse than the majority of such embryonic technical colleges throughout the country, for in the opinion of the Samuelson Commission, 'probably in no City in the Kingdom are these classes more flourishing or doing better work than in Liverpool'.

Many of the difficulties faced by the Liverpool School of Science were common to other similar bodies elsewhere during the nineteenth century. One unique feature of the Liverpool scene not shared by others was that the mechanics' institute was not the precursor of the technical college. In Liverpool the mechanics' institution, which was in competition with the School of Science as far as evening class provision was concerned, developed differently. Of its many initiatives it was the day school for boys which survived (as the Liverpool Institute High School for Boys, the leading boys' school in the City). This was clearly the result of not having an endowed grammar school, a gap which the Directors of the Mechanics' Institution filled so admirably. In other cities, Manchester, Bradford, Salford and Keighley, it was the mechanics' institute which formed the early nucleus of a technical college. This was the pattern in many parts of the country, particularly in the North of England.

Several of the mechanics' institutes were more fortunate, too, in gaining support from outside sources. Manchester Mechanics' Institute, for instance, was heavily in debt in the 1870s, but was rescued partly by the intervention of the City and Guilds of London Institute, which offered £200 a year for six years on condition that the Mechanics' Institute became a technical school. With this support and subscriptions by local firms a new Municipal Technical School was opened in 1883. At Bradford, likewise, a stimulus to the movement for a local technical college was a grant of £3,500 to the Mechanics' Institute for new buildings and an annual grant of £500 from the Clothworkers' Company of London, whereas at Oldham the School of Science and Art was well provided for by the Platt family.

But in other respects technical colleges suffered from the same handicaps as did the Liverpool School of Science: too much work was of an elementary character; studies were not systematic enough— provision consisted of specific classes rather than systematic courses; above all the stress on evening work with all its drawbacks was a handicap to students. Although most of the technical schools offered day courses numbers attending these were small, whereas the evening classes attracted clerks, warehousemen, shop assistants, mechanics and other kinds of workmen. Figures collected by the National Association for the Promotion of Technical and Secondary Education in 1889 revealed the disparity between day and evening attendance; day and evening enrolments at Bradford Technical College were 314 and 1,337 respectively and at Keighley Technical College 214 and 983 respectively. Evening class provision included elementary classes, commercial classes, Department of Science and Art classes and City and Guilds classes; they were offered on a piecemeal basis and not as connected units of a planned course of study.

Technical education abroad

In his Report[27] to the London County Council, J. C. Smail, Organiser of Trade Schools for Boys, after a visit to France and Germany in 1914, defined technical education in terms of three levels: *lower technical education*, intended for those with an elementary education only or for those engaged in or about to be engaged in trades, the object of this education being to train capable workmen; *middle technical education* for those with a more advanced general education or for those who had already had some trade or workshop experience, the object being to train draughtsmen, designers and foremen; and *higher technical education* for those with a thorough secondary education who were to become technical experts and managers.

It is clear from the foregoing that no such clear lines of demarcation existed in practice in the English system. Little regard was paid to higher technical education on a systematic basis until the emergence of the civic university colleges in the final quarter of the nineteenth century. Germany, on the other hand, had created a separate institution for higher technical education in the form of technical high schools. A discussion of the relative merits of these and the engineering faculties of universities is more appropriate to the following chapter.

It was comparatively easy for Smail to describe German technical education in these three neat compartments for 'Germany possessed a national organisation with definite national objectives'. In Britain Smail found overlapping between the three levels of education; often the same institution attempted to attain all three objectives within its programme. Germany systematically dealt with each problem separately and gave particular attention to the training of teachers for technical work and to the problem of apprenticeship. In England the system of apprenticeship left much to be desired; it had been allowed to lapse into 'one of the most unsatisfactory of vexed questions'. In Germany it was tackled by statute; after leaving school the apprentice was obliged to attend continuation classes for up to nine hours a week, the employer being responsible for his regular attendance on pain of fine. After some years of trade experience the apprentice could enter day trade schools which served the building and engineering industries. These provided five half-yearly courses which could be taken successively or interspersed with intervals—a 'sandwich' system. (Such sandwich schemes were hardly known in England.) These trade schools were scattered widely all over the country and the students found no difficulty in obtaining posts on leaving.

In England, according to Smail,

schemes which require five to seven years are generally drafted to secure a limitation in entry to the trade. The apprentice is not always placed in charge of someone competent and willing. Boys are allowed to pick up the technology of their trade as they please. The number who do this seriously from the beginning of their apprenticeship is extremely small. . . . The realisation of lost opportunities frequently comes at eighteen to nineteen years of age. . . . To sum up it may be said that the English system of single subjects and freedom of choice of subjects for young students has led to excessive expenditure for mediocre results, excessive equipment, discouragement of teachers, falling away of students and a want of belief in education on the part of employers. Against this must be set the great help that has been afforded to individual students of ability and perseverance, although it is probable that these would have profited equally by a more definitely organised curriculum.

Middle technical education was considered to be very important in

Germany. This was essentially day study on a systematic basis, although evening and Sunday classes were available. The view in Germany was that, though evening class instruction 'is only of limited value . . . attendance at full-time day courses is regarded as necessary if such training is to be secured as will enable a worker to proceed to a higher grade of employment'. In England the day system was not well established, evening classes being the norm:

The attitude of education authorities in Britain in providing evening classes with an object probably more philanthropic than patriotic has led to a mixture of types of students with a variety of aims and with widely varying standards of attainments. A generation of freedom of choice of subjects – often used capriciously and from alternative motives of trade advancement, general information or hobbies – combined with a possibility of dropping a subject at any moment when circumstances or mood might render its continuance doubtful has not been a good preparation for sounder methods.

Smail further backed up his strictures on the ineffectiveness of evening study by providing figures for Berlin and London and concluded:

The significance of these figures lies not only in the fact that more individuals are being educated in Germany, but that those in Berlin, who are being educated at approximately the same cost per head as those in London, are receiving from 4 to 5 times as much education. In London the number of student hours per enrolment per session amounts to 45.7 (evening school only); in Berlin about 90 per cent of attendance is secured for six hours per week over a session of 40 weeks, or an effective 216 hours per session per enrolment, a ratio of nearly 5·1 in favour of the Berlin student.[28]

A deputation from the Technical Instruction Committee of the City of Manchester which visited Austria and Germany in 1897 was likewise impressed by the zeal and thoroughness with which the governments of those countries supplied the resources for technical training. They were particularly interested in textile schools, with a view to incorporating one in the new Municipal Technical School then being built in Manchester. At Crefeld they visited the Textile School built by the Prussian Government. This included a Dyeing and Finishing Department

in accordance with the practice abroad which is to equip their finishing schools on a scale approaching the works themselves so as to give students trained in them a practical and effective knowledge of the processes employed. . . . Indeed it is plain that the better education of the dyer is a matter of far more vital moment in Manchester than it can possibly be in Crefeld; and yet the means of securing it here on an adequate and effective scale can scarcely be said to exist.

The lesson they took back with them was that:

It is to variety and excellence in respect of workmanship, colour and design that Lancashire must look to maintain and increase its supremacy and reputation as a manufacturing centre. . . . It is interesting to note with what discrimination and judgement that the educational authorities of Prussia pursue their object in this regard.[29]

Smail summed up the different approaches and attitudes between England and Germany: 'Germany', he said, 'has come to believe that workshop training alone is insufficient to make a sound industrial training; it must be reinforced by adequate education specialised to trades.' There was a difference of ideals — Germany was aiming at benefiting the nation by training all the workers through specialised courses whereas in contrast 'Britain is organised so that individuals may secure what they think best for their own advancement'.[30]

Smail's views on technical education found support in the Report of a Canadian Royal Commission on Industrial Training and Technical Education which had also been studying technical education on the Continent that same year. Its main conclusion was that:

In France, Germany, Switzerland and the United States, the power and influence of technical education of the highest types appeared to be greater than in the United Kingdom or Canada. In England the opinion most frequently heard was to the effect that hereafter the industries must somehow secure the services of more men of the highest scientific attainments with thorough technical training, or her manufacturers and merchants will not be able to hold their own against foreign competition.[31]

Chapter 5

Science and higher education

Higher education in the first half of the nineteenth century

In 1830 there appeared a controversial work by a Cambridge mathematician, Charles Babbage (1792–1871). Babbage invented the principle of the automatic computer and was instrumental in founding the British Association for the Advancement of Science and other scientific societies; his book *Reflections on the Decline of Science* referred to a state of affairs which had existed for over half a century. Its publication was precipitated by administrative malpractices in the Royal Society, ruled at that time by a coterie of dilettantes. Babbage gave no real indication of the state of science generally, but his book helped to air the grievances of those who were concerned at the absence of scientific institutions and the neglect of scientific instruction in higher institutions of learning. His contention was that in England the pursuit of science did not constitute a distinct profession. Trained for the law, the Church and medicine, English scientists with few exceptions were largely amateurs devoting the greater part of their time to their chosen professions.

It was to Scotland that England looked for the production of the 'professional' scientist. Scotland in the eighteenth century had developed a distinctive educational system of its own; at the age of fifteen students entered university for four years of a general education which included philosophy, classics and science. After this general education they undertook a specialist training. England owed much to the products of the Scottish universities in the fields of medicine, science and engineering throughout the nineteenth century. Professor Morgan, in an address entitled 'Medical education at the universities' in 1875, pointed out that of 3,241 graduates in medicine practising in England in 1875 no fewer than 2,829 (87 per cent) were products of the Scottish universities. In contrast those graduates at Oxford, Cambridge and Durham numbered only 230 (7 per cent).[1] Edward Turner, first Professor of Chemistry at University College, London, was trained at Edinburgh; so was his successor Thomas Graham ('father' of colloid chemistry). Among other distinguished alumni of the Scottish universities who emigrated south were David Brewster (experimental work on polarised light) and Clark Maxwell (electromagnetic wave theory).

In England the nearest approach to higher education in the eighteenth century was to be found in the dissenting academies. The revival of the 1559 Uniformity Act in 1662 and the allied legislation known as the

Clarendon Code (1662–65) with the demand that clergymen and university tutors should conform to the liturgy of the Church of England led to the exclusion of those other than Anglicans from teaching posts at Oxford and Cambridge colleges. The response of the dissenters was to set up their own academies. Created primarily to provide higher education for those entering the ministry, their curricula also included natural and experimental philosophy, mechanics and hydrostatics, geography, astronomy, French and German, as well as navigation and commercial subjects.

Oxford and Cambridge, deprived of many of their most able and vigorous dons, fell into decline; the curriculum was narrow, standard of tuition low and posts were limited to the clergy. Towards the end of the first decade of the nineteenth century the *Edinburgh Review* launched a sustained campaign of bitter criticism at the ancient universities. In 1810 it published a scathing attack on the concept of scholar upheld at the universities:

A learned man! A scholar! A man of erudition! Upon whom are these epithets bestowed? . . . Are they given to men who know the properties of bodies and their action upon each other. No! This is not learning. The epithet of scholar is reserved for him who writes on the Aeolic reduplication. . . . His object is not to reason, to imagine, to invent but to conjugate, decline and derive. . . . Would he ever dream that such men as Lavoisier were equal in dignity of understanding to, or of the same utility as Bentley and Heyne.[2]

At Oxford the subjects of the BA degree course were ancient history, Latin, Greek, poetry, philosophy, logic and mathematics. There was no chemistry taught at Oxford, and though Cambridge included chemistry in its curriculum, neither Oxford nor Cambridge had laboratories. Scientific lectures were being given at Cambridge as early as the 1800s by Professor Vince, who illustrated his lectures in mechanics with practical demonstrations, using apparatus which quickly became obsolete. In the 1820s Professor Airy, Lucasian Professor of Mathematics, delivered a course of lectures on pneumatics, optics and mechanics. Later Professor Farish, Jacksonian Professor of Experimental Philosophy, concentrated on the teaching of machinery, a practice that his successor, Professor Willis, continued and extended by lecturing on the nature of weaving, steam engine models and machines. George Liveing, Professor of Chemistry at Cambridge, in giving evidence to the Devonshire Commissioners later claimed that 'the results (in physical science) are very small compared with the noise which has been made about them'.[3] These early attempts at scientific instruction were spasmodic, as witnesses to the Devonshire Commission pointed out; they led nowhere, each innovation collapsing as soon as the innovator moved on.

The credit for pioneering the physical sciences and technologies at university level belongs to University College, London, and King's

College, London. University College was intended for those members of the middle class unable to enter Oxford and Cambridge, and also to provide opportunities for the study of subjects not available at the older universities. Opened in 1826, it was modelled on the University of Berlin. From the outset full scope was given to the sciences and engineering. Two years later King's College was established. This also adopted a progressive attitude to science and engineering, indeed the governors were determined to make engineering a distinctive feature of the college.

Before mid-century it was customary for those wishing to pursue a systematic course of advanced study in chemistry to seek it in Germany – at Giessen or Heidelberg or Marburg. Leading public figures came to the conclusion that a national college of chemistry was an urgent requirement. Thus was founded in 1845 the Davy College of Practical Chemistry, under a Council whose President was HRH Prince Albert. Although it was to be devoted mainly to pure science, at the same time in order 'to meet the exigencies of this country, and to adopt the latest improvements in the Continental schools an appendage will be provided, devoted to the Economic Arts, where inquiries relating to Pharmacy, Agriculture and the other Arts may be pursued'.

As a result of the personal intervention of the Prince Consort, Dr August Wilhelm von Hofmann was appointed to the post of Professor of Chemistry, being granted two years leave of absence by Bonn University. Under Hofmann's inspiration teaching and research flourished, the college attracting students of diverse backgrounds:

Almost all classes of society have been represented in the laboratory – gentlemen following chemistry as a profession, or as an object of scientific taste, chemists and druggists, medical students and medical men, agriculturists, manufacturers in almost all branches of the chemical arts, copper smelters, dyers, painters, varnish makers, soap boilers, brewers and sugar makers have been working side by side.[4]

Although the venture had not been lacking in guaranteed support, the College nevertheless was in financial difficulties by 1847, for subscriptions had fallen off considerably. The debt was partly cleared by twenty-three members of the Council contributing £50 apiece. Developments were seriously affected and financial sacrifices were necessary from all, including Hofmann:

Dr Hofmann voluntarily gave up in succession – first a portion of his salary, then his share of the students' fees and lastly his house; yet during this trying period he never in the slightest degree relaxed his efforts to establish the reputation of the College. He not only gave up the money which was his due, but, out of his extreme devotion to the educational objects of the College, abandoned for some years what to a German savant is of still greater importance, his original research investigation.[5]

Meanwhile in 1839 the government had founded the Museum of

Economic Geology. Here students received instruction in mineralogy, analytical chemistry and meteorology. Following a report by a committee of the House of Lords which expressed concern at the lack of facilities for mining education, the Museum of Economic Geology became in 1851 the 'School of Mines and of Science Applied to the Arts'. Instruction was designed to enable the student 'to enter with advantage upon the actual process of mining or of the Arts which he may be called upon to conduct'.[6] Thus in the quarter of a century 1826–51 four colleges had been established in London which between them provided an admirable range of scientific and technological studies.

What made higher education and in particular scientific and technical instruction at university level widely available across the country generally was the emergence of the 'civic' colleges during the last quarter of the century. Manchester led the way with the creation of Owens College in 1851 by means of a legacy from John Owens, a wealthy merchant of the city, who left £100,000 in trust for the express purpose of founding a college open to all, irrespective of creed. Owens College continued the trend begun by King's College and University College of providing studies relevant to the commercial and industrial needs of the country. The growing awareness of these needs led to six new colleges being founded between 1871 and 1881 all of which were later to acquire university status.

Oxford and Cambridge after 1850

Throughout the nineteenth century Oxford and Cambridge were favourite targets for the numerous critics of the scientific scene in England. The ancient universities were a perpetual thorn in the flesh of those who viewed with concern the rise of the German universities and technical high schools. In the view of such critics Oxford and Cambridge, with their continued adherence to traditional studies and neglect of science, were an insidious influence, a stumbling block to progress.

Although professional studies such as law, medicine and theology were of importance at Oxford and Cambridge in the early nineteenth century, they merely formed the superstructure, the foundation for which was a 'liberal' education firmly based on the classics. Only a minority of students pursued a professional course, the majority being content to confine their studies to classics. A significant innovation at Cambridge during the early nineteenth century was the emphasis given to mathematical studies. Under the influence of Sir George Airy and Dr William Whewell mathematics flourished at Cambridge, but there was no parallel movement at Oxford. However, these studies were not intended to lead to the production of professional mathematicians or to the training of such personnel who would apply their mathematics within another profession. For instance, between 1800 and 1850 no fewer than forty-three men who subsequently became bishops were

successful in the Cambridge Mathematical Tripos.[7] The real significance of this development was that the concept of 'liberal studies' had
now been redefined so as to include mathematics. The philosophical
foundations for such a view were to appear in Whewell's 'On the
principles of English university education', published in 1837, a theme
taken up by Newman in 'On the scope and nature of university
education', published in 1852. According to Whewell the virtue of
mathematical study was not that it lead to increased knowledge or that
it was useful as an instrument for other purposes, it lay rather in its
power to provide 'intellectual discipline'. The study of mathematics, he
said, 'induces solid and certain reasoning', and he argued that 'some
insight into the progressive sciences [i.e. mathematics] is an essential
part of a liberal education . . . the man of mathematic genius who . . . is
led to become familiar with the best Greek and Latin classics becomes
thus a man of liberal education'.[8]

In the view of these advocates then, mathematics was as essential a
part of liberal education as classics. In arguing thus Whewell and
Newman would have had the support of such theorists as Huxley and
Spencer, but when Whewell wrote that 'the State of Germany . . . has of
late years been unfavourable to the intellectual welfare of its students'
Huxley would have been in strong disagreement, for he was an advocate
of the German 'model' of higher education with its emphasis on
professional teaching and acceptance of science.

This was at the heart of the controversy which focused on Oxford and
Cambridge during the middle decades of the nineteenth century.
Witnesses to the Devonshire Commission in the 1870s stated that in
England there was a great gulf between the 'literary man' and the
'scientific man'. But this was to over-simplify matters. Perhaps John
Stuart Mill can be taken as a representative of the literary man on the
one hand and Huxley as the best representative of the scientific man on
the other. But such a polarisation obscures a wide spectrum of differing
viewpoints. Newman, for instance, supported mathematical studies but
did not go nearly as far as Whewell, and both stopped short of the
acceptance of science as an element of culture. Mill, in his inaugural
address as Rector of St Andrews University, claimed that universities
were not the place for professional education,[9] the purpose of university
education being to inculcate a noble and courteous bearing in the
conduct of life and to produce 'capable and cultivated human beings'.
Newman, like Mill, opposed professional studies and wrote of
university education in terms of the acquiring of 'delicate taste' and the
cultivation of the mind.

Such attitudes were challenged by Huxley. With a boldness
characteristic of 'Darwin's bulldog' Huxley expressed radical views
about scientific education. He called for theoretical studies of
technologies such as engineering, agriculture and industrial chemistry to
be included within university studies:

There can surely be little question that instruction in the branches of science which lie at the foundation of these arts ought to be obtainable by means of a duly organized Faculty of Science in every university. The establishment of such a Faculty would have the additional advantage of providing in some measure for one of the greatest wants of our time and country, I mean the proper support and encouragement of original research.[10]

Support for the importance of research came also from within the ancient universities. The Reverend Mark Pattison, Rector of Lincoln College, Oxford, in his seminal work 'Suggestions on academical organisations', wrote 'There remains but one possible pattern on which a University can be constructed. . . . This is sometimes called the German type . . . the Professor of a modern university ought to regard himself primarily as *learner*, and a *teacher* only secondarily.'[11]

This was diametrically opposed to Newman's view which was that the universities should not be concerned with research but only with teaching and education. Huxley's advocacy of technological studies, too, was far removed from Newman's narrow view, but it was Huxley's ideas that were to prevail. His desire for technological studies such as engineering, industrial chemistry and agriculture was to find realisation in most universities, including Oxford and Cambridge, by 1914.

Whatever the respective merits of 'liberal' education and 'scientific' education there was a growing dissatisfaction with the ancient universities. Many felt that there was an almost total neglect of science, facilities for scientific study were very inadequate and scholarships and fellowships in science were few. The student intake was largely from the public schools and certainly too exclusively from one sector of society. A further adverse factor was that lecturers had to take Holy Orders, but above all the most universally condemned feature was the dominant influence of the colleges. These possessed far greater wealth than the universities and were generally disinclined to appoint professors in new subjects and promote new disciplines. Royal Commissions were appointed to 'inquire into the state, discipline, studies and revenues of the universities and university colleges'. That on Oxford reported in 1852 and recommended the abolition of the then existing monopoly of the halls and colleges over the University; professors should be appointed to certain colleges and be assisted by lecturers, so as to break the hold that tutors then had on instruction. Further, the colleges should contribute out of their revenue towards university expenditure. The report advocated the building of a great museum for physical science which should be amply endowed with equipment. The Cambridge University Commission proposed similar changes. It was of the opinion that the university, which had already instituted a new tripos in Natural Science,[12] was ready to enlarge its circle of studies.

Partly because of these outside pressures and partly because of the reforming zeal of certain key figures within the two universities reforms were quickly implemented during the 1850s and 1860s and brought about a somewhat healthier position as far as science was concerned. Nevertheless, throughout these two decades great disquiet persisted over the state of scientific education at the universities.

The Devonshire Commission examined their work very thoroughly. Several witnesses who appeared before the Commission were highly critical of the state of science both at Oxford and at Cambridge. J. C. Adams, Lowndean Professor of Astronomy and Geometry at Cambridge, considered that 'science had largely been neglected hitherto'. At Oxford, N. S. Maskelyne, the Professor of Mineralogy, confessed he had only three students and 'Mineralogy is hardly pursued at all at Oxford and geology is only very imperfectly pursued'. G. M. Humphreys, Professor of Anatomy at Cambridge, thought the Natural Science Tripos, despite being in existence for twenty years, had not flourished as well as it might have done; the average number of candidates (mainly medical students) was twelve. The fact that the standard was not high was significant, as 'the route through the Natural Science Tripos was an uncertain avenue to a Fellowship'. The Rev. James Challis, Plumian Professor of Astronomy and Experimental Philosophy, wondered whether 'we perhaps have not made the advance [in physics] that we might do, considering what has been done outside the University'.[13]

The Devonshire Commissioners wrote to the Heads of the Oxford and Cambridge colleges to ascertain what sums had been spent on science. Several refused to reply and many others had spent no money on it. At Christ Church, Oxford, however, there had been an encouraging development. As a result of alterations to the Lee's Trust (set up by the will of Dr Matthew Lee in 1755) a sum of £1,360 had been set aside for encouraging scientific study, of which £900 had been spent on the appointment of readers in chemistry, physics and anatomy. At Oxford there was one fellowship each at Queen's College, Merton and Pembroke, while at Cambridge there were two exhibitions at King's College, two science scholarships and a laboratory at Sidney Sussex, a chemical lecturer and a small laboratory at St John's, and a lecturer in natural science at Downing. But in the fellowships 'league' classics and mathematics still dominated. Of a total of 449 at all the colleges no fewer than 212 (46 per cent) were in classics and 125 (27 per cent) were in mathematics; seven only were in natural science.

In the view of the Devonshire Commissioners:

The principal professions for which extensive preliminary scientific studies are required are the professions of medicine, consulting and manufacturing chemistry and civil, mechanical and telegraphic engineering. It is our opinion, therefore, that the universities should provide to the fullest extent for theoretical instruction of such professional students.[14]

Yet R. B. Clifton, the first Professor of Physics at Oxford, pointed out that most students taking science spent very little time on scientific study for they were taking another subject seriously and had little time to spare:

Those who work longest in the laboratory are intending either to go into the medical profession, or they are studying with a view to going to the bar, where it is thought that a knowledge of science may be useful; or to engineering or some branch of engineering where science may be useful. But by far the largest part are intending to become teachers.[15]

Several witnesses to the Devonshire Commission emphasised the research function of the universities but at the same time expressed great dissatisfaction as to the neglect of research at Oxford and Cambridge. Clifton thought Oxford did very little in that direction:

The professors' time is so taken up with teaching now that it is impossible for them to do anything more than teach, and in fact not to do that as thoroughly as they would wish. . . . One main duty of a university is to promote research and another is to supply the country with the very best teachers . . . the number of teachers now employed is so small that one of these aims must be neglected.[16]

Sir Benjamin Brodie, Professor of Chemistry at Oxford, also told the Commissioners that in the sciences the university had to supply elementary teaching, a situation which, according to the Master of Sidney Sussex College, also prevailed at Cambridge. The teaching was at an elementary level because those entering for science were not the best material and had been inadequately instructed in the schools. Teaching loads were high because there were so few appointments in science and consequently research was neglected. The Devonshire Commissioners provided lists of science lecturers at Oxford, Cambridge and Berlin and concluded that 'it is impossible not to be impressed with the evidence which the list affords of the abundance and variety of the scientific teaching given in Berlin by professors of great eminence'.[17]

The plurality of professorial appointments in any one subject was a key factor in the promotion of research. The Devonshire Commissioners illustrated it by quoting from the evidence of Sir Henry Roscoe, Professor of Chemistry at Owens College, Manchester, and J. G. Greenwood, principal of the College, who in 1868 had been on a conducted tour of the German universities. They claimed that

the number of teachers in Germany is considerably larger than in the English universities . . . Provision is thus made for the effective instruction of students and for the zealous prosecution of original research . . . the number of skilled assistants attached to each professorship is greater than we have in England. . . . In some cases the assistants are professors who lecture on special subjects . . . one great expense in working a laboratory is the cost of the apparatus and

materials and this is specially paid for in German universities by the state
. . . In England the greater part of this charge falls on the professor.[18]

Greenwood and Roscoe urged on the Commissioners the 'importance
of the principle that the existence of a plurality of teachers is an
indispensable prerequisite both for breadth and depth of instruction',
and where there were several teachers in one discipline 'the teachers are
also induced by the opportunity of lecturing on special subjects, to
engage in profounder investigations'.[19]

Witnesses to the Devonshire Commission agreed that the funds
provided by the universities were 'lamentably deficient' and professors
complained bitterly that they had to provide their own apparatus and
pay demonstrators out of their own pockets. Yet at Cambridge the
annual income of the colleges was estimated to be £180,000 whereas the
income of the university from endowments was a mere £2,000. A similar
situation existed at Oxford. Despite, therefore, the University Royal
Commissions of the 1850s the development of the universities lay largely
in the hands of the colleges; the final verdict of the Devonshire
Commissioners was that scientific teaching was 'inadequate in amount'
at the ancient universities.

Statistical data bear out the evidence presented by the witnesses to the
Royal Commissions as to the position of science at mid-century. The
class lists issued by the public examiners at Oxford show that there were
101 successful candidates in classics and 28 in mathematics. At
Cambridge 38 had passed the Classical Tripos and no fewer than 131 the
Mathematical Tripos; by this time success in the Cambridge Mathematical Tripos had become one of the highest honours attainable and to
be Senior Wrangler represented the apex of achievement, a distinction
eagerly sought after by clerics among others.

At Oxford there were fifty professors of whom ten were in science
(excluding mathematics). This certainly gives the impression that
science was not neglected, but taken on its own it is highly misleading for
while there were professors in geology and mineralogy the earlier
evidence of the Profeesor of Geology to the Devonshire Commission
points out that the number of students was few. Further, to put it into
perspective, there were two chairs in Arabic and one each in Chinese and
Sanskrit, but there was only one in the growing field of biological
sciences. It is very likely that the science professors were entirely
engaged in teaching medical students. At Cambridge the total number
of professors was far fewer: twenty-three, of whom four were in science –
in chemistry, physics, botany and mineralogy. Outwardly it would
appear that Oxford with its ten science chairs was in a far stronger
position than Cambridge with its four chairs, but this is negated by the
testimony of witnesses to the Devonshire Commission who invariably
pointed to the greater prominence of the sciences at Cambridge. Such
judgements, however, may have been coloured by the eminence of
Cambridge mathematics. It is difficult, therefore, to arrive at an

objective assessment of the relative strengths of science at the universities in 1850.

Whatever this may have been in 1850, by 1900 a radical shift had come about in their respective positions. This is illustrated in Table 5.1. At Cambridge out of a total teaching staff of seventy there were now eighteen (26 per cent) in the sciences. Comparable figures at Oxford were fifteen out of eighty-four (18 per cent). Technology at Cambridge was represented by the chair of Mechanical Sciences and the recently founded one in agriculture. At Oxford there had been no appointments in technology additional to that in rural economy which had existed in 1850. In mathematics and physics, if not also in chemistry, Cambridge was now clearly ahead. This impression is further strengthened by a survey of student numbers. At Cambridge the successes in Part I of the various Triposes were in 1900: Natural Sciences 136; Classics 126; Mathematics 82; History 49; Law 46; Languages 25; Mechanical Sciences 18; Theology 13; Moral Sciences 9. Thus, while classics still held a dominant position it had by now been surpassed by natural sciences, while theology had been totally eclipsed. At Oxford the position was very different. In the class lists issued by the public examiners classics led the field with 154 successes, closely followed by history with 148. Natural sciences came next with 37, nearly equalled by theology with 31, whereas there were only 26 successes in mathematics.

The data strongly suggest that Cambridge was by now the leader in science and it could certainly take a pride in its facilities. Between 1863 and 1900 museums of zoology, of botany and of mineralogy had been built, and in addition to the Cavendish Laboratories of Physics, opened in 1871, chemical laboratories had been established in 1887 and engineering laboratories in 1894.

Quantitatively and qualitatively by 1914 Cambridge may be said to have become more progressive than Oxford (see Table 5.2). At the latter while staff resources devoted to science actually fell from 18 per cent to 15 per cent, classics improved from 7 per cent to 13 per cent; the arts dominated, with nearly half the staff being employed in those subjects. At Cambridge, on the other hand, the decline in the importance of theology, classics and law had continued while the arts, medicine and science flourished. Science, with a quarter of the teaching staff, now held equal place with the arts and medicine; a significant development was that technology claimed over one-tenth of the total, and exceeded the combined strength of the staff in classics and theology. Science and technology now claimed 37 per cent of the total staff, the equivalent figure for Oxford being 18 per cent. To put these figures into perspective it should be pointed out that at Cambridge science and technology exceeded the arts while at Oxford the science and technology total was less than half that of arts and only a little more than classics alone. Such dramatic changes had come about not by the creation of chairs, which remained remarkably constant over the whole period from 1800 to 1914, but by the appointment of readers, lecturers and demonstrators – a

Table 5.1 Staff at Oxford and Cambridge

Oxford

	1850				1900			
	Professors	Others	Total	Percentage of total	Professors	Others	Total	Percentage of total
Theology	5	—	5	10	7	1	8	10
Classics	5	—	5	10	4	2	6	7
Law	4	—	4	8	5	1	6	7
Arts	19	—	19	36	22	17	39	46
Medicine	6	—	6	11	6	4	9	11
Science	13	—	13	25	11	4	15	18
Technology	1	—	1	—	1	—	1	1
	53	—	53	100	56	29	84	100

Cambridge

	1850				1900			
	Professors	Others	Total	Percentage of total	Professors	Others	Total	Percentage of total
Theology	6	—	6	19	6	—	6	9
Classics	3	—	3	10	5	—	5	7
Law	3	—	3	10	4	1	5	7
Arts	9	—	9	30	14	7	21	30
Medicine	3	—	3	10	9	4	13	19
Science	7	—	7	21	12	6	18	26
Technology	—	—	—	—	2	—	2	2
	31	—	31	100	52	18	70	100

Table 5.2 Staff at Oxford and Cambridge

Cambridge	1900				1914				1900–14
	Professors	Others	Total	Percentage of total	Professors	Others	Total	Percentage of total	Number increase
Theology	6	—	6	9	6	—	6	5	0
Classics	5	—	5	7	3	3	6	5	+ 1
Law	4	1	5	7	4	—	4	3	– 1
Arts	14	7	21	30	16	21	37	27	+16
Medicine	9	4	13	19	6	25	31	23	+18
Science	12	6	18	26	13	21	34	25	+16
Technology	2	—	2	2	3	13	16	12	+14
	52	18	70	100	51	83	134	100	+64

Oxford	1900				1914				1900–14
	Professors	Others	Total	Percentage of total	Professors	Others	Total	Percentage of total	Number increase
Theology	7	1	8	10	7	3	10	8	+ 2
Classics	4	2	6	7	11	4	15	13	+ 9
Law	5	1	6	7	4	5	9	7	+ 3
Arts	22	17	39	46	21	31	52	43	+13
Medicine	5	4	9	11	5	9	14	11	+ 5
Science	11	4	15	18	14	5	19	15	+ 4
Technology	1	—	1	1	3	1	4	3	+ 3
	55	29	84	100	65	58	123	100	+39

move advocated as far back as 1852 by the Royal Commissioners and belatedly put into effect after 1900. Technology at Cambridge illustrates well the benefits of such changes; between 1900 and 1914 readerships were created in forestry and metallurgy; lectureships in agriculture, mechanical engineering, electrical engineering, forestry and petrology, and demonstrators were appointed in forestry, mechanical engineering and petrology.

Table 5.3 Students at Oxford and Cambridge

| Cambridge | Passes in Part I of Triposes | | | | |
| | 1900 | | 1914 | | |
Subject	No.	Percentage of total	No.	Percentage of total	Change in no.
Mathematics	82	16	112	16	+30
Classics	126	25	112	16	—14
Moral sciences	9	2	10	1	+ 1
Natural sciences	136	27	152	22	+16
Theology	13	2	19	3	+ 6
Law	46	9	34	4	—12
History	49	10	132	19	+83
Oriental language	3	1	3	2	0
Medieval and modern languages	22	4	33	4	+11
Mechanical sciences	18	4	43	9	+25
Economics	—	—	28	4	+28
	504	100	678	100	+174

| Oxford | Class lists issued by public examiners | | | | |
| | 1900 | | 1914 | | |
Subject	No.	Percentage of total	No.	Percentage of total	Change in no.
Classics	154	34	133	22	—19
Mathematics	26	6	16	2	—10
Natural sciences	37	8	87	14	+50
Law	40	9	77	13	+37
History	148	33	191	31	+43
Theology	31	7	42	7	+11
Modern literature	—	—	29	5	+29
Oriental languages and literature	—	—	2	0	+ 2
English literature	14	3	37	6	+23
	450	100	614	100	+164

With regard to student successes similar changes can be seen at Cambridge (Table 5.3). While numbers in classics fell slightly those succeeding in the Mathematics Tripos increased from 82 to 112, in

Natural Sciences from 136 to 152, and Mechanical Sciences from 18 to 43. Perhaps the most significant change of all at Cambridge was the growth of History from 49 to 132. Thus Cambridge was now dominated by Natural Sciences and History. History had been a leading subject at Oxford even in 1900, and between 1900 and 1914 successes in it increased by a further 43, there was also a fairly spectacular growth in Natural Sciences from 37 to 87. Classics meanwhile fell from 154 to 133.

These changes can be further emphasised by the ranking order of student successes. At Oxford in 1900 the percentages were: classics 34; history 33; law 9; and natural sciences 8; by 1914 the percentages had become 22, 31, 13 and 14 respectively. At Cambridge in 1900 the ranking order was: natural sciences 27, classics 25, mathematics 16, and history 10; by 1914 the percentages had become 22, 16, 16, 19. Thus both at Oxford and Cambridge there had been both an actual and relative decline in classics as it gave way to other disciplines. If one combines science and technology at Cambridge this combination led the field with 31 per cent of the successes. There were no technology examinations at Oxford and the science successes accounted for only 14 per cent of the total. But at Oxford and Cambridge together there were still more successes in classics than there were in the sciences.

Cambridge was ahead of Oxford in other respects, too, for in 1875 it had instituted diplomas; by 1914 there were diplomas in Agriculture and Forestry as well as in more traditional academic subjects. By now, too, there was a place for research students (the most famous of these was Rutherford) and between 1897 and 1914 there were 153 research students at Cambridge, the largest number (72) being in physics and chemistry. A disappointing feature even at Cambridge continued to be the paucity of fellowships and scholarships in science. This was one feature which had not been significantly remedied over the period 1850 to 1914.

The civic colleges and universities

Between 1871 and 1881 six new colleges were founded: the Armstrong College of Physical Science, Newcastle (1871), the Yorkshire College of Science, Leeds (1874), the Firth College, Sheffield (1874), the Mason College of Science, Birmingham (1880), University College, Nottingham (1881) and University College, Liverpool (1881).[20]

University College, Liverpool, came into existence following a public meeting convened by the Mayor at the Town Hall on 28 May 1878, when a resolution was passed to the effect that it was

desirable to provide such instruction in all the branches of a liberal education as would enable residents in the town and neighbourhood to qualify for degrees in arts, science and other subjects, at any of the universities granting degrees to non-resident [and also] to give such technical instruction as would be of immediate service in professional and commercial life.[21]

The idea of 'practical utility' in the sense of providing instruction leading to university degrees, particularly in the sciences and in technology, stands out in this resolution. Furthermore, it is clear from the titles given to three of the colleges above that the fostering of scientific studies was their principal aim. That science was to be of dominant importance in the work of the college at Liverpool was further stressed by Principal G. H. Rendall in his inaugural address:

This is indeed in intellectual progress the age that science may justly call her own . . . for the present age and for life's daily needs, science bids fair to occupy the larger place; it is invading every department of life; and it is in purveying and disseminating this side of knowledge that the College will probably find its most special work.[22]

This statement can also be taken to present the philosophy underlying the formation of the other colleges.

The credit for pioneering the physical sciences and engineering belongs to University College, London (1826), King's College, London (1828), and Owens College, Manchester (1851). University College, London, achieved the distinction of being the first to appoint a professor of civil engineering when in 1840 it created a chair in this subject.[23] In 1847 a second chair, mechanical engineering, was added. In chemistry a chair was established when the college was founded and a second, in practical chemistry, was added in 1844. An unusual move was the creation in 1878 of a chair of chemical technology. The governors of King's College were also determined to make engineering a distinctive feature of the teaching of their college, and departments of manufacturing art and machinery and of land surveying and levelling were set up; these were changed in 1866 to departments of mechanical engineering and civil engineering respectively.[24] The college was a pioneer in other directions, too, for it instituted the first university chair of metallurgy in 1879, and the first chair of electrical engineering in 1890. The most significant contribution of Owens College[25] lay in the field of chemical studies, for under Sir Henry Roscoe a reputable school of chemical research was established and Roscoe was instrumental in attracting Carl Schorlemmer, a German-trained PhD, to the college as a lecturer in organic chemistry. Later in 1874 Schorlemmer was appointed Professor of Organic Chemistry. This was the first chair of organic chemistry at an English university and the lateness of this appointment is indicative of the neglect of the subject in the universities, a neglect which is difficult to explain.

Turning to the newer civic colleges one feature they had in common was the slow rate of growth in the numbers of candidates taking degree courses. Several years usually elapsed between the establishing of degree courses and the first degree awards. It was not until the 1890s that substantial numbers of degree successes were recorded. To overcome the difficulties that students encountered in pursuing three-year courses of full-time study the colleges established a variety of shorter courses leading to the award of diplomas, certificates and college associateships, which at the same time met the needs of local industries. Thus there were diplomas in mining, engineering and naval architecture at Newcastle, diplomas in mining at Sheffield and Birmingham, and a diploma in brewing at Birmingham.

Despite the fact that the civic universities owed their origins to a common purpose, in practice the scientific and technological studies they offered differed at many points; these cannot be explained entirely in terms of the reflection of local conditions and a determining factor may have been the means by which new enterprises were financed.

At Newcastle,[26] the first of the colleges to be set up, engineering was one of the strong points and by 1905 courses were provided in marine and electrical engineering. The college also specialised in mining, metallurgy and naval architecture, and cooperated with over a dozen firms in the area in developing a six-year sandwich scheme of study, students spending fifteen months at the college followed by fifteen months at the works. They then returned to college for two years and completed their course with eighteen months at the works. It was the practice for students to pay premiums to the firms for the privilege of training; these were as high as fifty guineas a year, a condition which must have considerably restricted the entry into the profession.

The Yorkshire College at Leeds[27] (science was dropped from its title in 1877) made a valuable contribution to local industries by establishing a wide range of relevant courses in mining (1877), textiles (1874), dyeing (1880), agriculture (1891), leather processing (1891), electrical engineering (1899) and coal gas and fuel with metallurgy (1906). The new technological subjects were not recognised as honours subjects of the Victorian University of Manchester to which the college was admitted in 1887, the college instead bestowed the title of associate on those who passed the final examinations at the end of a three-year course in a technological subject.

A special feature of the work of Firth College, Sheffield,[28] was the study of coal-mining. Saturday morning and evening classes in mining were held at the college from 1882 onwards. Later an attempt was made to take mining instruction to the miner, and centres were established in collaboration with the local authorities in Nottinghamshire, Derbyshire and the West Riding. These short lecture courses were put on a more systematic basis following the appointment of a professor of mining in 1892, and a further step forward was taken in 1903 when a new diploma in mining was established, which brought into the department a number of full-time students for the first time.

The Mason College, Birmingham,[29] like the Firth College, Sheffield, emphasised the study of mining and metallurgy. A professor of mining was appointed in 1882 and a lecturer in metallurgy in the following year, when a Department of Coal Mining and Colliery Management was set up. Unfortunately the Department of Mining was allowed to lapse and was not properly reorganised until 1902. The popularity of mining began to pick up shortly after this and twenty-six students obtained a BSc degree in mining and eighteen a diploma in mining between 1906 and 1913.[30] A remarkable innovation at Birmingham was the establishment of a Department of Brewing in 1899 following a donation of £28,000 by the local brewers. A diploma in brewing proved to be quite popular, no fewer than thirty-six candidates being successful in obtaining the diploma between 1901 and 1913.[31]

At Nottingham,[32] as at Birmingham and Sheffield, one of the most significant developments was the teaching of mining. Evening lectures on mining were given from the early days of the college and these were put on a full-time basis in 1906, but it was not until 1911 that a chair was established. This, together with the setting up of a full department, was made possible by the offers of support from the royalty owners and colliery proprietors of the district. The college also gave full support to the teaching of engineering. A chair in mechanics and engineering was established three years after the foundation of the college; chairs in engineering and technology and in mechanical engineering were added in 1890 and 1905 respectively, but there was no chair of electrical engineering until 1933.

When University College, Liverpool,[33] was founded in 1881 five chairs were created of which three were in the sciences, these being in mathematics and physics, chemistry and natural history. The scientific staff of the college doubled between 1890 and 1900 and doubled again between 1900 and 1910, by which time the college had been granted a university charter. By 1914 there was a scientific staff of sixty, thirteen of these being at the professorial level.

The first appointment in engineering was made in 1885 when H. S. Hele-Shaw was made a lecturer in civil engineering. This appointment had been made possible by a five-year guarantee fund set up by William Rathbone, merchant, Alfred Holt, marine engineer, and Sir John Brunner of Brunner Mond. As late as 1900 the engineering staff comprised only three members, a professor and two lecturers, but the next decade brought momentous changes. In 1889 a lectureship in electrotechnics had been established and in 1903 the holder, E. W. Marchant, became the first holder of the Chair of Electric Power Engineering, one of the earliest chairs of electrical engineering in English universities. An event of even greater significance was the innovation of appointing several associate professors from among the leading engineers of the city. Thus John Alexander Brodie, the borough engineer, was made an Associate Professor of Municipal Engineering; J. A. F. Aspinall, the manager of the Lancashire and Yorkshire Railway, was made an Associate Professor of Railway Engineering; A. B. Holmes, the borough electrical engineer, became Associate Professor of Municipal Electrical Engineering and A. S. Lyster, engineer-in-chief of the Mersey Docks and Harbour Board, was made an Associate Professor of Docks and Harbour Construction. This seems to be a development without a parallel in the other civic universities; indeed, no other university appears to have followed Liverpool's example in the years before the outbreak of the First World War. These titles were not merely honorary; they carried with them specific teaching duties which provided an exciting range of optional topics in the engineering curriculum related to the particular expertise of these associate professors.

At Liverpool another innovation was the creation of a chair in naval architecture along with a separate honours school in that subject. This chair was included in the Faculty of Engineering which had been set up in 1903, a faculty which comprised four full professors – two in civil engineering, one each in electrical engineering and naval architecture – together with the four associate professors. A notable omission was that of a chair in mechanical engineering. Nevertheless, starting from modest beginnings in 1886, by 1914 the university had succeeded in establishing an imaginative curriculum embracing a wide range of topics. In the field of chemical studies the most serious defect at Liverpool was the absence of a chair in organic chemistry. It is true that the subject formed part of the curriculum but it did not receive the emphasis and status that it deserved. Physical chemistry fared better: a Department of Electro-Chemistry and Physical Chemistry was set up in 1884, a professor of physical chemistry was appointed in 1903 and splendid new laboratories were also built in that year.

At each civic university the first chair in engineering was either in civil engineering or in mechanics or mechanical engineering. Electrical engineering developed later in the century and many colleges appointed a lecturer in electrotechnics, some of which later became chairs: King's College (1890), Yorkshire College (1899), Liverpool (1903), Birmingham (1905), Newcastle (1907), Sheffield (1917). Owens College, quite progressive in other branches of engineering, lagged behind in this, merely appointing a lecturer in electrotechnics in 1912.

The appointment of a professor at Liverpool in the new discipline of biochemistry (1902) was unique; most universities did not have such chairs until very much later in the century. Strictly speaking, the distinction of being first in this field should go to Birmingham, for in 1897 it created a Chair of Brewing and the Biochemistry of Fermentation. But what is so remarkable about the general development of chemical education is the neglect of organic chemistry and the lateness in the recognition of physical chemistry as a subject in its own right. As late as 1900 there was only one full professor of organic chemistry (Owens College). Liverpool, Yorkshire College and Firth College had lectureships in this subject and the chemistry of dyeing was included at Owens and Yorkshire College. As for physical chemistry there was only one appointment other than the chair at Liverpool up to the outbreak of war and that was a special lecturer in the subject at Sheffield.

It may be that a fuller investigation would reveal perfectly valid reasons for all the inconsistencies and divergencies revealed in a study of the scientific staff of the civic universities. One single factor which would account for many of them is lack of funds, something all the colleges had in common. While college councils might have wished to put in hand certain developments, the possibilities open to them in practice were often dependent on their benefactors. Thus at Leeds the Clothworkers' Company donated £15,000 for the textile department and £2,500 for the dyeing department. At Sheffield, Sir Thorpe Mappin, MP, a local cutler, gave £2,000 for the founding of a technical department and the Drapers' Company gave £4,000 for a similar department at Nottingham which also benefited from the local coal owners' guarantee of £300 a year for a mining department. At Birmingham the local brewers gave £28,000 for the chair in brewing.

Nevertheless, a careful examination of the sources of support at Liverpool reveals that not all the puzzling features can be accounted for on the basis of lack of finance; for instance it is not possible to account in this way for the low priority given to geology by the college.

The original laboratories at Liverpool were built at a cost of £20,000 made up from donations from several leading citizens. In 1886 Sir Andrew Walker (of Walker's breweries) gave £23,000 for engineering laboratories and this gift was exceeded in 1909 when the shipowners T. Fenwick Harrison, J. W. Hughes and Heath Harrison, donated £41,000 for additional engineering laboratories. Meanwhile, in 1905, Dr Edmund Muspratt had given £17,000 for physical chemistry laboratories. Up to 1914 donations for sites and buildings in science and technology exceeded £500,000; by comparison the amount the university received from government sources during the same period was a modest £170,000.

It was not only buildings and laboratories which depended on the generosity of local groups and individuals, but also the creation of chairs. These were sometimes the outcome of the fancies of wealthy individuals. At Liverpool the policy was that the creation of a chair required a specific endowment, usually to the value of £10,000. The financing of chairs from general college funds was not attempted prior to 1907, presumably because of the precariousness of the general financial position, and when such a policy was implemented the three unendowed chairs lapsed after twelve months. Between 1889 and 1893 endowments were provided for chairs in botany, physiology, pathology and anatomy, but there was no endowment for geology until 1916. Sir John Brunner, influenced no doubt by his industrial experiences, endowed a Chair of Physical Chemistry, and another chemist, Edmund Muspratt, provided new laboratories to go with this. A year earlier William Johnston, a local shipowner, had endowed the Chair of Biochemistry, but no one came forward to offer an endowment for organic chemistry.

Although wealthy industrialists, manufacturers and merchants were prepared to endow chairs, sometimes perhaps for reasons of prestige, the appointment of lecturers and demonstrators was financed out of general college funds. Such funds were rarely in a hea;thy state (the accumulated debt at Liverpool in 1901 was £11,000[34]) and this meant that junior posts were spread thinly. At Liverpool in 1895 the ratio of junior to professional posts was 1.6 : 1, many departments consisting only of a professor and one assistant; the ratio for all science and technology posts in the civic colleges in 1894 was 1.7 : 1.[35]

Despite all the generous donations from its supporters the college at Liverpool was forced to make a further appeal to its friends for additional annual subscriptions and these formed a special sustentation fund. Ramsay Muir, a young lecturer at the college, later a professor, considered that 'this forms a precarious and undignified means of supporting a great institution. A university should not have to depend upon charitable subscriptions. . . . Even with the Sustentation Fund, however, it is found impossible to make both ends meet.'[36]

One consequence of the small number of staff in each subject as at Oxford and Cambridge was that teaching duties tended to be heavy, with the result that research was neglected. One department, namely Biochemistry, was able to devote more attention to research than the others. There were always at least ten workers engaged in research in the department and in the session 1906–07 no fewer than sixty papers were published. But even in this department it was only the salaries of three members of staff and the building itself which had been catered for by the endowment. The equipment and day-to-day running costs had to be met in other ways. Professor Moore, the first holder of the Chair of Biochemistry, complained in 1911 that:

After the unavoidable expenses of cleaning, gas light and water there remains to defray the cost of material and chemicals for research an annual sum of £120. Even when most economical types of work are chosen the average annual expenses of a worker in a laboratory works out at £20. It follows that for about one-third of each year all funds are lacking for even the most ordinary materials.[37]

The endowment provided by Johnston for Moore's chair was unique for it was specifically intended for a research chair, the only one of its kind in the university. In all other cases professors and lecturers were appointed to teach, research being fitted in whenever possible. Moore saw this as a great weakness in the university design:

It is much to be regretted that in the financial system of our universities no separate provision is made for the endowment of research apart from ordinary undergraduate teaching. Even where the Charter of the University insists that it shall advance arts, science, learning and education, no provision is made for any separate endowment of research. . . . The result is a perpetual struggle between teaching and research for the partition of a sum of money inadequate to supply completely the needs of both, and in such a struggle research, though equally or even more important, comes off worst because it is usually regarded by administrators as a luxury, whereas teaching is deemed an essential function in the work of a university.[38]

Research scholarships were few: in 1907 there were twenty-five science research students and five research students in engineering, and in that year the college Report commented that 'research work has been retarded by the excessive demands of teaching'. Up to 1914 fewer than a hundred research scholarships had been awarded, but by that time research was beginning to play an increasingly important role and in 1914 over a hundred papers were published by members of the science and technology staff.[39]

The first students attending the new college at Liverpool in 1881 were able to study for the degrees of London University, but after 1884 when University College, Liverpool, became part of the Victoria University of Manchester, a new option was open to them and very quickly the Victoria University degree replaced that of London in popularity. The first success at the London BSc general degree examinations was recorded in 1885, but by 1889 the Victorian degree was taking over and although for a number of years there was usually the odd student who chose the London degree, up to 1898 there had only been twelve successes in the London examinations.[40] Few students ventured on an honours degree, the first successes recorded being mathematics (1888), engineering (1888), chemistry (1890) and physics (1894). Successes in the honours examinations did not become numerous until about 1910.

College reports were constantly drawing attention to the poor standard of the student entrants and in the early days many of the college classes were pre-matriculation classes, so that much of the effort was devoted to the equivalent of school work. That few students entered the lengthy and rigorous courses was not surprising in view of the lack of provision of entrance scholarships – initially there were only four scholarships and by 1900 there were still only fifty.[41]

Being a student all too often involved a substantial degree of financial hardship and many were effectively barred from full-time study or could only embark on a limited period of study. The college authorities recognised this and at Liverpool, as at all the other civic universities, in many disciplines a number of alternative courses were provided at different levels so that students were not obliged to enrol for a complete degree course. For instance the Mathematics Department in 1884–85 had junior, intermediate, senior and higher advanced courses. The first of these was an introductory course of a standard equivalent to the fourth-form work of a present-day secondary school. The intermediate course prepared candidates for the Cambridge Higher Local Examination. The senior course 'was adopted for the London BSc degree' and the higher advanced course prepared students for the honours BSc degree. In chemistry there were no fewer than twelve courses at different levels.

In addition to its provision of day classes the college arranged a programme of evening classes in a wide range of subjects. During the first session the Registrar was able to announce that over 500 students attended the college classes but fewer than a hundred had registered for the day classes. The evening classes, which were open to both sexes for a charge of six shillings per session, continued to flourish throughout the period 1881–1914. In 1889 subjects offered in the evening included mathematics, physics and chemistry, electrotechnics, technological chemistry, oceanography and geology. The physics course spread over twenty weeks was entitled 'Scientific principles of the electric telegraph'; there were also twenty weeks of elementary practical physics and twenty weeks of electrotechnics. In engineering there were classes in vibration and balancing of machinery, applied mechanics and theory of machine design. A special feature of the evening programme at Liverpool was the classes in mechanical drawing and engineering drawing at the Walker Engineering Laboratories; these classes given, by Professor Hele-Shaw, were attended by large numbers of artisans (often 200 or more) for a charge of one penny per evening. But Liverpool was far from being unique in emphasising evening instruction, and similar programmes of evening classes may be found in the calendars of most other civic universities. Thus Leeds in 1914 had classes in textile industries, dyeing, leather industries, book-keeping and shorthand in addition to the conventional arts and science subjects. In that year at Leeds there were 457 day students, and 411 evening students.[42]

The government played little part in the origins and development of the provincial civic universities; financial support was not forthcoming until 1889 when the first Treasury grant in aid was awarded. Government aid in England was concentrated instead on the two London institutions – the Royal School of Mines and the Royal College of Science[43] – despite the pleas of industrialists to the effect that it was not in London that centres of science and technology should be placed but in areas such as Newcastle and Sheffield, in close proximity to the major centres of industry. In 1907 these two colleges were amalgamated with the City and Guilds' Central Technical College founded jointly by the London Livery Companies and the Corporation of the City of London in 1884. The result of this merger was the Imperial College of Science and Technology, a cooperative venture involving the Government, the London County Council and the City and Guilds. It paid off handsomely, for it soon became the leading centre of science and technology and by the outbreak of war had nearly forty professors. Its impact can best be seen in the field of engineering for the number of candidates successful in the London Honours BSc in engineering rose from a mere five in 1903 to sixty in 1910, the college contributing 50 per cent of the successes.[44] Between 1903 and 1910 the City and Guilds' College had a clear dominance over all other colleges, producing 128 successes. Its nearest rivals were University College, London (43) and King's College, London (33). The East London Technical College – formerly the Finsbury Technical College founded by the City and Guilds – had 15 successes.[45]

The subjects taught at the Royal College of Science before the amalgamation of the three colleges had been mathematics, physics, chemistry and biology, and at the Royal School of Mines geology, metallurgy and mining. The School of Mines was the first institution to include metallurgy and mining in its curriculum, lecturers being appointed in 1851. The Central Technical College concentrated on engineering; following the reorganisation it became the Engineering Faculty of the Imperial College. Students at the three colleges were able to study for the BSc degree of London University but each of the colleges had established separate three-year and four-year courses leading to the award of College Diplomas. At the School of Mines the Diploma of Associateship of the Royal School of Mines (ARSM) was awarded to successful students after four years, students studied mining, metallurgy and geology but specialised in one of them. In 1870 there were only seven successful candidates but numbers rose gradually and by 1910 there were thirty-eight. The Royal College of Science provided a three-year course in the sciences in which students specialised in one subject. They were awarded the Diploma of the Associateship of the Royal College of Science (ARCS). As with the ARSM, numbers completing the course successfully were initially few; the first success was not until 1882, but in 1910 fifty diplomas were awarded, sixteen of them in chemistry. The Central Technical College, too, at the time of its foundation inaugurated three-year courses in civil and mechanical engineering, electrical engineering and in chemistry and these courses led to the award of the Diploma of the Associateship of the City and Guilds' Institute (ACGI). In 1910 there were no fewer than eighty-five diplomas awarded in engineering. In addition to degree and diploma students others labelled 'occasional students' were allowed to enter and study one or more special branches of science or technology.[46]

It has been seen that considerable numbers of students succeeded each year in obtaining diplomas of the three colleges after rigorous three- or four-year courses in which students specialised in one subject. Because of the length and rigour of the courses and because of the illustrious staff attracted to the colleges – Sir Norman Lockyer (physics), John Percy (metallurgy), Thomas Huxley (biology), Sir Lyon Playfair and Sir Edward Frankland (chemistry), and Sir Warington Smyth and Sir Clement Le Neve Foster (mining) – there is justification for including these diploma students among those listed as honours graduates in Table 5.4: the ARSM students are included in honours metallurgy or honours mining; the ARCS students in the subject in which they qualified and the ACGI students among the honours chemistry or honours engineering students.

It has been demonstrated that graduate scientists and technologists represented but a small fraction of all those who received some measure of university training. The graduates were the elite, or the fortunate, or perhaps merely the 'fittest', for many students entered full-time courses at the universities after years of evening study at technical colleges and universities only to abandon their studies at a later stage. By no means all students entered degree courses, for other courses had a wide appeal; among those on degree courses the numbers graduating were only a small proportion of those who began the course.

Scientific manpower and the English civic universities

During the greater part of the nineteenth century there were few openings in industry for scientists, and opportunities for research, both at university and in industry, were rare. For many the opening up of the Dominions and South American countries offered more attractive prospects than were available in England and this accounted for the high 'brain-drain' of trained manpower. To some extent this was offset by an influx of trained scientists from the continental countries, particularly Germany. With the establishment of the new civic colleges, the growth of technical colleges and the gradual change in the attitude of the schools to science, opportunities in teaching and lecturing became increasingly available. The attitude of industry changed also, for while earlier there had been no very great demand for scientists there was a greater readiness at the end of the century to undertake organised research and this coincided with the rapid increase in the number of trained scientists. One result of the availability of English-trained manpower was that progressive firms such as Crosfields of Warrington, who had earlier employed German-trained scientists, were now able to replace these with men trained in the English universities.

During the second half of the nineteenth century the leading technological centre in England and the institution most likely to produce the managerial technologist and scientific research worker was the combined Royal College of Science and Royal School of Mines. From a survey of the careers of 850 former students,[47] it is possible to draw certain conclusions. Of these 850 students, whose careers spanned a period of forty years, only 170 (20 per cent) had entered industry at some stage in their careers. It is not unreasonable to assume that no other institution contributed as many. Of those who spent some time in industry the majority entered mining and brewing and frequently they held positions not in management or research but in the inspectorate. Some 32 per cent went abroad, either immediately after qualifying or at later stages in their careers and 28 per cent entered the teaching profession. Some indications of research publications are given and from these it would seem that no more than seventy-five (9 per cent) engaged in research.

Another source of information regarding careers of graduates is Professor Schuster's account in *The Physical Laboratories of the University of Manchester* published in 1906.[48] Arthur Schuster was educated at Frankfurt Gymnasium and later studied for a PhD degree under Kirchhoff at Heidelberg University. He was appointed Professor of Applied Mathematics at Owens College in 1881, and his account contains a record of the careers of those who studied at the physical laboratories during the period 1881 to 1906. The increasing opportunities for physicists following the founding of the civic universities, the development of technical education and the integration of science into the secondary school curriculum is demonstrated by the fact that of 115 individuals listed no fewer than thirty-three obtained some appointment on the staff of a university department, eighteen became lecturers in technical colleges and twenty-one took up school teaching. Fewer than twenty entered industrial firms and of these several went to Mather and Platt or British Thompson Houston as heads of various divisions.

The membership of the Institute of Chemistry in 1901 totalled 683 Fellows. The *Proceedings* of that year contains a survey of this membership but unfortunately no information is given for 340 of them; of the remaining 343 it is clear that the majority were engaged in academic rather than industrial spheres. No fewer than 66 had the degree of PhD which indicates the strong connections between training in chemistry and the German universities; (Table 5.7 shows that in 1890 there were only 38 honours degrees in chemistry from English universities); 33 were on university staffs and 23 in technical colleges; 50 went abroad and 84 were employed in laboratories of various description. These included the laboratory of Somerset House and public laboratories such as the railways and borough council laboratories.

An analysis of past students of the Liverpool University Engineering Society from 1885 to 1912 reveals that there was a considerable braindrain of graduates to the Dominions; some 35 per cent went abroad, which corresponds very closely to the 32 per cent that went from the Royal College of Science.

Perhaps the most comprehensive source of information is E. Fiddes, Registrar of Manchester University, in his Register of Graduates of the Victoria University of Manchester (see Table 5.7). His survey included all graduates of the closing years of the nineteenth and early years of the twentieth century, and reveals that the rate of emigration was slowing down. Opportunities in industry for chemists and engineers were improving, but it was still true that the major proportion of graduates, either through choice or force of circumstances, entered the teaching profession.

In conclusion it would appear that the numbers of fully-trained scientists and technologists in England fell far short of what was desirable in the last quarter of the nineteenth century. In 1910 the number of university students of science and technology was about 3,000 whereas the corresponding figure in Germany was 25,000.[49] On the one hand there was a considerable wastage of latent talents and on the other too many partially or inadequately trained scientists were produced.

One of the main objectives behind the creation of the civic universities was the training of the cadres of scientists and technologists the country needed. The blame for not tackling this problem earlier may be attributed to industry, for not creating a demand for scientists; to the ancient universities, for paying too little attention to the physical sciences; and to successive governments, for their failure to establish an efficient unified educational system. It is certainly true that the intake of scientists into industry was not great, but it may well have been that many firms had every wish to employ scientists but were unable to find enough men of the highest calibre. It seems, therefore, that, while industry should not be entirely exonerated, the major portion of blame should fall on the government, for the civic universities were left to

Table 5.4 Graduate manpower 1870–1910 (figures represent numbers graduating in the stated years)

	1870	1880	1890	1900	1910
Science					
*BSc Honours Mathematics	1	1	8	22	44
*BSc Honours Physics	0	7	16	25	39
*BSc Honours Chemistry	3	1	26	48	126
*BSc Honours Geology	3	3	9	9	14
†BSc General degree	6	26	77	200	577
Total science	13	38	136	304	800
Technology					
‡BSc Honours Engineering	0	0	11	46	183
§BSc Honours Mining	3	6	13	14	31
§BSc Honours Metallurgy	3	11	3	3	10
BSc Technology (Honours)	0	0	0	0	12
BSc Engineering	0	0	0	0	137
BSc Mining	0	0	0	0	6
BSc Metallurgy	0	0	0	0	3
BSc Technology	0	0	0	0	9
Non-degree technology awards	0	0	3	11	40
Total technology	6	17	30	74	431
Total science and technology	19	55	166	378	1,231

* Includes Associates of the Royal College of Science
† Includes Associates (of Science) of the Armstrong College, Newcastle
‡ Includes Associates of the City and Guilds Central Technical College
§ Includes Associates of the Royal School of Mines

Source: Calendars of:
 (a) *Universities*
    London, Durham, Manchester, Liverpool, Leeds, Sheffield, Birmingham, Bristol
 (b) *Colleges*
    Imperial College of Science and Technology; Owens College; Yorkshire College; Armstrong College of Science; Mason College, Birmingham; University Colleges of Sheffield, Liverpool, and Nottingham.

Note: If Oxford and Cambridge are included the additions to the figures in the final total for science and technology are: 1870 (150); 1880 (148); 1890 (177); 1900 (160) and 1910 (189). The lack of variation in these figures reflects the dominance of mathematics at Cambridge. Mathematics graduates at Oxford and Cambridge accounted for 90 per cent of all English university science graduates in 1870 and 80 per cent in 1890.

Table 5.5 Non-degree courses in technology at English universities

College/University	Title of course	Year of first award
Newcastle College of Physical Science	Associateship in Science	1892
	College Diploma in Engineering	1899
	College Diploma in Naval Architecture	1903
	College Diploma in Mining	1903
	College Diploma in Marine Engineering	1914
	College Diploma in Agriculture	1912
Yorkshire College	Certificate of Proficiency in Engineering	1881
	Certificate of Proficiency in Dyeing	1888
	Certificate of Proficiency in Textile Industries	1894
	Certificate of Proficiency in Leather Industries	1894
	Certificate of Proficiency in Agriculture	1894
Firth College, Sheffield, and Sheffield University	Associateship in Engineering	1893
	Associateship in Metallurgy	1898
	Diploma in Mining	1910
Mason College of Science, and Birmingham University	Diploma in Engineering	1887
	Diploma in Mining	1904
	Diploma in Brewing	1907
University of Liverpool	Certificate in Engineering	1905
	Diploma in Engineering	1911

struggle on as best they could, facing immense difficulties in their attempt to achieve their objectives. More government money at an earlier stage, improved primary and secondary systems of education, and a national system of scholarships along the lines of the Whitworth Scholarships could have eased their task. Neither the Devonshire nor the Samuelson Commission[50] produced a cogent analysis of England's long-term needs for scientific manpower, and the picture that emerges from this survey of the civic universities reflects the absence of planning. At the core of the problem was the lack of a blueprint based on national objectives. The Imperial College of Science, in which the government played a full part, showed what could be done if the problem were tackled in a systematic way.

German higher education

The German universities, unlike their English counterparts, were state-sponsored institutions, being a direct responsibility of the Minister of Education. By the beginning of the nineteenth century some twenty universities had been founded throughout the states which later became unified to create the modern Germany. These universities were based on a four-faculty structure embracing law, medicine, theology and philosophy; the last of these being a late addition, being first established at Göttingen in 1737. It was through the philosophy faculties that the

Table 5.6 Cumulative totals of graduate scientists 1870–1910 (figures represent numbers graduating in or before the stated years)

	1870	1880	1890	1900	1910
Science					
*BSc Honours Mathematics	17	33	85	213	443
*BSc Honours Physics	0	16	87	286	640
*BSc Honours Chemistry	24	49	179	675	2,430
*BSc Honours Geology	30	76	113	189	271
†BSc General degree	6	172	614	2,577	7,126
Total science	77	346	1,078	3,940	10,910
Technology					
‡BSc Honours Engineering	0	0	60	440	1,553
§BSc Honours Mining	28	91	151	312	558
§BSc Honours Metallurgy	22	75	140	202	291
BSc Technology (Honours)	0	0	0	0	47
BSc Engineering	0	0	0	0	570
BSc Mining	0	0	0	0	26
BSc Metallurgy	0	0	0	0	30
BSc Technology	0	0	0	0	56
Non-degree technology awards	0	0	18	90	289
Total technology	50	166	369	1,044	3,420
Total science and technology	127	512	1,447	4,984	14,330

*Includes Associates of the Royal College of Science
†Includes Associates (of Science) of the Armstrong College, Newcastle
‡Includes Associates of the City and Guilds Central Technical College
§Includes Associates of the Royal School of Mines

Source: Calendars of:
(a)   *Universities*
       London, Durham, Manchester, Liverpool, Leeds, Sheffield, Birmingham, Bristol
(b)   *Colleges*
       Imperial College of Science and Technology; Owens College; Yorkshire College; Armstrong College of Science, Mason College, Birmingham; University Colleges of Sheffield, Liverpool, and Nottingham.

German universities attained their greatest eminence; this was attributable in large part to the role the universities played in fostering science studies which formed part of the philosophy faculties.

At a time when German morale was low following defeat at the battle of Jena, Wilhelm von Humboldt conceived the regeneration of the German state as coming through the schools and from the universities through a combination of teaching and research. Influenced by the work of the French chemist, Gay-Lussac, von Humboldt did much to introduce empirical science into the philosophy faculties of the German universities and spread the ideas and methods of French science in Germany. Berzelius exerted a strong influence, too, by his writings but the most significant contribution was made by Justus von Liebig

(1803–73), one of Gay-Lussac's first students, when in 1826 he established a chemistry laboratory at Giessen. Chemistry, especially organic chemistry (Liebig's special contribution), was to become the pre-eminent German science. Liebig's laboratory became a world-famous international training school and a model for others that followed.

Table 5.7 Occupation of graduates of the Victoria University, Manchester

	(a) Secondary Schools %	(b) University Technical college Training college %	%	Emigrated %	Other %
BSc Finals	31	13	11	7	38
BSc Honours Mathematics	36	40	0	2	22
BSc Honours Physics	41	31	9	3	16
BSc Honours Chemistry	21	29	28	12	10
B English	0	22	32	20	26

Source: E. Fiddes, *Chapters in the History of Owens College and of Manchester University, 1851–1914*. University of Manchester Publications, number 254, Historical Series, number 74, Manchester, 1937.

German universities during the nineteenth century were noted not only for the excellence of their scholarship but also for the lavish sums spent on them. The most generous of the states was Prussia which as early as 1805 spent £15,249 on universities – a sum exceeding the first grant to English universities in 1889. By 1880 Prussia was spending £350,000 on its six universities.[51] Berlin University seems to have been the university best supported by any of the German states; in 1876 it received 91 per cent of its income from state sources. The corresponding figures for Halle and Heidelberg were 65 per cent and 41 per cent, the average figure for all universities being 71 per cent.[52]

The excellence of the German universities must be seen against the background of the remainder of the educational system, in particular the schools. Like the universities these too were state institutions established only with the state's knowledge and consent; patronage of Church or private persons was rare. The foundations of a highly structured and well organised educational system in Prussia was laid down as early as 1808 by von Humboldt when he was placed at the head of the Prussian Education Department. Nothing approaching the extent of provision nor the degree of organisation of the Prussian system was to be found in England until 1902. There was no doubt in the minds of a deputation from the City of Manchester visiting Germany in 1896 that the key factor in Germany's rise to industrial eminence lay in the school system:

It is by no means a difficult matter [it said] to trace to the influence of the schools and the system of education generally, the improvement which has marked the manufacturing progress of Germany. . . . It is high time the effort was made in this country to give our youth the educational advantages which are enjoyed by their rivals abroad.[53]

The Samuelson Commission set up to inquire into technical instruction in England examined the school system in Germany. In its Report it stated: 'Secondary instruction of a superior and systematic kind is placed within the reach of the children of parents of limited means, to an extent of which we can form no conception in this country.'[54] The same lavish expenditure that one observes in regard to the German universities is found applying to the school system; again, particularly in Prussia. But it was not merely a question of setting aside certain sums of money; it was allocated according to predetermined needs as Dr Frederic Rose, the British Consul at Stuttgart, recorded: 'The Prussian Education Ministry maintains that state aid must be regulated by the needs of various localities and must not be simply a question of the even distribution of a certain amount laid aside for educational purposes.'[55]

Universities formed only a part of the German system of higher education; it also encompassed technical high schools and academies of technology specialising in particular fields. In contrast to the English universities, technical studies at university level were to be found not in the universities but in the technical high schools which were part of the German higher education system. These *technische Hochschulen* were created between 1840 and 1890 by converting small trade or technical schools established earlier in the century. The first technical high school, that at Carlsruhe (1867), had its origins in an institute founded in 1825 and modelled on the French École Polytechnique. That at Berlin was founded as a technical school in 1821, becoming a trade and building academy in 1871 and ultimately a technical high school in 1881. The technical high schools at Stuttgart (1870) and Darmstadt (1883) were founded originally as trade schools in 1836 and 1840 respectively. Between the formation of Carlsruhe in 1867 and Dresden in 1890 nine of these technical high schools were established: Aachen, Carlsruhe, Darmstadt, Dresden, Hanover, Berlin, Stuttgart, Munich.

In most cases it was merely a question of converting or extending existing premises, albeit at considerable expense to the authorities; in other cases entirely new buildings were erected. Stuttgart founded as a trades school in 1829 extended its buildings in 1879 at a cost of £75,000. New buildings were provided at Dresden (1875) and Hanover (1879), and at Aachen where a new chemistry laboratory was built in 1870 at a cost of £45,000. The Munich Technical High School cost the state £157,000, that at Hanover £350,000 and a new building at Berlin £450,000. The running costs, too, were largely provided by the states; the school at Berlin for instance received 90 per cent of its income from the state in 1876. The actual extent of state support varied from one school to another; in 1876 this ranged from 25 to 93 per cent.

The motive underlying this vast expenditure was simple; the technical high schools according to the Samuelson Commissioners were to impart 'a scientific training with its practical applications so that by this means a body of men might be educated in such a way as to make it possible for Continental states to compete with the workshop-trained engineers of England'.[56] As well as a full range of science and engineering disciplines the technical high schools included special subjects in their curriculum: naval architecture (Berlin), mining (Aachen), forestry (Stuttgart) and agriculture (Munich).

There was nothing comparable to them in England and any assessment of them must be set against the relative neglect of higher technical instruction in English universities and the difficulties encountered in establishing technical studies within the English universities. By 1900 there were over 13,000 students attending the technical high schools which without exception had highly qualified staffs.[57] There were over 4,000 students in attendance at Berlin alone in 1903. This school – Königliche Technische Hochschule at Charlottenberg – was perhaps the prize among the technical high schools. It was a state institution under the direction of the *Cultur Minister* (or Minister for Ecclesiastical, Educational and Medical Affairs). The school provided through a four-year course a specialised training in industrial subjects founded on a preliminary scientific education. Students came well prepared, having previously been required to attend a *Real Gymnasium* for a nine-year course and passing successfully the rigorous and demanding school-leaving examination. Students at the school in 1903 included: architecture 739, civil engineering 689, mechanical engineering 1,499, electrical engineering 321, naval architecture 259, marine engineering 123, chemistry 181, metallurgy 180, and officers and engineers from the navy.[58] To cope with such a large student body required a staff of over 400 – professors, private *dozenten*, assistants and construction engineers. In chemistry alone there was a staff of 55; staff in other subjects were mechanical and electrical engineering 115, architecture 89, civil engineering 56, science 66 and naval architecture. There was nothing quite approaching the scale of such an institution in English higher education.

Observers consistently pointed out that German education at all levels was characterised by a systematic thoroughness and zeal. The positive results that this bore in higher education can be illustrated by a single statistic: whilst the numbers of students of science and technology grew from about 3,000 to 4,000 in England and Wales (a 25 per cent increase) in Germany in the same period they increased by 40 per cent, from 15,000 to 25,000. Table 5.8 provides a detailed picture of the extent of the system in the session 1912/13 and Table 5.9 indicates how the universities, technical high schools and the higher academies of technology between them provided for German industry an elite corps of highly trained scientists and technologists far greater in number than that available to British industry.

Table 5.8   Students in German higher education 1912/13

	Number of institutions	Fully qualified students	Others	Total
Universities	22	59,312	9,965	69,277
Technical high schools	11	11,003	5,415	16,418
Mining academies	3	617	121	738
Forestry academies	4	273	54	327
Agricultural high schools	4	1,414	279	1,693
Veterinary high schools	5	1,241	99	1,340
Commercial high schools	6	2,326	5,311	7,637
Others	55	76,186	21,244	97,430
	110	152,372	42,488	194,860

Source:
Appendix to *Trade and Technical Education in France and Germany*, Report by J. C. Smail, Organiser of Trade Schools for Boys, London County Council, 1914, p. 22.

Table 5.9   Number of students studying technology in Germany, United States and Great Britain 1901–02

	Germany Technical high schools	United States Institutes for higher education	Great Britain Universities, technical schools and colleges
Agriculture	42	2,852	411
Architecture	1,440	459	—
Civil engineering	2,257	3,140⎫	
Mechanical engineering	5,503	4,459⎬	2,259
Electrical engineering		2,555⎭	
Chemistry and Metallurgy	1,180	*	667
Naval architecture	318	†	33
	10,740	13,465	3,370

*Chemistry not given separately, but probably included in 'General science courses', the number attending being 10,925.
† Included in mechanical engineering.

Source:
W. E. Dalby, 'The Education of Engineers in America, Germany and Switzerland', *Proceedings of the Institution of Mechanical Engineers*, 1903, Parts 1–2, pp. 281–349.[59] Figures for Great Britain and Germany taken from a schedule published by the Association of Technical Institutions.

Chapter 6

Industry, education and training

The entrepreneur, industrial management and education

'It is essential for the progress of the industry of this country that those to whom is entrusted the management of large concerns should have generally a higher class of education than that which they possess at the present time.'[1] Thus spoke Isaac Lowthian Bell, a leading steel manufacturer, in presenting evidence to the Royal Commission on Scientific Instruction in the 1870s. Industrial leaders and technological innovators in the Industrial Revolution had been largely self-educated men such as Nasmyth, Bramah and Stephenson, but as Britain moved into the era of steel, chemicals and electrical industries her failure to match others in the rate of increase of productivity focused attention increasingly on the quality of management. Lack of education and appropriate training was thought to be a key factor.

The transition from iron to steel occurred during the second half of the century; while British production of pig-iron trebled between 1850 and 1900, steel production increased from 60,000 tons to 5 million tons. The significant technological discoveries were of British origin but British steel production, despite an enormous initial lead, was overtaken by that of the United States and by that of Germany by the end of the century.

In the production of chemicals prior to mid-century the field was dominated by 'heavy chemicals', a cluster of products—alkalis, bleaching materials and inorganic acids—based on a group of processes centred on the alkali industry which mainly served the needs of the textile manufacturer. Until the final quarter of the century the main method of production of alkali was that discovered by the Frenchman Leblanc. In this field, to which chemical science had hardly been applied in a systematic way, British manufacturers led both in production, in exports and in industrial inventions.

This position was transformed by the discovery in 1865 of another method of alkali production by the Belgian Ernst Solvay. Because of favourable patent laws this could be taken up more quickly by continental manufacturers than by British; the latter were up against severe competition. Until 1875 England had supplied the entire home, United States, and much of the continental demand for caustic soda, soda ash and soda crystals, but after 1875 the rate of establishment of new factories declined. In 1883 *The Times* went so far as to declare the alkali industry a 'dying industry'. The position was exacerbated by the

McKinley (1890) and Dingley (1899) tariffs in the United States which reduced alkali exports to that country by a factor of five in the 1890s. This led to a number of the smaller factories going out of business, the Leblanc manufacturers finally being forced to amalgamate in November 1890 to form the United Alkali Company, a merger involving forty-eight factories and three saltworks with a productive capacity of 15 million tons. This represented a unification of the greater part of Britain's older chemical industry. Fourteen of the constituent concerns of the United Alkali Company were located in Widnes, ten of the twenty-three members of the original Board being Widnes industrialists.

Meanwhile the initiative had passed to Germany in organic chemistry, particularly in the production of synthetic dyes from coal tar which replaced the traditional dyes from natural sources. The first of these artificial dyes, indigo, was discovered by W. H. Perkin at the Royal College of Chemistry in 1856 and for the next twenty years the initiative was to remain with England. This changed with the discovery of synthetic alizarin in 1875, as profits from alizarin became an important source of funds for the German dye industry. This factor, together with the ready availability of qualified chemists from her universities and technical high schools, led to Germany becoming the site of the principal dyestuffs discoveries and developments after the 1870s.[2]

Towards the end of the century England became increasingly dependent on Germany for dyestuffs, intermediates and chemical plant. There was a certain irony in the situation, for with the outbreak of war in 1914 imports from Germany ceased and there was not sufficient dye available for the uniforms of soldiers. As one contemporary observer remarked: 'England produces immense quantities of benzene, the greater part of which goes to Germany, there to be converted into aniline dyes, a considerable quantity of which goes back to England.'[3] In 1880 the range of organic compounds numbered 15,000; by 1910 it had risen to 150,000. A whole new range of products—fertilisers, explosives, cyanides and pharmaceuticals—had been developed. Dyestuffs, textile auxiliaries and photochemicals as a group formed what became known as *petite industrie chemique*.[4] Other branches of chemistry had also come to the fore; physical chemistry, hardly established in 1875, by the end of the century was making a great impact, and electrochemistry too had by 1900 an established place in industry.

The electrical industry hardly existed in 1880 but by 1913 was of increasing importance, embracing telegraphy and electrical power generation and distribution. In this field a considerable part of the large plant for power stations was imported from Germany, much of British factory electrification being done by the German firm of Allgemeine Elektrizität Gesellschaft. Thus during the second half of the century new industries had made their appearance; products, industrial activities and techniques were both more extensive in range and more sophisticated than those at mid-century, calling for skills and knowledge not required by earlier industrial leaders.

The new demands that industry made on its leaders are exemplified in the person of Henry Bessemer. Self-educated he operated within an industry which called for greater scientific knowledge than the iron industry it was in part replacing. According to Michael Sanderson:

If there was a symbolic pivot in the transition of technology passing into the sphere of science it was Sir Henry Bessemer. A non-university man himself, he was increasingly forced by the middle of the century to rely on people like Dr Henry, Dr Percy and Dr Ure for scientific knowledge of which his own lack of higher education had left him ignorant. Bessemer's experience showed that it was becoming increasingly difficult to pursue the career of inventor independent of university expertise.[5]

Around this time 'innovation in a range of industries passed from men outside universities to those working in universities or who had benefited from university training':[6] in steel Darby, Cort and Bessemer gave way to Thomas and Siemens; in thermodynamics Watt, Stephenson, Trevethick and Joule gave way to Rankine (Glasgow); in metallurgy Sorby and Hadfield gave way to Arnold (Sheffield) and in hydraulics Rennie gave way to Reynolds (Manchester).

Bessemer was not alone in lacking formal education, nor in being partly dependent on others who had been trained. At mid-century, if not later, the majority of the industrial leaders were men who had entered firms as apprentices. Such was the case with William Armstrong, William Mather, Joseph Whitworth and William Fairburn. Traditional training for engineers had been an apprenticeship in factories, naval dockyards and railway workshops; in 1911 eleven of the knighted naval engineers had started as dockyard apprentices under the Admiralty Dockyard scheme. The same connections with apprenticeship are found in the chemical industry. Among the leaders of the Merseyside chemical complex of Liverpool, Warrington, St Helens and Widnes, William Gossage, Henry Deacon, Holbrook Gaskell and James Hargreaves had been apprenticed to druggists in early life. Others such as James Muspratt, John Hutchinson and Josias Gamble had even lacked such a start as this, embarking on an industrial enterprise with hardly any previous industrial experience. William Hesketh Lever went into soap-making in the 1870s because as a grocer he was being charged too much for soap; by 1900 he had become the leading soapmaker in England. Likewise William Pilkington, the founder of the glass firm, with little background went into partnership with others to form the St Helens Crown Glass Company; by 1900 Pilkingtons was the leading glass firm in England. Alfred Holt, after an apprenticeship with the Liverpool and Manchester Railway Company, could not get a post as railway engineer so decided to enter Lamport and Holt, the shipping firm, as a clerk. There he took up the study of marine engineering and his innovative skills in this field eventually won him the Watt Medal and Telfer Premium of the Institution of Civil Engineers. Setting up the Blue

Funnel line in partnership with his brother, Philip, he succeeded in solving the combined problems of the screw propeller, iron construction and compound engine, making it possible for large oceangoing steamships to operate economically.[7] Countless such examples were to be found throughout the United Kingdom during the nineteenth century; exceptions of course were the German born immigrants such as Ludwig Mond (Cassel Polytechnic and Heidelberg University), William Siemens (Göttingen University) and Ivan Levinstein (Berlin Technical High School and Berlin University).

A survey of industrialists and manufacturers active in the third quarter of the century on Merseyside reveals that of twenty-one individuals four only had received a university education, three of the four being educated in Germany or Switzerland. Nine of this group were born in or near Merseyside. It is not clear whether any of the British-born members received a secondary education, whereas ten of the next generation of industrialists on Merseyside were educated in secondary schools. Further, in contrast to the earlier generation half of the later generation were university educated.

A charge that was sometimes directed against industrial leaders in the nineteenth century was that they imitated the professional classes and gentry in sending their sons to public schools and the ancient universities, thus either directing them into non-industrial careers or unfitting them to manage the family firm adequately. One such criticism was made by Sir Swire Smith, a woollen manufacturer and member of the Royal Commission on Technical Instruction. In his inaugural address at Dundee Technical Institute in October 1888 he claimed: 'The wealthy manufacturer sends his son to a classical school to learn Latin and Greek as a preparation for cloth manufacturing, calico printing, engineering or coalmining. . . . After his scholastic career he enters his father's factory absolutely untrained.'[8]

Among Swire Smith's acquaintances there may have been some to whom this applied. Such a charge, however, has no validity with regard to Merseyside industrialists, among whom an awareness of their own educational shortcomings seemed most acute. An outstanding example is, of course, James Muspratt. After meeting and befriending von Liebig, the originator of the first university research laboratories, Muspratt sent his four sons, none of whom went to a public school, to Giessen to study under Liebig. All four returned to Merseyside, three of them entering their father's firm and making distinctive contributions to its success. Josias Gamble sent his son David to University College, London, to study science and engineering. He returned to his father's firm, eventually becoming its manager and the outstanding manufacturing chemist of St Helens. Sir John Brunner, of Brunner Mond, sent both his sons to Cheltenham and thence to Cambridge to study natural science, one going on to study at Zurich Polytechnic. Like the Muspratt family, later generations of the Pilkingtons, too, carried on in the family firm. William Pilkington's brother Richard was a trained engineer and his son William Windle served an apprenticeship in the firm in the 1860s. William's own sons William Roby and Thomas both entered the firm, the latter on the commercial side and the former eventually becoming factory superintendent. George Pilkington, who trained as a chemist at the Royal College of Chemistry, also returned to join the firm as its chemist. Elsewhere firms like Cadburys, Bibbys, and W. H. Allen sent their sons to the university generation after generation, even if they were the only graduates the firms employed.

It is clear that industrial leaders who had lacked a scientific education were aware of their deficiencies and were anxious to ensure that their own sons benefited from such an education. This concern often extended to their workmen too. At Crosfields of Warrington most managerial appointments were made from among men who had been brought up in the firm. After entry from school and training in the laboratories and works departments many continued their education, with the directors' strong encouragement, in the evening classes of the local technical colleges. Examples of such men in top positions in the firm in 1907 were F. Smith, a practical soap boiler with little academic knowledge who was manager of the soap-boiling department, F. J. Burton, the chief engineer who had started as a draughtsman, and G. Dale, originally a boilerman who had worked his way up to become manager of the fuel, gas and water departments.[9]

Leading industrialists were equally aware of the importance of pure science to industrial success. Replying to a circular distributed by the National Association of Technical Education in 1889 Sir William Mather, head of a large engineering firm in Oldham, wrote that 'in the technical schools the means should be provided to pursue science in the abstract for purposes of scientific research'. Ivan Levinstein in his reply insisted that what was needed were better trained chemists. Earlier, Lowthian Bell, in giving evidence to the Devonshire Commissioners, had expressed the hope that higher education institutions would be established in the industrial towns and cities so that men of pure science would settle in manufacturing districts and come into contact with the 'great industrial questions of the day'. The Devonshire Commissioners themselves concluded that 'much has to be done which will require continuous efforts on the part of the administration unless we are content to fall behind other nations in the encouragement which we give to pure science, and as a consequence to incur the danger of losing our pre-eminence in regard to its applications'.[10]

It was a reaction to the fear of foreign competition engendered by the visit of Leeds businessmen to the Paris Exhibition of 1867 and the apprehension that the French were outstripping them with the quality of their textiles which led to the foundation of Yorkshire College, Leeds, in 1874.[11] Recognising that Oxford, Cambridge and the public schools were not the answer to their needs and having little faith in the central administration, the manufacturers and industrialists adopted a policy of self-help on a massive scale; they turned their efforts to the creation of institutions of higher education which would provide the kind of scientific and technical training they themselves manifestly lacked. The movement for 'civic colleges' would not have gained the success it did were it not for the support of merchants, manufacturers and industrialists.

Josiah Mason founded his College of Science at Birmingham in 1880 as he was 'deeply convinced from his long and varied experience in different branches of manufacture of the necessity and benefit through systematic scientific instruction especially adapted to the practical mechanical and industrial pursuits of the Midland district'. [12] Later Sir James Chance, head of the Birmingham glass firm, gave £50,000 for engineering. The same pattern was found in many other cities. In Manchester the engineers of the city raised £10,000 in 1866 to found a chair of engineering at Owens College. In Liverpool leaders of industry and commerce contributed some £500,000 between 1881 and 1914, while the government in the same period gave only £150,000. [13] One of the greatest single gifts at Liverpool was that of £41,000 by Fenwick Harrison and J. W. Hughes for the construction of engineering laboratories specialising in engines, oil and gas for marine propulsion. At Newcastle a special committee was set up as early as 1852 with a view to establishing a science college; this committee included among its members four chemical manufacturers, four mining engineers, two civil engineers, one iron manufacturer, glass manufacturers, a shipbuilder and a shipowner. A college was opened in 1871, by which time young men of the area had for some time been going to Germany for a preparation for business and industrial life. [14]

The same general picture of initiatives taken by commercial and industrial leaders accompanied by a large measure of financial support is found at Sheffield, Nottingham and Bristol. As a number of scholars have pointed out this was actuated by self-interest; industry mainly supporting universities which gave them some expectation of return. Be that as it may, it was through this expectation of return that the country obtained the facilities for higher education in research in metallurgy (Sheffield and Birmingham), electrical engineering (London and Liverpool), mining (Birmingham, Newcastle and Nottingham) and naval architecture (Newcastle).

The concern of industrial leaders with science and technical training did not stop short at higher education – it extended to all levels. During the first half of the century in particular they were patrons of the mechanics' institutes. They later gave their support to the 'science and art' classes movement. At Warrington George Crosfield, who took the initiative in founding the School of Science, was chairman of the local Science and Art Classes Committee; likewise Henry Roscoe and Edmund Muspratt became chairmen of the local committees at Manchester and Liverpool respectively. The latter was profoundly influenced by this scheme and put his finger on its fundamental weakness when he observed:

I saw the evils resulting from the South Kensington system, which proceeded on the same lines as London University which granted degrees to all comers, provided they passed an examination only, without reference to their education and training. From this experience, together with the evils of the system of payment-by-results in elementary education I had come to the conclusion that there must be a radical change in our whole system of education.[15]

Enlightened firms took an interest in the further education of their employees both within and outside the firm. A notable example was Crosfields, which provided regular lectures, both scientific and popular, and a library of technical books and journals. An enquiry in 1907 revealed that of 123 youths employed by the firm only 27 attended night classes; to encourage better attendance the directors decided to pay a sessional fee of five shillings each and to offer an additional five shillings as a bonus for passing the examinations. Attendance greatly improved and was then made compulsory for all under seventeen years of age. To facilitate study in 1908 it was agreed to allow employees to leave work half an hour earlier on four days a week.[16]

At Bootle the firm of Johnsons at one time sent all their boys to the technical school for instruction in chemistry and other subjects but found that for the majority of cases it was 'a pure waste of time owing to the lack of general education'.[17] The firm consequently decided to hold special classes at the works itself, the instruction being provided by the head chemist. Attendance was voluntary, but nearly all the boys and men went through the course. Furthermore, boys who wished to attend continuation school were let off work and had their fees paid.

Manufacturers and industrialists sought to overcome their own educational deficiencies and to keep abreast of increasing specialised knowledge through the formation of technical and professional associations. On Merseyside a local branch of the Society of Chemical Industry was set up in 1882 shortly after a national society of the same name was formed. The membership of the national society included alkali manufacturers, chemical engineers, analytical chemists and assayers and university professors; 11 per cent came from Merseyside. All the leading manufacturers and chemists from alkali works, soap works and sugar works joined the local branch, whose first chairman was E. K. Muspratt. The committee included Holbrook Gaskell, Frederick Gossage, Ferdinand Hurter (later to become chief chemist to the United Alkali Company), J. C. Brown (Professor of Chemistry at University College, Liverpool) and Norman Tate (see chapter 4). In this body were forged the essential links between teachers and academics on the one hand and manufacturers and industrial chemists on the other. The national society produced a fortnightly journal and in 1887 another journal made its appearance – the *Chemical Trade Journal*. Such developments as these were not of course confined to chemistry. Each developing field was 'professionalising' itself in the same manner as evidenced by the formation of the Institution of Mechanical Engineers (1847), Institution of Gas Engineers (1863), the Iron and Steel Institute (1869), the Institute of Mining Engineers (1889) and the Institute of Mining and Metallurgy (1892).

The early generations of managerial leaders could not be blamed for their almost total lack of formal instruction in pure and applied science for until 1850 or so such facilities did not exist apart from those at the two London colleges. Many industrialists did what they could to ensure that their own sons did not lack scientific instruction and sought to create facilities with sparse aid from the government. There is little doubt that they had positive progressive attitudes towards the importance of pure science, technical training and research.

The three studies that follow of chemical education, engineering education and mining education demonstrate that the responsibility for the deficiencies in education and training can be attributed principally to the governments of the day.

The chemical industry and higher education

The technical initiative in the chemical industry passed to Germany in the final quarter of the century. This, according to Hardie and Pratt, 'was not a matter of commercial or indeed government concern; the philosophy of laissez-faire and Smilesean "self-help" governed trade and enterprise'. The dominance was most clearly marked in organic chemicals, in particular in dyestuffs. Did Britain's dependence on the German dye industry really matter? Certainly in terms of direct earning power the dyestuffs industry was not of crucial importance. 'After all', argued Hardie and Pratt, 'the value of the dyes was about 1 per cent of the textiles to which they were applied.'[18]

Although the value of exports of all chemicals from the United Kingdom fell from £9 million in 1890 to £8.6 million in 1900, while those of Germany increased in the same period from £4.5 million to £6.5 million, too much cannot be made of this as these figures were dwarfed by earnings from coal, steel, textiles and machinery. Hohenberg concedes that 'surprisingly, even the German industry was of limited importance as an exporter. In 1908 chemicals represented only 3.6 per cent of German merchandise exports', and he concludes that 'there is little evidence of spectacular gains to the economy from growth in chemicals . . . the chemical industry did not exert any great influence on growth by stimulating the demand for other products, or, more generally, by raising the level of economic activity'.[19]

During the latter part of the century the German chemical industry, the universities and technical high schools were the objects of frequent visits by deputations and observers from England. The visitors were invariably impressed by all they saw. Around the turn of the century Dr Frederick Rose, HM Consul at Stuttgart, attempted to relate the German investment in higher education with the progress of the chemical industry, or, in his words, attempted 'to show to what extent the German chemical industries have benefited by the sums expended by the German states on chemical instruction'. His findings are worth examining in some detail. The field of chemical research and investigation, he said, was so dominated by Germany that 'a knowledge of German is essential – the best manuals are in German and two-thirds of the world's annual output of chemical research work comes from Germany'.[20]

A survey by Professor Fischer of all the larger chemical works and 80 per cent of the smaller revealed that Germany possessed 4,000 works-based chemists who had passed through universities or technical high schools.[21] Some of the larger works employed between 20 and 105 chemists and no fewer than thirty-three employed between 6 and 20. The Baden Aniline Dye and Soda Works alone employed more than 100 academically trained chemists.

The figures given in an earlier chapter show that production of honours chemists in English universities and university colleges from 1860 to 1897 totalled only 859. In 1902 a Committee of the British Association circularised the Society of Chemical Industry. Of 502 replies 107 were graduates; of 167 industrial chemists 43 had a degree. A similar survey of the Institute of Chemistry membership revealed that 30 per cent were graduates.

By 1897 German production of chemicals amounted to £50 million, but there was no complacency. In the view of the Society for the Protection of Chemical Industries: 'It is absolutely indispensible for the further progress of chemical industries that the necessary sums for thorough reorganisation of chemical industries be forthcoming.'[22]

Between 1820 and 1899 state aid to universities in Prussia multiplied tenfold; in 1897 the total income of Prussian universities amounted to £563,584 of which the state gave £412,683. Sir Philip Magnus estimated that in the 1880s the total capital cost of technical high schools in Germany amounted to some £3 million with a further annual running cost of £250,000. The investment of such vast sums, a considerable proportion of which went on chemical instruction, was in Rose's view justified: 'Sums expended on chemical instruction have been amply repaid . . . it is universally recognised that the efforts made hitherto must be increased and more carefully and judiciously applied, if the German chemical industries are to maintain and strengthen their position in the future.'[23]

The contrast between higher chemical education in Germany and that in Britain was striking, particularly in regard to the measure of support it received from the state and the way it was organised. The chemical industry on Merseyside and its relationship with the University of Liverpool serves as an illustration of this.

As the chemical industry in and around Liverpool grew in the second half of the nineteenth century Merseyside became a major centre of the industry. On the formation of the United Alkali Company in 1891 no fewer than fourteen of the constituent firms were situated in Widnes and ten of the original members of the Board were Merseyside industrialists. Further, the man appointed to be chief chemist of the United Alkali Company, Ferdinand Hurter, was chief chemist of the Widnes firm of Gaskell and Deacon; born in Schaffhausen Hurter was educated at Zurich Polytechnic and Heidelberg. In the period 1850 to 1890 profits in the chemical industry soared, but the wealth accumulated by Merseyside chemists did not match that made by Liverpool shipowners and merchants in the early part of the century. Nevertheless, the chemists were a source of constant support to the fledgling university from its foundation as a University College in 1881. The names of Brunner, Muspratt, Gaskell and Gossage constantly recur. Such support was very necessary in view of the tardiness of the government in assisting the college.

To start with £80,000 was collected by public subscription, which enabled the college to open, thereafter subscriptions and donations were the main means of financing it; in 1895 for instance they formed 35 per cent of its income. But in addition a special Sustentation Fund had to be established in order to enable the College to continue in being; Brunner, Muspratt and Gossage all contributed sums of £100 a year for ten years to this Fund. In 1906 the annual income amounted to £64,000 of which government grants accounted for £13,200 and local authority subsidies for £2,400. In the same year Brunner and Edmund Muspratt gave £6,666 and £5,700 respectively for specific purposes; together these amounted to 20 per cent of the annual income and exceeded government grants on the one hand and authority subsidies on the other.

Financial hardship was a constantly recurring theme of the college prior to 1914. In the Annual Report for 1887 the Principal stated:

No one realises to what hole-and-corner shifts the College is reduced to for getting through the needed work. Every fragment of space, corridor or closet, heated or unheated, has been pressed into service, single rooms are curtained off into double, no Professor can regard any lecture room as his own, and equip it accordingly and lecturers and demonstrators have no room at all.

Chemistry was as hard hit as any subject. 'The requirements of advanced technological and honours students', wrote the Professor in 1892, 'are met with difficulty, they work in scattered rooms designed for accessory purposes and neither in supervision, ventilation or economy of teaching strength can such a system be regarded as otherwise than defective.' The intentions of the College towards chemistry at its opening had been admirable; indeed one of the six chairs created was in chemistry and the first building erected was the first section of the chemistry laboratories. But intentions with regard to the development of organic chemistry and technological chemistry could not be put into effect for lack of facilities. To relieve the tremendous pressure on the inadequate chemical laboratories a subscription appeal was launched, as a result of which it was possible in 1896 to erect the extensions originally proposed in 1881.

Contributions for these, the William Gossage Laboratories, came from his son F. H. Gossage and his partner F. S. Timmins (£7,000), and from John Brunner, E. K. Muspratt and William Lever who each gave £1,000. Brunner, Muspratt and Gossage also provided the equipment for these laboratories, together with extensions for metallurgy. To complete the chemical facilities of the new college, for which £29,000 had already been contributed, Muspratt in 1905 donated a gift of £17,000 for laboratories of physical chemistry. This followed Brunner's gift of £10,000 to create a Chair of Physical Chemistry two years earlier. With these additions the University placed itself in the forefront of university chemical education. According to Ramsay Muir:

These are the only laboratories of their kind in England. Mr Muspratt, himself a scientific chemist, knew that this branch of chemistry was to become of increasing importance to the industry of England, and he ensured that his own city should be ahead of all England in meeting this new need. This has placed Liverpool in the forefront of English cities in the provision of the most complete facilities for advanced studies, especially for those studies upon which national efficiency depends.[24]

In the absence of research endowments and fellowships such research as did take place in chemistry was carried out by members of staff. In 1886 the chemistry staff consisted of three; this number increased to five by 1893 and subsequently to six (1896), eight (1897), nine (1908), eleven (1909) and twelve (1913). They were few in number and weighed down by extensive teaching duties, so that research tended to take second place. But from the early days there were individual members of staff who engaged in research at a time when research publications figured less prominently in promotions than they were to later. By 1913–14 there were thirty-one research papers (involving twenty individuals), none of which seems to have had any relevance to industry.

As far as research is concerned the university in its early days seemed to have been of little value to local industry. But it must be borne in mind that the academic priority in the minds of the founders was 'scientific instruction'.

To cater for the various needs of students at the undergraduate level the college had implemented a number of different courses; by 1906 these spanned general chemistry, physical chemistry, organic and advanced organic chemistry, metallurgy, engineering chemistry and the alkali industries. Entries were fourteen, thirty-four and twenty-four respectively for general chemistry, organic chemistry and physical chemistry, but disappointingly only three students enrolled for the alkali industries class and two for the metallurgy. Even at this relatively late stage there were only two successes in the honours BSc degree examinations and twenty-two in the finals BSc. It is clear that the honours degree examination presented a major obstacle which few students attempted, numbers rising only slightly between 1900 and 1914. In the decade 1880–99 there were thirty-three successful candidates in the BSc finals degree examination (about three per year); between 1900 and 1909 there were 205 (twenty per year) and from 1910 to 1913, 179 (forty-five per year). In the period as a whole between 1881 and 1914 there were in all some 350 successful finals degree students.

Chemistry was but one of many options open to candidates; assuming that as many as one-third of the successful candidates had studied chemistry this represented no more than about 120 graduates spread over a thirty-year period and at a conservative estimate at least 50 per cent of these went into teaching. One can safely say that over the period not more than some fifty to a hundred graduates were available to fifty or so chemical firms on Merseyside. Without detracting from the contribution the civic colleges made to the technological progress of the country it can be argued with some justification that the chemical industry did more for the university than the university was able to do to service the needs of industry.

There was a paucity of British chemists working in industry in the 1870s and their growth in numbers was slow. Edmund Muspratt, convinced that some knowledge of metallurgy was necessary, found that Edward Frankland at Owens College could teach him nothing so 'I got a textbook on assaying and worked by myself in the basement as there was only one other worker in the region'. It was the same with organic chemistry; W. H. Perkin recalled the circumstances in which his father, the discoverer of the first aniline dye, abandoned the industry in 1874: 'Inquiries were made at many of the British universities in the hope of discovering young men trained in the methods of organic chemistry but in vain.'[25]

It is sometimes claimed that there was little incentive for the graduate to enter industry and that industrialists viewed the academic graduate with suspicion. If anyone can be said to represent the views of both industry and the academic on Merseyside it was Edmund Muspratt. In 1870 he had been some sixteen years in charge of the family's Widnes alkali works and writing of that year later in his autobiography he observed that

having so many new processes in hand I thought it advisable to engage a well-educated chemist as head of the laboratory at Widnes. It was difficult to find at that time a suitable man in England and in Germany owing to the war which had taken so many young men for service in the army, it was difficult to find a young chemist willing to come to this country. After some correspondence with Professor Knapp of Brunswick Polytechnic I engaged a Dr Jurisch who had been educated at Berlin University.[26]

Fortunately the deficiencies in the ranks of chemists both on Merseyside and nationally could be made up by bringing over German chemists. An additional factor was that English graduates could supplement their training by a spell at a German university. Most leading British chemists spent a period under Liebig or Bunsen or

Kekulé or Kolbe; they included Henry Roscoe (Heidelberg), Lyon Playfair (Giessen), Edward Frankland (Marburg and Giessen), William Ramsay (Heidelberg and Tubingen), A. W. Williamson (Heidelberg and Giessen), H. E. Armstrong (Leipzig) and E. K. Muspratt (Giessen, Heidelberg and Munich).

The attractions of studying under one of the outstanding German chemists apart, there were other inducements to go to Germany. Fees at the Royal College of Chemistry were £30 to £40 a year whereas German semesters cost only £5, laboratories were £6 and board and lodging were cheap. Foreign students thus benefited from the large state subsidy to German higher education. Rose in 1901 estimated that Germany spent £60,000 educating foreign students who then went back to their own countries and increased foreign competition.[27] There was a qualitative difference, too, for the German PhD was research-based compared to the three-year British undergraduate degree through lectures and examinations. 'The Germans with their Lern und Lehrenheit are on true lines whilst we are hindered by examinations, are too apt to ignore in our old system the essential aim of all university life – the advancement of learning.'[28]

Muspratt's solution to his problem, namely the employment of a German chemist, was one adopted by many manufacturers, none more so than the Warrington soap firm of Crosfields. The arrival of Karl Markel at that firm in 1890 initiated a 'new era'. But Markel had originally been brought over by Ludwig Mond to tutor his children. Mond, educated at Cassel Polytechnic, at Marburg University under Kalbe and under Bunsen at Heidelberg, came to Manchester with a sulphur extraction process for alkali production by the Leblanc process but later went into partnership with John Brunner thus creating the firm of Brunner Mond set up to produce alkali by the new Solvay process. Mond, who was never satisfied with 'rule of thumb', had high regard for German chemists. His first works chemist, Mebus, had also studied under Kolbe and Bunsen. English chemists in Mond's view were 'less rigorously schooled'. He had occasion to change his opinion after engaging the services of Watts, an English chemist; Mond at first refused to employ him on the grounds that he only employed German chemists, whereupon Watts offered to work for nothing until he had proved his worth. Mond was so impressed by Watts that he reversed his earlier policy and encouraged Roscoe to send him graduates from Owens College. But the policy of bringing key men over from the Continent was continued for 'it was on his German assistants that Mond most heavily relied'.

Mond's favourable attitude to German chemists could not be ascribed to prejudice for the same policy was found at Crosfields where Markel so impressed the firm that he was appointed works manager. He thereupon proceeded to recruit a brilliant team of German chemists. According to George Crosfield 'Markel set to work to apply scientific knowledge where there had been merely common practical manu-

facturers without any chemical knowledge'. Each production department was put in the charge of a trained chemist, but clearly this did not
meet with approval in English eyes, Crosfield's judgement being that 'he,
Markel, was obsessed with the idea that no good chemist came out of
England and the consequence was that we began to get an overdose of
German scientists in-the works'.[29] It was 1907 before Markel's German
scientists were replaced by English graduates.

Read Holliday, the Yorkshire dyestuffs firm, used mostly Germans as
did Mortons of Carlisle. In fact the English dye industry as a whole was
highly dependent on Germans, and the best native firm, Levinsteins, had
been founded by a German emigré in 1864. Its chief innovator after
Perkin, Peter Griess, was also a German.[30] Pilkingtons, by 1900 the
leading glass firm in England, also sought Germans. The firm enquired
after and obtained a German chemist at the Royal College of Chemistry,
probably through the influence of George Pilkington, who had been
trained there.

It was the same with appointments to university staff, the best known
being Carl Schorlemmer whom Roscoe brought over to Owens College
in 1874 to promote organic chemistry. Shortly after, in 1878, J. J.
Himmel, a graduate of Zurich Polytechnic, was appointed to be the first
instructor (and later professor) of the Dyeing Department at Leeds. At
Liverpool C. A. Kohn was appointed demonstrator and assistant
lecturer in 1886. Kohn was the first of what appear to be several
German-trained PhDs to join the staff; of twenty-eight members of staff
appointed between 1881 and 1913 no fewer than ten were in this
category.

Although the direct economic benefit to Germany from investment in
the chemical industry was minimal there were substantial other
advantages. In Haber's view of all the industries, both British and
German, 'the German chemical industry appeared to be the most
dynamic'. This was due to the financial ability of management, the
concentration of the industry in large and medium sized firms, but
above all to the fact that the day-to-day business was being directed by
chemists and scientifically-oriented managers.

The Samuelson Commissioners on visiting the Baden Works at
Ludwigshafen and other firms in Germany and Switzerland found large
numbers of chemists employed by the firms together with a variety of
laboratories in each firm. Their conclusion was that: 'The first principle
which guides the commercial heads of all the Continental colour works
is the absolute necessity of having highly trained scientific chemists, not
only at the head of every department of the works. . . . this stands in
absolute contrast to the method adopted in this country'.[31]

Professor Paul Hohenberg in his study of the chemical industry
concluded: 'The most striking characteristic of the early German firms
was the willingness of entrepreneurs to entrust the operation of the firm
to technical men and gradually to shift the focus of decision-making
away from the factory towards the laboratory.'[32] German firms, he

found, 'made considerable use of technical and scientific personnel in a managerial capacity – Non technical entrepreneurs were willing to hire and promote these men – and to allow the operations of the firm to grow and change in response to the new technology being developed'.

Professor David Landes of Harvard University has called the attitude of German entrepreneurs 'a commitment to technical efficiency, largely independent of any economic calculus concerning the relative merits of change and the status quo'. The 'spin-off' of these attitudes, according to Hohenberg, 'was the magnitude of the research efforts, and frequent expansion and diversification dictated by the results of this effort. Capital followed where science led, and funds were not begrudged even when profits seemed distant and uncertain.' The result was that by 1914 'a major factor in Germany's short run advantage was her "installed capacity" for technical effort'.[33]

A commitment, then, to technical effort and research and the effective use of scientists and technical experts at all levels – in the research laboratory, on the production side, in management – was the foundation of the success of the German chemical industry. A policy of heavy investment in universities and technical high schools meanwhile ensured the supplies of the necessary experts. Perhaps of equal importance was the fact that German firms made use of highly trained technical salesmen who were instrumental in consolidating existing markets and winning new markets abroad.

The education of engineers in England and abroad

During the second half of the nineteenth century a radical change had been effected in English society, one which involved a rapid and increasing trend towards 'professionalisation'; although characteristic of several occupational areas of life this was especially marked in engineering.

The censuses of 1841, 1861, 1881 and 1911 provide information which illustrates this trend. The census of 1841 listed only clergy, lawyers and medical men as 'professional persons', and these were found to number 54,000. The census of 1861 admitted civil engineers to the professional ranks. By 1870 the *Contemporary Review* was citing the Church, the Bar and the army and navy as 'higher' professions; civil engineers, along with medical practitioners and solicitors, were considered to be 'lower' professions. According to the census of 1881 professional men had increased to some 115,000 of whom 9,400 were engineers (civil and mining). They were very much in the minority among professional men for there were 45,000 clergy, 20,000 lawyers and 21,000 medical men. The same general picture is to be found in 1911 with engineers accounting for only 17,000 out of a total of about 170,000.

Small as this may seem as a proportion of professional men it is nevertheless true that engineering was becoming increasingly recognised as a 'respectable' profession. It had become organised into a number of distinct professional bodies, the membership of which increased by leaps and bounds between the time of their formation and the end of the century. The first of these professional institutions was the Institution of Civil Engineers founded in 1818. By 1900 it had a membership of over 6,000. Other major bodies were: the Institution of Mechanical Engineers (107 members in 1847 – 3,000 by 1900); the Institution of Electrical Engineers (110 members in 1871 – 3,660 in 1900); and the Institution of Mining Engineers (founded 1889 – 2,400 members by 1900).

Thus a remarkable transformation had taken place both in society as a whole – that of late Victorian England becoming increasingly professional and technological – and within the field of science and engineering where the dilettante amateur had been replaced by the qualified professional, a move which was accelerated by the institutions' strict adherence to qualifications and standards of entry. The engineers themselves were aware of the victory they had achieved, namely, acceptance by society of engineering as a profession suited to the middle classes and even perhaps to gentlemen. This was a hard-won achievement despite the lip-service continually paid to the engineering marvels of the new technological and industrial society. Continually charged as the profession was with the accusations of 'rule of thumb' and 'trial and error' it was inevitable that the whole question of education and training should rank as a high priority in the deliberations of the professional institutions.

The earliest and numerically the strongest in terms of membership of the professional institutions was the Institution of Civil Engineers. This showed an understandable concern over the problems of education, training and status. Indeed the Council of the Institution itself made two extensive analyses of the education of engineers, in 1868 and 1903, which were later published as reports.[34]

The first analysis was made through the issue of a circular which asked for details of the general system of engineering education, list of establishments, and diplomas or certificates awarded in several countries. In addition the Council invited suggestions from any person willing to help. The Council began its report by pointing out that in England the profession of engineering was entirely unconnected with the government and further that there was no public provision for engineering education.

Every candidate for the profession must get his technical, like his general education, as best he can; and this necessity has led to conditions of education peculiarly and essentially practical, such being the most direct and expeditious mode of getting into the way of practical employment. The education of an engineer is, in fact, effected by . . . a simple course of apprenticeship, usually with a premium, to a practising engineer, during which the pupil is supported, by taking part in the ordinary business routine, to become gradually familiar with the practical duties of the profession.[35]

It was conceded that it was not the custom to consider theoretical knowledge as 'absolutely essential' but that the practical education available in England was the most perfect possible, and that: 'This thorough proficiency in practical matters tends to largely compensate for – in many cases to outweigh – the deficiency in theoretical attainments, and it is undoubtedly this, influenced in some degree by the natural self-reliance and practical common sense inherent in the English character, which has given such a high standing to the profession in this country.'[36]

The Council found that in most parts of the Continent in contrast the status of civil engineers differed markedly from that obtaining in England. In almost every country of Europe there existed a state corps of engineers, educated and supported by the government and whose function it was to construct and superintend the public works of the nation.

In France, where the best example of this system was found, there were two divisions of Government Corps of Engineers, namely, the Ingénieurs des Mines and the Ingénieurs des Ponts et Chaussées. After a three-year course at the École Polytechnique students passed on either to the École des Mines or to the École des Ponts et Chaussées for at least three years. The education obtained at all these institutions was mainly at the expense of the government, for the students' fees were very modest. For practical education students were sent on 'missions' to various public works. Engineers, other than those for government service, did a three-year course in the École Centrale des Arts et Manufactures which, although founded as a private establishment, was, in 1870, under state control. Students paid moderate fees and at the end of the course were awarded a Diploma of 'Ingénieur des Arts et Manufactures'. The Polytechnique was itself a feeder school for more specialised studies in selected branches of engineering, the so-called 'écoles d'application' comprising the École des Ponts et Chaussées, the École du Génie Militaire (moved from Mézières to Metz), the École d'Artillerie, the École des Mines, the École des Ingénieurs Geographes, and the École des Ingénieurs de Vaisseaux.

In Prussia master constructors (Baumeisters) were employed by the state and their education was rigorous. After a thorough education in a gymnasium and a year spent with one of the construction officers of the state a student was admitted into a special government educational establishment in Berlin, the Royal School of Construction (Königliche Bau Academie) where he spent two years studying science, engineering and architecture. At the end of this if he passed his first state examination he entered practical paid employment in a subordinate capacity. After three years he devoted two more years to study and then sat a second state examination. If successful he was considered fully qualified for a government appointment. Thus the complete education of the government official engineer occupied eight years from the time of his leaving the preliminary school. But a feature of this education was that four years were devoted to practice, and in this it contrasted to the French system; in fact it combined the best characteristics of the English and French systems. The systems pertaining in Austria and Switzerland were similar to the Prussian system whereas that in Russia was practically the same as in France.

The Council drew the obvious conclusion that:

The education of foreign engineers is strongly contrasted with that in England in every particular. Practical training by apprenticeship is unknown; the education begins at the other end, namely, by the compulsory acquirement of a high degree of theoretical knowledge, under the direction, and generally at the expense of the Government. Partly with this, and partly afterwards, there is communicated a certain amount of information on practical matters; but this is imparted in a way differing much from the English plan, and probably with less efficient results. Thus, while the English engineer is launched in his profession with the qualification of a considerable practical experience, but with perhaps little or no theoretical knowledge, the foreign one begins with a thorough foundation of principles, but with a limited course of practice; a deficiency, however, which tends to correct itself with time.[37]

The 1870 Report of the Institution of Civil Engineers contained suggestions offered to the Council by various professional engineers. The most devastating and at the same time constructive analysis of the English system was given by Professor Fleming Jenkin of Edinburgh. Jenkin pointed out that abroad, as well as the central schools of Berlin and Paris, where competition was severe and standards high, there existed polytechnics at Zurich, Hanover and Dresden, offering an education only a few degrees less severe than that at the École Polytechnique yet the numbers attempting to gain admission were considerable. In England, on the other hand, 'Young men, at the age of about eighteen, enter the office of a civil engineer. Usually few questions are asked as to previous training . . . the pupil is a sort of nuisance in an office, only tolerated in consideration of the fee which accompanies him.'[38]

From personal experience I can declare, that most pupils are so ignorant of algebra that they cannot apply the simple formulae which are given in engineers' pocket-books. Their arithmetic is very shaky, and a knowledge of physics, chemistry, geology, or the higher mathematics is wonderfully rare. . . . These young men during three years have the run of the office or workshop. . . . No-one teaches them anything. . . . Abroad, competitive examinations keep out incompetent men, in Britain they are weeded out by the result of the struggle for existence.[39]

Despite his trenchant criticisms Jenkin did not wish to see the English system of apprenticeship or pupilage removed but rather that the defects of the system be eliminated and to that end he urged a great improvement in the teaching of the sciences in the secondary schools and 'the establishment in some large towns, such as Liverpool and Birmingham, of colleges on the Scottish model, i.e. well endowed colleges giving chiefly general scientific training, with a few special technical chairs'.[40]

In 1903 the Council of the Institution showed its continuing concern with the state of engineering education by setting up another committee to consider the best methods of training for all classes of engineers on the principle that the education of an engineer 'must include both practical experience and scientific training'. This Committee under the chairmanship of Sir William H. White, President of the Institution of Civil Engineers, included representatives of the Institution of Mechanical Engineers, the Institution of Naval Architects, the Iron and Steel Institute, the Institution of Electrical Engineers, the Institution of Gas Engineers and the Institution of Mining Engineers. The conclusions of its Report can be taken therefore to represent a wide range of opinions and experiences.

The Committee found that 'at present a considerable proportion of students enter technical institutions ill-prepared, and at least one year has to be devoted to instruction which ought to be secured beforehand'.[41] The main recommendation of the Committee was to the effect that all boys entering engineering should stay on at school until they were seventeen years of age, and should be given a broadly-based education with emphasis on mathematics and science. After this thorough scientific education half of the training was to be practical and half devoted to theoretical studies including post-graduate work 'facilities for which should be considerably increased'. Thirty-five years had elapsed between these two major reports; after that considerable period of time for reflection what the committee was in effect recommending was the German system of engineering training.

It is no mere coincidence that in the same year (1903) as the committee of representatives of all the Institutions was appointed a lengthy paper was read to the Institution of Mechanical Engineers by Professor W. E. Dalby on 'The education of engineers in America, Germany and Switzerland'.[42]

Professor Dalby began by reminding the members that long before Britain's foreign competitors had any engineering industries at all, Britain had gained a monopoly of world trade

partly due to the fortunate possession of coal and iron, but chiefly due to the genius, inventiveness, perseverance, shrewdness and business acumen of the great British engineers of the last century. . . . As the industries developed, the method of training apprentices gradually took form and became a system, and probably most of those present have served an apprenticeship under some form of this system, namely a seven or five years' apprenticeship in the works. With scientific progress, changing methods of manufacture, and the advent of electricity as a necessary part of the engineering equipment of every mechanical engineer, there has been scarcely any change in the recognised method of training engineers.[43]

Dalby was of the opinion that the weak point in British training was basic scientific instruction. This detracted from the success of the multiplicity of courses which had been established at colleges and universities for 'much time is wasted at colleges here on teaching things which should have been taught at school'. The training provided at Charlottenberg and Zurich, on the other hand, was too academic, though he conceded that 'one thing is certain, the American, German and Swiss student starts his course with a far better education on which to build than is the case with us'. The Reports of the Institution of Civil Engineers had stressed that any reforms had to have the full cooperation of employers; in Dalby's view the latter were the key to the situation: 'The great defect in the English method of training engineers . . . is the want of coordination between the colleges and the employers. If the employers will concern themselves with this question their attitude will speedily change.' 'Employers', stated Dalby, 'still look askance at college-bred youths.'[44] Abroad it was a very different story.

Dalby's solution to the problems besetting English engineering training was a 'sandwich' system; he advocated that the winter months be spent in college and the summer months in the works. He conceded that this scheme would be a novel concept to many in England although it was common practice abroad and was not unknown in Britain. 'This alternating system must not be regarded as experimental. The Admiralty have had something very similar in operation for forty years and it has been of benefit in the education of marine engineers – the Scottish universities lend themselves too to the system.'[45]

Dalby's paper, read on 24 April 1903, formed the focus of a long debate on the subject of the education of engineers in which much support was expressed in favour of the 'sandwich' system. Professor Archibald Barr of Glasgow spoke in favour quoting from many letters he had received. In his view, which was also, he claimed, the unanimous opinion of engineers in the Glasgow district, it was preferable for all students to spend a year in the workshops before going up to university. J. A. F. Aspinall, a Vice-President of the Institute of Mechanical Engineers and later appointed Associate Professor at Liverpool University, believed there was a great deal of truth in Dalby's remark that 'many employers look askance at college-bred youths'. In his view, 'many youths quite deserve it' for 'often young men who go to college first without having any workshop experience, do not, when they come to the workshop, do as well as they should, and were very apt, on account of their superior airs, to give a great deal of offence to those with whom they were working'.[46]

It is perhaps not altogether surprising that Aspinall took this view for as a young man he himself had been an apprentice and it was only by means of a Whitworth scholarship had he later been able to study. This prejudice against the college man and college training was common to a number of the engineers most of whom had reached the top through apprenticeship and evening classes. Sir Arthur Rucker, Professor of Engineering at London University, complained that 'in this country a degree did not carry any very great weight in the engineering world'. That such a view prevailed after the great studies which had been made in engineering education at university level was a poor reflection on the profession and practice of engineering.

Following the lead given by University College, and King's College, London, all the later civic colleges gave a special emphasis to engineering education; though the most complete provision of engineering education was to be found at Glasgow, which had instituted the first chair of civil engineering in 1840 and pioneered the 'sandwich' system. The first attempt to produce a 'technological university' in England was the creation in 1884 of the Central Institution at South Kensington. This, as pointed out in an earlier chapter, was the brainchild of the City and Guilds of London Institute for the Advancement of Technical Education formed by the Livery Companies of London. The City and Guilds had shortly before spent £36,000 on the erection of Finsbury Technical College, one of the first purpose-built and well-endowed technical colleges to offer systematic and extended day courses. By the end of the century there were a number of such colleges, together with the Royal Indian Engineering College, Cooper's Hill (established 1871) and the Crystal Palace School of Practical Engineering (established 1872).

On the face of it, with some dozen university engineering departments and another dozen or so intermediate establishments, it would seem that facilities for engineering education were fairly adequate, giving the lie to the repeated assertions of the engineering institutions that theoretical instruction was undervalued. But the mere existence of these institutions alone does not answer the case. There were in 1900 still fewer than twenty engineers who were entitled to be addressed as 'professor', and the total strength of the academic staff of all engineering departments did not exceed a hundred; at that time the Charlottenberg Technical High School in Berlin alone had a staff of thirty in its engineering 'department', while the Munich, Hanover and Stuttgart Schools had fourteen, thirteen and fifteen respectively. From the mid-1880s onwards there were about a hundred university-trained entrants to the engineering profession together with some 100 to 200 entrants from one of the other institutions.

The 1870s and 1880s witnessed many developments in engineering education; the civic colleges referred to this period as a 'new era' in engineering. One would expect that by 1890 engineering graduates would have been produced in considerable numbers. In fact by 1890 English universities had produced fewer than a hundred graduates with a BSc general degree and of these only a small proportion, perhaps one-fifth, studied engineering. As to honours graduates there were three only produced in 1890 – at Owens College – and the total number produced up to that date still fell below twenty. Thus engineering was not a graduate profession even at this late date.

With Liverpool, Leeds, Birmingham and Sheffield all attaining independent university status in the 1900s (when that was also a rapid multiplication of chairs in engineering) a more promising picture could be expected in 1910. The number of honours graduates produced in that year was nearly 150 and the total number of graduates was over 1,000. The trend at London illustrates well the rapid growth: between 1903 and 1910 the numbers of honours graduates each year were 5, 4, 18, 27, 32, 44, 55 and 60 respectively. The older colleges of University College and King's College were outpaced by the Central Technical Institution, which produced 128 graduates compared to University College's 43 and King's College 33. This is of great significance in view of the fact that the Institution was the country's first and only technological university comparable to the German technical high schools, and points the moral that such an institution, and indeed more than one institution, should have been created very much earlier in the century. It had been left to the City and Guilds of London Institute to take this vital initiative, a matter which should have been the responsibility of the government.

By 1910 the Central Institution was the leading school of engineering and had achieved a dominant position; it is also interesting to note in passing that the East London Technical College – formerly the Finsbury Technical School and another creation of the City and Guilds – was producing several honours graduates in engineering. In fact the London colleges now dominated the scene and provided nearly 50 per cent of the honours graduate manpower, Cambridge and Manchester being the only other significant schools. The first honours graduate at Liverpool was in 1888, at Leeds 1891, Birmingham 1905 and Sheffield 1909.

But even had there been a flow of highly qualified graduates leaving universities it is doubtful whether there would have been sufficient openings in industry offering inducement to newly qualified applicants. Would industry have been receptive enough to them and would the rewards have been tempting enough to keep them in England? A survey of 235 engineering graduates of the Victoria University of Manchester around the turn of the century shows that no fewer than 20 per cent went abroad, and a study of the occupations of the past students of the Liverpool University Engineering Society between 1889 and 1912 reveals that 39 went abroad, 17 took up educational employment, 17 entered public employment, and only 34 entered industry. There were at this time more lucrative openings in the colonies and in America than in England, and it is probably true that higher education in England in 1910 presented better opportunities for the highly qualified graduate than did industry.

For the greater part of the nineteenth century apprenticeship remained the main avenue into the engineering profession. Evening class instruction in a local science or technical institute supplemented this as the standard education of most English engineers. Liverpool's engineers, whether engaged in municipal and academic life or in industry, had risen to the top through apprenticeships from which many were enabled to proceed further by means of the Whitworth scholarships. Not one had received a conventional education of secondary school followed by university (as would be the case in Germany and Switzerland) and only one had been to a grammar school. What did they think of this system? Their opinions are to be found in the several discussions on the question of technical education conducted by the Liverpool Engineering Society (founded in 1876) and the Liverpool Polytechnic Society (founded in 1838 for the encouragement of useful arts and inventions), societies which were as concerned about this problem as were the national engineering institutions.

In 1868 George Sander read a paper to the Polytechnic Society entitled 'On engineering education' in which he described the English scene at the time:

Hitherto our workmen have been left to do for themselves . . . although engaged from 6 a.m. to 6 p.m. at their daily work, they manage to attend evening classes, where these are available, and where they are not, they tread their way along, picking up what scraps of information they can find in the nearest lending library and by their dint of British pluck – get sufficient knowledge to fit them for foremen and managers.[47]

A more valuable contribution was that of Dr William Rickard in 1871, a paper on 'Technical education'. We had become rich, he asserted, because of our vast mineral resources and absence of competitors but during that time improvements in manufactures were more often the result of accident than of design, and trial and error was our main guide. Many of our engineers were ignorant of basic principles, while the government looked on complacently; 'the British workman unaided by the government had thus far educated himself'. But now it was time to educate technically those who were to perpetuate our success.

In opening the discussion Norman Tate confessed that in the past results had been obtained by 'rule-of-thumb' methods and that workmen, foremen and often the masters were totally ignorant of the simplest scientific principles. He pointed out that he himself taught operatives in the evening classes and attendance, after being regular at first, quickly fell. He asked one of the men the reason and was told it was 'impossible to learn chemistry, if one had to do with multiplication' for 'these men were not able to follow scientific instruction for want of elementary education'. Professor Osborne Reynolds of Owens College was present at the meeting. The system of pupilage had afforded very successful results, he said, so far as practical instruction went, but it involved a great waste of time and labour unless scientific instruction preceded it. G. F. Deacon mentioned that after receiving the ordinary course of classical education in a grammar school he had passed into the workshop of a Glasgow firm, where he had found himself lamentably deficient in theoretical knowledge.

One of the most worthwhile papers presented to the Society was one by J. B. Jeffrey in 1915 on 'The education of a marine engineer'; this provoked a lively discussion. Jeffrey had pursued a course of technical instruction in Germany and had served an apprenticeship at one of the largest shipbuilding firms there. He contrasted the differing paths to a career as a marine engineer in the two countries and he concluded that the German system was more rigorous and better coordinated.

In the discussion that followed E. S. Forber said that he wished he had been born forty-five years later, for when he was a lad he had to start work at 6 a.m. and finish at 5 p.m., only to have to go home to Walton and get back to his classes in the city by 7 p.m. He was able to follow the teacher up to a certain point, beyond which he might as well have stopped away for the rest of the course. B. G. Oxford argued that conditions had changed little for not long ago an engineering apprentice had perforce to rise at 5 a.m. in order to be at the workshop by 6 a.m. He reached home tired by 6 p.m., washed and dressed and was back at his classes by 7.00 or 7.30 p.m., to listen to two lectures if he could keep awake. He left at 9.45 p.m. and was home at 10.15 p.m. to snatch six hours sleep. This he did on three evenings a week; on the other evenings he did homework, for even if he passed the examinations he would not receive the certificate if he had not done sufficient homework.

Although he was unable to be present, A. Laslett submitted his views by correspondence in which he said that his recollections of the system in vogue thirty years earlier were not pleasant. There were long arduous days in the workshop followed by three to four hours at the technical school, where the blackboard became gradually more and more dim to the sleepy eyes of the tired student. He pleaded for day-release schemes and stated that the remedy lay within employers and educational agencies. He quoted Robert Blair, the Chief Education Officer of the London Education Committee, who had written in a report, 'Are we not putting an unnecessarily severe strain on our very best material? In these days of international and industrial rivalry, can we afford to allow the "lad-o-parts" to sacrifice so much to the process of "coming through".'[48]

Although there were widely divergent views during these many discussions as to whether or not Britain was industrially on the decline, there was complete unanimity of opinion over the necessity for an improved system of technical training. Too much of the onus of obtaining theoretical training was left to the individual, the emphasis on 'night schools' and part-time education imposing a great strain on them. In the opinion of one critic, technical training was a matter of the 'survival of the fittest'.

Before the outbreak of the First World War the President of the Liverpool Engineering Society, Professor W. H. Watkinson, re-emphasised the deleterious influence of evening class instruction; he cited a lecture delivered by Charles Washburn at Worcester Polytechnic Institute, Massachusetts, in 1906. Washburn drew attention to the too great emphasis given to the value of 'evening classes' in England and its resultant effect.

[These] night schools [he said] are exceedingly common in England, so common that they have undermined the influence of the regular day schools, and have implanted the erroneous idea into the mind of the average young Englishman that he can work all day, go to school at night and still be successful in each case. ... The Germans have not made this mistake and emphasise the necessity of giving undivided attention either to educational work or to industrial work, but not to combine the two. ... When the Americans awakened to the need of better scientific training for their engineers, they did not come to this country but to Germany, to find their models for schools of engineering, and nearly all their great schools of engineering which have been built up in recent years, are founded mainly on the German system.[49]

In the debates conducted at the end of the nineteenth and in the opening years of the twentieth century the impact of the work of Darwin, Galton and Mendel is evident. A commonly held view was that Britain's technological achievements were due to 'our inherited instinct for engineering'. It is also clear that there was an imperfect understanding of the genetic term for while it was conceded that this country had relied in the past on this 'inherited instinct' the Germans were now 'acquiring it' by means of 'superior training'.

Mining education

Mining, in particular coal mining, figured prominently in Britain's export trade during the second half of the nineteenth century in spite of inadequate facilities for training at both management and worker level. At the time when the Devonshire Commission reported (1872) there were few facilities in England for higher education in mining, and unfavourable comparisons with the situation on the Continent were drawn. Successive governments had done little other than set up the Royal School of Mines in London (1837), and even this did not meet with the success expected. Mining areas such as Wigan and Cornwall had attempted to take matters into their own hands and established mining institutions, but these suffered from lack of financial support and other adverse factors, though at Wigan the mining school, after a shaky start, eventually prospered. In Newcastle the recently opened College of Physical Science gave particular emphasis to mining; a mining school at Bristol had existed for a short time but was saved only by being merged with the Bristol Trade School. As in engineering, training was based largely on pupilage schemes and in Britain mining did not become a recognisable discipline until the 1880s, the result being that only a handful of the industry's leaders received a rigorous scientific training prior to 1900.

The position was very different on the Continent. According to

Warrington Smythe, lecturer in mining and mineralogy at the Royal School of Mines, there were two mining academies, nine mining schools, and nine preparatory schools in Prussia alone. The system of training in England depended on apprenticeship rather than on higher academies. In colliery engineering, said Smythe, an engineer took in a number of pupils to his office where they received scant attention but paid handsomely for the privilege. When asked by the Devonshire Commissioners whether there was any continental mining district of equal extent to that of North and South Staffordshire without a mining school, his answer was most emphatic, 'No, certainly not!' British mine managers, he stated, were inferior in general acquirements to the Germans but had greater energy and practical acquaintance.[50]

The outstanding institution on the Continent was the Freiberg Mining Academy, founded in 1766; this was state-endowed and its professors received their salaries from the government. The Academy provided courses of lectures in all branches of science allied to mining and metallurgical processes. It had the advantage over London's Royal School of Mines of being sited in the centre of a mining district. Throughout Germany mining education was systematically organised and of a uniformly high standard. There was in each district a major mining school served by preparatory schools. Warrington Smythe was enthusiastic about the German system, but saw little hope of such a system being established in England without the direct intervention of the central government.

During the nineteenth century it was the common practice to obtain trained managers and experts from the Continent; this was so in chemistry, smelting, engineering and mining. When asked by the Devonshire Commissioners to account for this, Smythe pointed out that it was because owners could not get English trained experts; he referred for instance to Mr Vivian at Swansea who over the previous quarter of a century had been obliged to obtain his assistants from among those who had passed the courses at Freiburg.

The Royal School of Mines originated in 1837 as the Museum of Economic Geology following a suggestion made by Henry De la Beche (later Sir Henry De la Beche, Director-General of the Geological Survey) to the Chancellor of the Exchequer. A year later an influential committee of the British Association for the Advancement of Science recommended a National Depository for the preservation of documents and records relating to the mining operations of the country and in 1839 the Museum became the place of deposit for the Mining Records.

The Museum was opened to the public in 1841, pupils being instructed in chemistry, metallurgy and mineralogy. In the same year the Museum of Economic Geology and the Geological Survey were united under one government department. Sir Henry De la Beche was appointed Director-General of the Museum and his staff included Edward Forbes (palaentologist), Warrington Smythe (mining geologist), and Lyon Playfair in chemistry. The small attendance during the first and ensuing sessions was a disappointment to everyone, for it was expected that the mining districts at least would have sent students. Forbes suggested that the classes of people for whom it was intended could not afford the high fees or were not available for day instruction. The Museum of Economic Geology had been built according to the ideas of Sir Henry De la Beche, and its purpose was to apply the science of chemistry to agriculture – the great topic of the day. Trentham Reekes, Registrar of the School of Mines, confessed to the Devonshire Commission that the School of Mines had been grafted on to the Museum and 'the whole thing was an experiment, the Museum was built scarcely contemplating that the School of Mines would be established and proper preparation was not made'.[51] To meet the need for a school of mines the Museum of Economic Geology was moved from its cramped quarters in Craig Street to new buildings in Jermyn Street off Piccadilly in 1851 and subsequently renamed the School of Mines and of Science Applied to the Arts.

High hopes were held out for the School. Mr William Hopkins, in his presidential address to the Geological Society, said:

The Museum of Practical Geology cannot fail to exercise an important influence. The lectures will help to extend an abstract knowledge of geology and the allied sciences, and cannot fail to accord useful aids to some of the most important material interests of this country. Perhaps not one of these great interests has suffered more from want of scientific knowledge than that of mining.[52]

All seemed set fair, but the expected success did not materalise for some time. Isaac Lowthian Bell, iron manufacturer and colliery owner from Middlesbrough, saw the siting of the School in London as a fundamental weakness. Lionel Brough, Inspector of Mines for the South West District, was another who considered London an unsuitable centre. He agreed with the Commission that Merthyr Tydfil would have been a better centre for a mining school. In evidence to the Commissioners he stated he had not met any of the former pupils of the School as colliery managers, although he had come across several metallurgists. Brough, as Inspector of Mines for the South West District, was responsible for Monmouth, Somerset and Gloucestershire; Bell's experiences in the North East were similar. Warrington Smythe conceded that not a great number of former pupils had become mine managers. The reason, according to Brough, was that pupils had 'got scattered more abroad in the British Colonies, they have sought for employment abroad more than they have at home'[53] being attracted there by better employment prospects and higher remuneration.

For many years the numbers attending the School were small; not more than six students in any one year before 1869 gained the Associateship awarded for completion of a prescribed course of study, and double figures were not reached until 1876. Thereafter numbers increased fairly regularly, by the 1890s reaching forty per year. That support was forthcoming, albeit slowly, is indicated by the fact that in the two decades 1855–75 the School produced 99 Associates whereas in the following two decades some 400 Associateships were awarded.

One of the main objects of the School was 'to give a practical direction to the course of study, so as to enable the student to enter with advantage upon the actual process of mining, or of the Arts which he may be called upon to conduct'.[54] Unfortunately, although students could choose to study any combination of the three subjects, geology, metallurgy and mining, of the 500 or so Associates, less then half chose to study mining, either on its own, or in combination with one of the other subjects. A. W. Williamson, Professor of Chemistry at University College, London, in evidence to the Devonshire Commissioners stated that the School of Mines was more of a success as a school of 'science' in which role it did more good than as a school of mines. Of the students leaving the School only about 10 per cent entered mining as managers or mining engineers. Such a figure seems to support Lionel Brough's contention that students 'have sought for employment abroad more than they have at home'.

By 1900 other centres of advanced training in mining were to be found in five of the 'civic' colleges: Newcastle, Sheffield, Leeds, Birmingham and Nottingham. The first chair was created in 1880 at Newcastle, endowed by the local coal owners. The Newcastle Department developed rather more rapidly than did the other departments, by 1895 supplying more inspectors of mines than any other Institution.

There were no full-time day students until nearly the end of the century – in 1896 at Sheffield and 1906 at Nottingham. The position at the turn of the century was that graduates in mining or metallurgy produced by English universities numbered fewer than a dozen each year. There were in addition to degrees in mining, diploma courses at Newcastle, Birmingham and Sheffield, but numbers of students qualifying were few; at Newcastle between 1903 and 1912 only ten students gained the diploma in mining.

Earlier in the century a special sub-committee of the Lords of the Committee of Privy Council in considering the Royal School of Mines had expressed great faith in the role of local mining schools and had predicted in its Report (1862) that 'it is probable that besides the schools of mines of Cornwall, Bristol and Wigan already existing, mining schools will be gradually established in other parts of the kingdom'. Such schools did not emerge and furthermore the quality of work at the three schools already in existence left much to be desired. No school was more flourishing than at Wigan which, even so, led a precarious and peripatetic existence, being forced to close down for a number of years. (Among its temporary quarters were the Conservative Working Men's Club, the Town Hall and the Free Grammar School.) A totally inadequate building was erected in 1882 at a cost of £2,000. It was not until 1897 that £50,000 was raised through a 'new building appeal', the list of subscribers being headed by the Wigan Coal and Iron Company. The main provision of the school was classes arranged in conjunction with the Department of Science and Art. However the number of students in the mining classes were few compared to those studying magnetism and electricity or machine construction and drawing. The same charge that Professor Williamson levelled against the Royal School of Mines, namely, of being more a school of 'science' rather than of mining, was equally true of the Wigan school. For over thirty years after it was founded the school received no assistance from government other than the annual 'payments-by-result' to teachers averaging £100 to £300 a year.

In 1872, at the time of the Devonshire Commission Report, there were over 200 students at the Bristol Trade School. Of these two thirds were studying at an elementary level and the remainder spread their studies over drawing, mathematics, chemistry, mineralogy and geology, in addition to mining; only six were studying mining and in attempting to assess the extent of mining education there is no great value in citing the numbers of students under instruction in mining schools. According to the 1883 Report of the Department of Science and Art there were 435 students of mining in England and Wales, these being spread over establishments which included the Wigan Mining School, national schools and British schools, miners' institutes, mission rooms, colliery schools and mechanics' institutes. Perhaps the oddest of these was the Coffee Tavern at Maesteg, which accommodated the group of twelve students (the only group in Wales). The greatest number of students at any one institution was found at Wigan (70), but the leading region was Durham with 197 students despite the absence of a mining school. In Cornwall, there were only ten students, at Redruth; and there was an almost complete absence of students in Yorkshire, Northumberland, the Midlands and South Wales. In mining as in all other fields of technical education the government was obsessed with the education of the artisan and the worker. Despite the exhortations of Royal Commissions to lay greater emphasis on the education of mine managers, and despite the lip-service occasionally paid to it, the government, having set up the Museum of Economic Geology, and later the School of Mines, took little further part in mining education at the highest levels; this was left in the hands of local agencies such as colliery owners, industrialists and philanthropists. The result was that facilities for higher mining education were long delayed; there were few departments and staff, accommodation was limited and financial support was lacking. The absence of a system of scholarships, fellowships and grants made full-time day study difficult and inevitably the quality of study could not be of the highest. Original research was almost totally non-existent.

In the field of higher mining education where were mining engineers and mine managers to exchange ideas and learn of new developments and the introduction of new techniques? Fortunately this became possible through the activities of the Institution of Mining Engineers formed in 1889 with 1,239 members, and the Institution of Mining and

Metallurgy, formed in 1892 with 170 members. The immediate success of these two bodies pointed to the fact that there was enormous interest among the mining engineers and mine managers of the country in the profession and techniques of mining.

Industrial research

For a considerable part of the nineteenth century industry in England did not practise or promote research in any real 'scientific' sense. Paradoxically, despite this lack of research almost all the great improvements in the manufacture of iron and steel had come from Britain. Of the three figures who contributed the major developments in steel, Bessemer, Siemens and Gilchrist Thomas, it was only Thomas who fitted the modern concept of a research scientist. Bessemer was an inventor with no formal education and Siemens a trained engineer. Although Thomas was a police court clerk with a classical education he had a passionate interest in chemistry through attending evening classes at Birkbeck, and by diligent study and experimentation in his own laboratory he acquired a knowledge of chemistry which enabled him to demonstrate how steel could be produced from phosphoric ores: 'He alone analysed the whole problem and found a theoretical solution which was successful in practice.'[55]

With respect to research the iron, steel and related metallurgical industries seem to have been in a parlous state if sufficient weight can be attached to Lowthian Bell's evidence to the Devonshire Commissioners:

If an iron smelter wishes to inform himself at all upon the theories of iron smelting, or any other matter concerned with metallurgy he is obliged for original research to go abroad. He must either be able to read German or French, or both, or he must be content with some translations which have made their appearance in this country.[56]

English tradition was empirical, 'rule of thumb' and 'trial and error'. A jury at the Paris Exhibition observed that: 'the English in general are steeped in a narrow utilitarianism which has prevented them from engaging in pure research.'[57]

For evidence of research activity one must again turn to the chemical industry, for 'firms dealing with chemicals and metals tended to have laboratories to deal with routine testing, analysis and sampling of materials sent to them by customers or arising during production. These activities imperceptibly began to merge into innovatory research.'[58] The origins of truly scientific research in the chemical industry are to be found in aniline dye manufacture. In Professor Cardwell's words: 'The aniline dyes were the first of the synthetics which are now so common and they originated in scientific research organised on modern lines: they were as we can see the harbingers of present-day practice.' To trace the origins of industrial research is not easy as 'the industrial record is incomplete for it is common practice for firms to destroy their archives'.[59] Furthermore, the firms that exist today are those that were successful. Having sounded this cautionary note Cardwell suggests that the first industrial research laboratory in England was to be found at Read, Holliday of Huddersfield. This firm had been recruiting 'such scientists as they could find' – not surprisingly the majority were German – and by 1890 the firm had a research laboratory in which some four to five chemists were continuously employed in research.

W. H. Perkin, following the discovery of the first aniline dye at the Royal College of Chemistry, later set up in business on his own. During the 1870s he certainly employed some chemists in his works but 'he always reserved the research function for himself and the research laboratory was kept strictly private'.[60] To the United Alkali Company, therefore, goes the credit of creating the second industrial research laboratory. One of Hurter's first tasks as chief chemist was to review the laboratory resources of all the constituent firms which constituted the Company. Although researches of various kinds had been carried out in the small laboratories of the firms such as those of Gossage, Gaskell and Muspratt, Hurter found that not one of the existing laboratories was adequate to accommodate a research department. His original staff numbered 'half a dozen chemists, a general handyman and a confidential clerk'.[61] The first applicant to be appointed under Hurter was H. Aller, also a product of the Zurich Polytechnic. A contemporary comment in *The Times* was to the effect that 'the chemical industry owes nothing to the historic educational institutions of this country but a great deal to Zurich Polytechnic and the German universities'.[62]

German influences were also to be found at Brunner Mond, Crosfields and Levinsteins. There seems to be some uncertainty regarding Ivan Levinstein's personal attitude; according to Cardwell 'he did little research and was reported to have been a bad employer of scientific labour'[63] but Herbert Levinstein wrote that 'his father employed fourteen chemists – greater than any other works in England'.[64]

Ludwig Mond for many years after the creation of Brunner Mond was busily engaged in mastering the Solvay process and it was not until 1881 that he was able to turn to original research. He thereupon embarked on a scheme of research 'recruiting trained scientific staff on a scale that would have seemed a wasteful extravagance to his competitors'.[65] By the 1890s Mond's views about research had crystallised. He was now convinced that apprenticeships to an industry or even courses of technological study in special laboratories or institutions could never make a successful chemist. His commitment to research can be judged from the fact that he bought the house adjoining the Royal Institution and converted a number of rooms into small laboratories. He spent in all £45,000 on apparatus and £62,000 on the endowment.

Sanderson in his study of chemical research at Liverpool University concluded that the University 'does not seem to emerge as a significant research centre before 1914'. In attempting to account for this he suggests that 'it may have been less necessary since the great chemical works of the region had a larger tradition of research within the firm than any other sector of British industry'.[66] The implication is that industrial research was in a healthier state on Merseyside than elsewhere in the country but the evidence available indicates that little high-level research in any organised systematic sense was conducted on Merseyside. Crosfields was probably the most 'scientific' firm, followed closely by Brunner Mond and Gaskell Deacon. When William Hesketh Lever moved from Warrington to Port Sunlight in 1888 he took with him key staff from his Warrington factory. Among these were two or three technically trained managers supported by skilled men who had served apprenticeships in the firm. Until the early years of the twentieth century graduate scientists and engineers were confined to a handful of senior personnel. A proper research laboratory was not established until 1911; by 1914 this was employing sixteen graduates.[67] Such was the status of research in the largest soap firms in Britain.

Other sources, too, suggest that few graduates were employed on Merseyside during this period. A survey of former pupils of the Royal College of Chemistry and the Royal School of Mines[68] shows that of 850 over a forty-year period nine only seem to have had any connection with Merseyside industries. Among them were Charles Longuet Higgins, described as being a 'manufacturing chemist' at the Muspratt works in 1887, and John Saltmarsh, head chemist of Davis's Chlorine Process Plant, in Northwich in the 1890s. Other names were associated with the firms of Simpson, Maule and Nicholson, Ditton Copper Works, Broughton Copper Works and the Atlas Dye Works. Arthur Schuster's list of 115 former pupils of the Physics Department at Manchester University indicates that sixteen had an industrial career;[69] only one (Thomas Best) seemed to have entered Merseyside industry. Best studied under Schuster at Owens College between 1883 and 1886 then proceeded to Erlangen where he took his PhD. On returning he went to the Manchester Municipal Technical School but later joined Gambles at St Helens as their chief chemist.

The membership of the Royal Institute of Chemistry in 1891 included 683 Fellows; but the proceedings for that year provides information on only 343; of these eighty-four were in laboratories of all descriptions, but only a few were in industrial laboratories. Six names only are associated with Merseyside, these involve the firms of Bostock and Company, Lever Bros, Ditton Copper Works, the Alkali and Sulphur Company and Sutton Alkali Works. The Whitworth Register provides a list of fifty-eight names associated with Merseyside about whom information is given for forty-four.[70] All these were originally apprentices before taking up their scholarships, after which twenty-two entered higher education, thirteen only going back into industry. Five of these attained high positions, two being on Merseyside, J. H. Gibson becoming engineering manager at Cammell Laird and E. Godfrey rising to engineering development manager at the ICI General Chemicals Division. Finally, of 107 members of the Liverpool University Engineering Society between 1889 and 1912, thirty-four went into industry, nine of them on Merseyside.

'Stalwart graduate employers' in the late nineteenth and early twentieth century, according to Sanderson, included Pilkingtons, Crosfields, British Westinghouse, Levinsteins, British Thomson Houston, Parsons, Mather and Platt, and Tate (sugar). These graduates were drawn mainly from the 'civic' colleges of the North of England reflecting 'a fairly clear pattern of rise in the 1870s, fall in the 1880s, rise in the 1890s and sharp rise from 1910 to 1913'.[71] Manchester chemists (47.3 per cent entered industry in the years 1886–1900), Manchester physicists (48.3 per cent in 1890–99) and Newcastle graduates (36.3 per cent in 1890–99) figured prominently. The contribution from Oxford and Cambridge did not begin to pick up until the turn of the century. But the tendency for firms, especially business firms, to take Oxbridge arts men in greater numbers than scientists was still strong; of over fifty Cambridge men employed in the 1900s eight were mathematicians, eight scientists and five engineers, whereas nineteen had graduated in classics and fifteen in arts subjects.[72]

Many surveys indicate that the numbers of graduate scientists and technologists entering industry in the late nineteenth century were few. Teaching and higher education offered more attractive careers and a significant proportion of graduates went abroad. Of those entering industry not many were employed in a research capacity within a laboratory research setting. Thus a tradition had become established which British industry followed in the twentieth century.

Chapter 7

Did Britain go wrong?

There was little doubt in the minds of contemporary observers during the late nineteenth century that a decline had set in in Britain's industrial progress. This was reinforced by historians writing in the twentieth century and by the middle of the century it had become common practice to look back on late Victorian Britain as the beginning of Britain's industrial decline, the blame being placed firmly on Victorian management. An influential work in creating this climate of opinion was Hoffman's *Great Britain and the German Trade Rivalry*[1] in which the author, using indices of trade, painted a depressing picture of Britain's performance.

Serious reservations, however, are now being expressed. Contemporary observers and early historians based their assessments on statistics relating to industrial output and trade figures, which clearly indicated a 'relative decline' vis-à-vis Britain's competitors. Economic historians of recent times, on the other hand, in particular the econometricians, have attempted an assessment based on quantitative tests using a variety of more sophisticated mathematically-based economic measures. There may have been individual industries in which the quality of entrepreneurial leadership was deficient, but such a charge it seems may no longer be justified when applied to British industry as a whole. Indeed, one view, perhaps not entirely acceptable to all critics, is that 'there is little left of the dismal picture of British failure painted by historians'.[2] Although the performance of British industry is by no means a closed book, the spotlight has shifted somewhat to the conditions of international trade, to the availability and efficient use of capital and to other possible causes.

Over the years a multiplicity of factors have been advanced to account for Britain's 'assumed failure': managerial incompetence, tariff barriers, patent laws, labour problems and education; among these the last has always figured prominently. The theory of entrepreneurial failure is no longer as fashionable as it once was, but it is our belief that there was a marked failure in educational thinking and planning during the second half of the nineteenth century. Observers of the contemporary scene singled out education as the predominant factor in Britain's disappointing industrial performance. Although previous chapters have demonstrated that both the extent and quality of English education left much to be desired, we would hesitate to affirm that this was a major factor responsible for poor industrial performance. A scientific relationship between education and industrial productivity has yet to be established; it is at present a largely subjective matter. All that we would contend is that the influence of education may have been too readily dismissed.

Any judgement about Britain's decline can only be effected against the background of how Britain came to be the dominant industrial country by the mid-nineteenth century. The period encompassed within the years 1770 to 1840 has been commonly accepted to constitute the Industrial Revolution. This cataclysmic complex of events first occurred in Britain; later developments in France and Germany to a considerable extent mirrored the British scene. Recently historians have been seeking to identify a definite point in time at which the Industrial Revolution can be said to have originated. The argument has been advanced by Professor Rostow that in each country there is a long period of agricultural preponderance at the end of which conditions favourable to a 'take-off' are gradually assembled. Rostow's stimulating and controversial theory has been criticised on the grounds that economic development lacks the scientific orderliness of biological growth – in particular there are many elements of overlap and confusion between the stages of 'pre-condition' as opposed to 'take-off'.[3] In the final analysis one finds no consensus view as to an exact take-off point in Britain; at best one has to fall back on the more orthodox view of a fairly sharply defined period as characterising the Industrial Revolution.

Why did the Revolution occur at the particular time that it did? And why in England? There is no single answer to either of these questions. Professor Ashton distinguished a number of factors which taken together led to the Industrial Revolution.[4] These were: a rapid growth of population and output of commodities and a marked increase of capital. The latter factor was decisive, for 'industry had to await the coming of capital in quantities large enough, and at a price low enough, to make possible the creation of the "infrastructure" of roads, bridges, harbours, docks, canals and so on which is a prerequisite of a large manufacturing community'.[5]

According to Hobsbawm the social and economic condition for an industrial revolution existed in the eighteenth century. He rejects as exclusive or primary reasons many factors which have been put forward from time to time to explain why the Industrial Revolution occurred in Britain at the end of the eighteenth century rather than earlier and rather than in some other country. Such factors include: coal supply; a moist climate and suitable geographic conditions; good harvests in the early eighteenth century; the scientific revolution of the seventeenth century; and political factors. He also discounts population growth, for population was growing all over northern Europe. Population may have been a supporting rather than a causal factor because 'if in eighteenth century England a growing labour force assisted development, as it undoubtedly did, it was because the economy was already dynamic not because some extraneous demographic injection made it so'. The reason why the Industrial Revolution occurred in Britain at the particular time it did in Hobsbawm's view is not simple; it is related in a complex way to the European economy and world trade. It was a period characterised by an expanding network of trade and a vast and growing circulation of goods which provided a limitless horizon of sales and profit for merchant and manufacturer. Essentially: 'our industrial economy grew out of commerce, especially our commerce with the underdeveloped world'.[6]

Hobsbawm identifies three main sectors of demand in the genesis of industrialisation: *export trade* which provided the 'spark' and led to major improvements in sea transport; the *flourishing home market* which gave a broad base for a generalised industrial economy and created incentives for major improvements in inland transport; and *systematic government support* for merchant and manufacturer. He attaches considerable importance to the key roles played by the cotton industry and government, and regards the period 1750 to 1770 as the runway for the industrial 'take-off'. During these two decades home industries increased their output by 7 per cent and export industries by 80 per cent – 'if a spark was needed this is where it came from'. Cotton as the leading industrial sector was essentially tied to overseas trade, by 1805 it was exporting some two-thirds of its total outlay.[7] Rostow, too, emphasises the role of cotton as the leading sector in Britain's 'take-off', citing as his evidence spectacular increases in the input of raw cotton in the decades 1781–91 (31%) and 1791–1801 (67%).[8] The exact contribution of cotton to the national economy at that particular time is open to question, but there is little doubt that cotton together with iron [9] were making significant contributions to the economy in that period.[10] Indeed the fortunes of cotton and Britain's industrial progress seem linked, if not causally related:

When cotton expanded at the rate of 6 to 7 per cent in the twenty-five years after Waterloo British industrial expansion was at its height. When cotton ceased to expand as it did in the last quarter of the nineteenth century, when its rate of growth sank to 0.7 per cent per year, all British industry sagged. Even more unique was its contribution to Britain's international economy. In a real sense the British balance of payments depended on the fortunes of this industry, and so did much of Britain's shipping and overseas trade in general.[11]

The cotton industry states Hobsbawm 'ended as it had begun'. It had relied not on its competitive superiority but 'on a monopoly of the colonial and underdeveloped markets which the British Empire, the British Navy and British commercial superiority gave it'.[12] Contributing factors writes Hobsbawm were wars, the needs of the British Navy and the support of government. Wars and the navy contributed directly to technological innovation and industrialisation by creating demand, particularly for armaments, and successive governments adopted a policy which promoted trade through colonisation:

War and colonisation required – a government willing to wage war and colonise for the benefit of British manufacturers. In government 'the advantage of Britain over her potential competitors is evident. Unlike some of them such as France she was prepared to subordinate all foreign policy to economic ends. Her war aims were commercial and naval.'[13]

A rather different interpretation is provided by Flinn, who sees the Industrial Revolution as essentially a two-phase operation, the period of rapid change in the last two or three decades of the eighteenth century being preceded by long periods of moderate growth.[14] The Industrial Revolution cannot be explained in terms of a single prime mover; inevitably a wide range of factors is involved. Flinn reduces these to three groups of elements: accumulation of a set of necessary prerequisites – improvements in agriculture and transport, availability of capital and so on; a group of industrial sectors of steady expansion related to the diffusion of a 'growth mentality' among businessmen; thirdly, and most importantly, the critical timing of the onset of rapid economic development. This 'take-off' according to Flinn was due neither to population growth nor to expansion of home and overseas markets; the decisive factor 'both in increasing the scale and in changing the methods and location of production was *technology*'.[15]

Thus the key factor in the 'take-off' was, in Flinn's view, the adoption of new techniques of production which led to a flood of cheap textiles, the iron age, steam power as an aid to industry and the aggregation of large numbers of workers in a single unit of industrial production in urban areas – all facets of the Industrial Revolution. The three groups, argues Flinn, were all present in Britain in the late eighteenth century. The Industrial Revolution stemmed from the dynamic interplay between them. A further factor which enabled this to occur in Britain rather than in France, Germany or America was the freedom that British industry enjoyed up to 1775. In summarising the conflicting views advanced to explain the origins of the Industrial Revolution Flinn concludes that:

It is clear that the precise origins of the Industrial Revolution remain something of a mystery. This is hardly surprising as the origins themselves have been little studied compared with the copious descriptions produced by historians, each generation of whom have reflected the particular point of view of their ages. For the present generation of scholars the Industrial Revolution represents a more complex event than hitherto.

Consequently 'it is not to be expected that the study of the origins of the Industrial Revolution so recently begun should have led to any definitive conclusions'.[16]

Not only is it difficult to identify the causal factors of the origins of the Industrial Revolution and to specify its take-off point, it also appears that it is questionable whether there were clear discontinuities at certain historical points which serve as the boundaries for a distinct historical period. Phyllis Deane, for instance, poses the question: 'Is the Industrial Revolution a definite process to which we can assign a beginning and an end. . . . Can we date it?'[17] while Ashton pointed out that 'the term "revolution" implies a suddenness of change that is not, in fact, characteristic of economic progress – there is a danger of overlooking the essential fact of continuity'.[18] To Claude Fohlen the Industrial Revolution 'is a continuing phenomenon which is going on in front of our eyes in countries which have already in the past experienced a profound mutation. . . . We must recognise that the process once launched knows no limit and that the Revolution is rather a series of revolutions'.[19]

The view now appears to be that there has been a continuous industrial–economic process whose origin may be traced back as far as the early eighteenth century or even to the sixteenth or seventeenth century. Superimposed on this continuous process are fairly well defined critical events which characterise certain periods. Adopting this approach the Industrial Revolution in nineteenth-century England can be thought of as consisting of two separate phases or, indeed, even as two quite distinct revolutions. The first of these, centred on coal, iron and cotton, has been described traditionally as *the Industrial Revolution*. The second 'revolution' embraced the developments associated with the electrical industries, electrochemistry, organic chemicals and the internal combustion engine. Hobsbawm has argued the case for a second Industrial Revolution. 'The transformation of industry since the end of the Industrial Revolution', he states, 'has become continuous, but every now and then the cumulative results of these changes become so obvious that observers are tempted to talk about a Second Industrial Revolution. The last decades of the nineteenth century were such a time.'[20] Landes takes a similar line: 'The speed of advance and its consequences towards the end of the nineteenth century were far-reaching, and formed part of a much wider process of change, which included electricity, the internal combustion engine, and assembly-line production, in short a cluster of innovations that earned the name of the Second Industrial Revolution.'[21]

It was seen earlier that Flinn cites technology as a decisive factor in the origin of the Industrial Revolution. The distinctive feature of the second revolution, in marked contrast to the first, was its close connection with pure and applied science. According to Hobsbawm:

the major technical advances of the second half of the nineteenth century were essentially scientific; that is to say they required at the very least some knowledge of recent developments in pure science for original inventions, a far more consistent process of scientific experiment and testing for their development and an increasingly close and continuous link between industrialists, technologists and professional scientists and scientific institutions.[22]

Britain 'won' the First Industrial Revolution decisively, but it can be argued that she 'lost' the Second. The key to this may be found in the fact that 'the output of technological progress was a function of the input of scientifically qualified manpower, equipment and money into systematic research projects'.[23] Yet 'many industries continued to make progress in very much the old way – using science only as a desperate device when nothing else would serve'[24] and 'the typical inventor of machinery was usually a workman or amateur who contrived to find the most convenient arrangement of wheels, rollers, cogs and levers designed to initiate the movement of the craftsman at higher speed and using steam engines'.[25]

The relative decline in Britain's industrial progress

That there was a decline in the rate of increase of industrial production relative to competitors cannot be denied. The United Kingdom share of manufactured goods was 41.4 per cent of the world output in 1880, whereas in 1913 it constituted only 29.9 per cent; it still surpassed Germany's share which, nonetheless, during the same period had increased from 19.3 per cent to 26.5 per cent.[26] Between 1899 and 1914 Britain lost £360 million in annual manufacturing exports on account of competition, a loss of about 18 per cent of the actual value of her manufacturing exports in 1913, while Germany gained £330 million.[27] At one time it was authoritatively accepted that this was directly related to a failure by British industry to maintain the momentum it displayed in the first half of the nineteenth century.

The decline in Britain's fortunes must be judged against a broad backcloth which takes into account the changed circumstances operating in the second half of the century, the availability of capital and the emergence of powerful new competitors. It was 'probably inevitable that Britain should lose her predominant position in the older manufactures as other countries industrialised but she failed to secure a large share of the newer trades then coming into being'.[28] The British chemical industry in 1913 accounted for only 11 per cent of world output as against 34 per cent by the USA and 24 per cent by Germany, while the latter exported twice as much as did Britain.[29] The British pioneered electrotechnics, yet by 1913 the output of the British electrical industry was only a third of that of the Germans and its exports barely a half. Again in steel Britain dominated the early innovations but lost her pre-eminence in the 1890s. In motor cars by 1913 Britain ranked a poor second to the United States, and by the outbreak of war was short of khaki dye, acetone for explosives and magnetos for transport, as Germany had become the chief source of supply.[30]

With regard to traditional industries the picture is confusing. In the coal industry output per man per year declined in Britain after 1880 and by the early 1900s was only about half of that of the United States. But the reasonable explanation for this is the great depths of British mines;

American seams were also better and thicker and freer from faults. It appears that 'the case for a failure of masters and men in British coal mining before 1913 is vulnerable to a most damaging criticism: there was clearly no failure of productivity'.[31] Burns, the chief historian of the steel industry,[32] criticised managers for ignoring the use of phosphoric ores. He emphasised personal deficiencies, attachment to routine and inadequate education. Other critics since have taken a kinder view. McCloskey claims that the contrast between the apparent American vigour and British tardiness may be in need of critical re-examination. He argues that by the mid-1900s the British steel industry could do little better than it did.[33] Musgrove in comparing the British and German performances in the steel industry concluded that a major factor in the success of German industry was that large-scale operations had a higher status in that country; size of units in Britain tended to be much smaller.[34]

In engineering the development of machine tools was influential. Many writers have attributed the success of the American system of manufacture to the inventiveness and productive skill of its machine tools. No industry was more British in origin, yet, according to Hobsbawm, 'nowhere did foreign countries – and yet again chiefly the USA – leap ahead more decisively than in this field'.[35] Saul has studied the influence of machine tools at three different levels of the engineering industry: heavy, medium and light. He concludes that one cannot generalise about the machine tool industry. Apparently some sectors did well whilst others did not; where success varied it was often due to the 'peculiar condition of the market'. Market forces, too, appear to be Saul's answer to Sir John Habbakuk's statement that 'some lag in technology is reasonably well attested by contemporary comment and requires explanation'. The assumption that British engineering technology lagged behind is 'seriously misleading' in Saul's view. It was 'the victim of market forces . . . which the individual firm was powerless to alter. The classic engineering industries continued to enjoy marked technological progress but with their success limited here and there by peculiar market problems.'[36]

It is clear that British pioneer industries lost ground 'relatively' as the rest of the world industrialised; the earlier rate of expansion declined. The problem has been to explain this declining rate of growth of production which led to the deterioration in our international position: 'There is now general agreement that this period saw a slackening in the rate of growth of labour productivity in the economy as a whole, there is much less agreement on the causes of this slackening.'[37] Until recently it was axiomatic that the decline was accompanied by a 'genuine loss of impetus and efficiency'.[38] Entrepreneurs lost their drive and enthusiasm[39] so that leadership 'was not wrested from Britain, but fell from her ineffectual grasp'.[40] Habbakuk commented:

There is a widespread impression that this lag represents the onset of deep-seated and persistent deficiences. The changes are frequently presented in terms of rigidity and ossification – the characteristics of an old economy or a sociological explanation in which these technical deficiences are attributable wholly or in part to British entrepreneurs.[41]

The British industrialist, it has been argued, ceased to strive when early success led to his absorption and acceptance by his social superiors in the landed gentry. At a national level British industry, having attained top position, allowed an element of complacency and self-satisfaction to set in. Hobsbawm argues that the 'value of such observations is limited, if only because very many British businessmen did not conform to them. . . . Sociologically the incentive to make money fast was by no means weak in Victorian Britain.'[42]

McCloskey, in a penetrating paper, argues that there were three senses in which Britain could be said to have 'failed'. These were: output grew too slowly because of sluggish demand; too much capital was invested abroad; and productivity stagnated because of inept entrepreneurship. He produces arguments to dismiss the first two and reduces the case for Britain's failure to the third factor. Using national product estimates (including food) as a measure of 'productivity' he comes up with some surprising results. Thus his productivity growth rate (i.e. the growth of real product not attributable to the growth of capital and labour) is found to increase steadily from about 1860 onwards but after 1900 falls sharply. Thus although neither industrial production nor our exports were growing at a rate commensurate with our competitors 'real productivity' as defined by McCloskey was actually increasing in the very period that accusations of failure were so insistent and clamorous. McCloskey's conclusion, therefore, is that failure, if indeed failure there was, was an Edwardian phenomenon not Victorian:

'There was a dip of productivity in the 1900s but it was too short, too late and too uncertain to justify the dramatic description 'climacteric'. Nor does it support the notion that British businessmen were marking time from the 'seventies onwards. There is, indeed, little left of the dismal picture of British failure painted by historians. The alternative is a picture of an economy not stagnating but growing as rapidly as permitted by the growth of its resources and the effective exploitation of the available technology.[43]

Many factors have been advanced for Britain's assumed 'failure', among which the quality of entrepreneurial leadership and the impact of education stand out. Lesser factors include the supply of capital, labour problems, patent laws, the impact of tariffs and the attitude of the British government. Before assessing the significance of these factors some of the interpretations of Britain's decline by contemporary observers are examined. These contrast sharply with the conclusion of a 1970 conference of economic historians, namely that 'during the critical period 1870 to 1900 when the balance tilted from dominance to dependence, the British economy performed as one would expect a competitive and prosperous economy to perform'. The papers that were concerned directly with British entrepreneurs found them 'on the whole to have been responsive to the opportunities available'.[44]

The contemporary view of Britain's decline

There was little doubt in the minds of those living in the second half of the nineteenth century that Britain was declining as an industrial nation. Writing at the turn of the century Sir William Ashley commented that: 'all the older staple industries of Great Britain are either visibly declining or maintaining themselves with increasing difficulty'.[45] It seemed to Ashley that Britain's relative advantages were only to be found in coal, or in trades that depended on her resources of cheap labour; the rest was threatened by American mass production. He referred to the development of manufactures in countries previously supplied by Britain and observed that in many cases these manufactures were being conducted more efficiently than they were in Britain.

It was not only the traditional industries that were letting us down. An official report after the war found that in the years prior to 1914 the United Kingdom had taken a very limited share in the rise and expansion of the more modern branches of industrial production; 'as is evidenced by our relative weakness in respect of the electrical, chemical or chemico-metallurgical industries; and it is admitted that in a number of smaller trades foreign manufacturers had shown greater enterprise and originality'.[46]

Our trading position had worsened vis-à-vis our competitors, but equally significant the quality of our goods was not matching those of our competitors, with the result that goods which were formerly bought in England and which had been the pride of British industry were being bought elsewhere. Above all the bogy of German competition and efficiency lay over the land. Other nations, wrote Arthur Shadwell, 'have not only caught up with us from behind but have surpassed us'. In his view both Germany and the United States regarded England with 'a mixture of contempt and pity as a spent force'.[47]

In seeking the causes of such an attitude Shadwell carried out an exhaustive study of continental industry and education and analysed the effect of many factors. He found that English industry operated under severe handicaps of antiquated equipment and obsolescent plant, the protection tariffs imposed by other countries, and the government regulations and English factory laws which provided superior protection to workmen, particularly women and children. Shadwell was one of a number of leading English figures who travelled extensively on the Continent in an attempt to discover the root causes of the problem. Others, for instance, included Sir Swire Smith and Sir Philip Magnus, both members of the Samuelson Commission on Technical Education. In the findings of these observers the British worker is generally presented in a favourable light and is largely exonerated, his deficiencies, such as they were, being attributed to the English system of training and education which was heavily censured on several grounds.

The advance of German trade was no reflection of any inadequacy of the English worker. Working hours on average were shorter in England than in Germany but according to Shadwell, neither this fact nor higher wages were critical causal factors, a view shared by Magnus and the Samuelson Commission which affirmed that 'the English workman . . . notwithstanding his shorter hours and his higher wages is to be preferred'.[48] With few exceptions wrote Magnus the efficiency of labour was as good in England as it was in Germany. The British workman came in for praise too from Shadwell:

I have often seen technical education referred to by English writers on account of its value in producing skilled workmen, that is a delusion. Skilled workmen are not produced by technical schools anywhere . . . industrial skill is acquired in the mill and workshop. Nor are German workmen more skilled than the British. In some industries they are conspicuously less so.[49]

Swire Smith found that German success had little to do with the cheapness of German labour. On the other hand, it had a great deal to do with a general willingness to profit and learn from others for Germany had made great strides 'through importing English machinery and tools, engaging Englishmen and copying their methods'.[50]

It was this particular aspect, the attitude to change and innovation, which Shadwell highlighted as deleterious to industrial advance. Relationships between men and management bedevilled English industry as they did not on the Continent. In many industries he found that the manufacturers 'fully recognise the necessity of keeping abreast of the times', whereas the workmen on the other hand 'dislike and resent change, and even ridiculed foreign competition'. He took a serious view of the 'deep and abiding' suspicion between employers and employed: 'the habit of distruct is both a sign and a source of weakness in industrial matters . . . the standing objection of workmen to innovations and improvements is rooted in it, and the very large proportion of the dispute between capital and labour can be traced to nothing but mutual distrust'.[51]

The trade unions were often accused of restriction of output; of opposition to machinery; of interference with management; and with fermenting disputes. Shadwell found little real evidence to support such accusations. In Germany and the United States he had not heard 'a single word in favour of trade unions from any employer', whereas in England 'I have far more often heard from employers and managers fair and friendly expressions of opinion'. A leading industrial manufacturer confided to Shadwell that whilst some blame could be attributable to the trade unions, he himself had 'found the trade union leaders level headed and responsible . . . the greater fault is the manufacturer himself, he has been too supine and easy going.'[52]

The attitudes of the German worker and employer had been fashioned in the school system in which inculcation of duty and development of a national character were of supreme importance. In England wrote a 'German resident' in the *National Review* of June 1905 'a young man leaves the primary school with no idea of duty'. He was astonished to find that

the majority of your workers read little but the sporting press, and care for little but betting and sport. It is always a source of wonder to me after seeing the thousands who go to Lord's or to the Oval on some weekday, not a holiday, that any work at all is done in England – your workers are determined to level down, not to level up; they would drag down the industrial and energetic.[53]

Shadwell's assessment of the differing character of the English and German nations was that the English were an inventive people whose work was distinguished by solidity, durability and finish. The essential English weakness was in the application of this inventiveness and of native qualities.[54] The Germans in contrast were neither an inventive nor an adventurous people; they were deliberate, careful, methodical and thorough. Nevertheless, given a road marked plain before them they had an 'unequalled capacity for mapping it out in the right direction and following it steadily'. This quality had enabled them within the space of thirty years and while bearing the burden of an enormous system of military defence to build up from comparatively small beginnings a great edifice of manufacturing industry.

The industrial fortunes of Germany were clearly linked in the eyes of contemporary observers to the educational system – not only its importance in developing a sense of duty, a national will and determination, but also the inculcation of the requisite skills at all levels for industrial progress. To the Germans training and education were of paramount importance. 'The advance of German trade', stated Magnus, 'was due solely to the superior fitness of the Germans, due unquestionably to the more systematic training they received for mercantile pursuits.'[55] The Samuelson Commissioners on their visits to Germany found

that in nearly every instance we were able to trace the success of German firms to the scientific and artistic training of heads of departments, designers and skilled workers, and not seldom to the superior commercial knowledge and linguistic attainments of employers themselves . . . The Commissioners were satisfied that this and nothing else explained the growing success of Germany.[56]

To Philip Magnus the advance of German trade was due 'solely to the superior fitness of the Germans, due unquestionably to the more systematic training they received for mercantile pursuits' whereas England in the matter of education was particularly deficient. 'Much of the industrial success of the German people', wrote Magnus in his autobiography,

is due to the excellence of the primary instruction – to the evening continuation schools in which they build upon early education a sure foundation for higher specialised instruction, to the well-organised system of secondary education, and to the general appreciation of a love of learning, which, owing to the existence of these educational agencies, is diffused through all grades of society, and has produced habits of thought and aptitudes for work which unfortunately are at present wanting among the same class of our own people.[57]

Magnus's assessment of both the German and the English educational system was shrewd. The particular strengths of the German system were the commercial schools, the evening continuation schools, the gymnasia but especially the technical high schools which emphasised science in its application to industry. 'To the technical schools the Germans rightly ascribe, to a great extent their industrial success, to which they pointed with pride and satisfaction. Without having seen one of these institutions it is almost impossible to realise their vast extent, the beauty of their construction, the completeness of their arrangements and the luxury with which they are fitted.'[58]

Shadwell draws similar conclusions. The special value of these schools to Germany, he pointed out, were not that they produced better workers but that they rendered a service to industries by training 'officers' rather than 'rank and file'. 'In the application of science to which the future belongs, they, the Germans, easily beat both England and the United States.'[59]

In England, Magnus found little wrong with the elementary schools and evening schools though 'all else is chaotic'. The fundamental weakness in England was secondary education:

Our entire secondary education needs to be remodelled and for the first time properly organised. It is the defects of our secondary education which are affecting the trade interests of the country. . . . It is not only because of her commercial schools that Germany sends forth hosts of well trained young men to occupy the best posts in foreign commercial houses, and to establish trading stations in all parts of the globe. It is mainly because her secondary education is adapted to the wants of her people.[60]

But there was no room for complacency in Magnus's view. We could not rely any longer on material advantages in wealth. As far as education was concerned the remedy was clear. 'The state must step in and help', he roundly declared. He called for the general guidance and control of some central body in the form of a Department of Education and a Minister to preside over all education from primary to university education. 'Government supervision', he wrote, 'may prove an advantage if properly directed in securing a high standard of efficiency in educational institutions . . . many of the anomalies that now exist would disappear and much uselessly expended energy would be avoided.' It was only in recent years in England that the state had interfered with the educational system of the country whereas in Germany such had been the case for many years. The advantages were there for all to see: 'There is probably no country in the world in which national prosperity has been so clearly incubated as in Germany. . . . To the lessons learnt in school has been due much of the assiduity, the perseverance, the devotion to duty, the power of work which have enabled the Germans to succeed as a nation.'[61]

The pessimistic picture of Britain's industrial progress built up by contemporary observers has been one supported by historians until recent times, but the certainty and confidence with which conclusions were drawn during the period in question have given way to uncertainty, hesitation and some confusion. Criticisms are mounting of the economic naïvety and lack of scientific rigour of earlier assessments. 'To refer without qualification to Britain's "failure to mechanise" and "failure to modernise plant" or to adopt new processes is to confuse modernity and machinery with profitability.'[62] Professor West writes:

Observers living in the 1870s who complained of the danger of economic failure did not of course employ evidence of national aggregates of output, labour and capital. Such statistics were not available. Their case rested on international comparisons of productivity in specific industries. Here their information was impressionistic and confused.[63]

Some critics have been tempted to go further than merely to point out the inadequacy of the tools of measurement on contemporary observers. For instance, Professor Landes writes that 'the evidence is biased to a degree that is hard to assess. Contemporary observers emphasised the failures of British entrepreneurship and the imminent danger of German competition – this was clearly one of the popular dirges of the day.'[64] These criticisms may, of course, be valid with regard to economic assessments made by contemporary observers and the conclusions and assumptions drawn from them; they bring into question the whole thesis of Britain's failure and the causes of such failure. But what they do not do is invalidate the criticisms levelled by contemporary observers at the English educational system. In any case there was such unanimity of opinion regarding the deficiencies of English education that it cannot be too lightly dismissed as being the result of naïvety or bias: 'The flood of documents although prejudiced were not entirely inaccurate for the more scholarly and analytical accounts contained similar conclusions . . . There must have been an element of truth since informed opinion was almost unanimous on the question.'[65]

The modern assessment

The theory of entrepreneurial failure. The belief that Britain's industrial decline was partly, if not mainly, attributable to bad management was espoused by contemporary observers and has been advanced by numerous critics down to the present day. In particular during the 1940s and 1950s economic historians argued that the keystone of Britain's industrial decline was the performance of the Victorian entrepreneur. This case was argued forcibly by David Landes in the *Cambridge Economic History of Europe* in 1965[66]; the contrast between German and American success on the one hand and British failure on the other was attributable to entrepreneurial and technological creativity by the former and incompetence by the latter. The case against the entrepreneurs was damning: they had failed to adopt new techniques of production ranging from ring-spinning and automatic weaving in cotton to the mechanical cutter and electrification of mines in the coal industry; they had neglected research, investing too little in laboratories and technical personnel; they continued for too long to invest in the traditional industries of cotton and iron at the expense of the newly emerging industries – chemicals, electrical engineering and automobiles – and they had lost export markets through the inefficient use of salesmen.

The hypothesis of entrepreneurial failure embraces many familiar accusations: amateurism, indifference and complacency; incompetent and indifferent salesmanship involving the unwillingness to try new products; a stubborn refusal to suit goods to the needs of potential clients or to engage technical salesmen with a facility in foreign languages; lack of managerial dynamism and adventurousness; technical and organisational lag within individual firms; conservatism in the face of new techniques and a reluctance to abandon individuality and tradition. Because England industrialised earlier, English entrepreneurs were often second or third generation entrepreneurs in the critical period 1870 to 1900, and were more likely to be distracted from business by social life. Furthermore, their lack of formal training told against them – they lacked technical expertise and were less able to judge the commercial prospects of particular innovations.[67]

Professor Allen in *The British Disease* sought to explain the slackening in Britain's industrial growth by examining the problems of labour supply, financial organisation and the effect of German cartelisation. Failing to draw any satisfactory conclusions from his analysis, he concluded: 'We are led back to the proposition that industrial progress depends primarily on the quality of industrial leadership and we have to consider whether the quality had deteriorated since the great days and if so for what reasons. Evidence must be sought in managerial recruitment, social attitudes and education.'[68] He listed complacency, disdain of trade, anti-manufacturing snobbery, the cult of the amateur and the pervading influence of the public schools as detrimental to the quality of Britain's industrial leaders.

Postan, in his survey of the industrial manager in Europe, argued that industrial leaders of the type classified as 'parochial' or 'traditional' had established themselves as the predominant type in most of the older British industries.[69] Charlotte Erickson in her study of the social origins and careers of British business leaders pointed out that many of the pioneers in the nineteenth-century steel industry despatched their sons to public schools; often these sons married into the landed and professional classes and acquired their outlook. Thus high achievement in industry and commerce, it is argued, came to be regarded as a route to the satisfaction of social aspirations. Consequently, Britain was ceasing to produce in the older industries a class of leader who found adequate satisfaction in his business.[70]

With regard to management in the newer industries emerging at the end of the nineteenth century, Allen points out that 'many of the entrepreneurs in the newer lines of production at that time did not come from the well-established firms in those industries which might have seemed the most likely parents'. He cites the larger engineering firms as being 'sceptical of the prospects of the motor vehicle, the development of which they left to pioneers from electrical engineering, cycle making, tinplate manufacture and sheep shearing manufacturers'.[71] Likewise, rayon manufacture was introduced not by any of the major firms in the great textile industries but by a specialist silk weaver who happened at a critical moment to have in his employment an imaginative chemist.

Professor Landes's work in the *Cambridge Economic History of Europe*, together with the persuasive arguments of Derek Aldcroft, represented the culminating point of the vilification of the Victorian entrepreneur, thereafter economic historians using new forms of economic measurement have developed a more sympathetic picture of the problems besetting the entrepreneurs and in consequence several have vindicated the efforts and performance of Victorian management. One leading critic considers that 'the hypothesis of "entrepreneurial failure" has been put on the defensive' and another that it has 'taken quite a beating'.[72] A consideration of the specific problems faced by industrial firms has led to the view that 'one can seldom fault the solution arrived at in the light of available information at the disposal of the entrepreneur'.[73] A general verdict of '*not guilty*' has been arrived at over the alleged deficiencies of British entrepreneurs in the coal and steel industries: 'late Victorian entrepreneurs in the iron and steel industries did not fail. By any cogent measure of performance in fact, they did very well indeed.'[74]

The same is true to a lesser extent in machine tools, whereas in shipping British performance was creditable.[75] The industry which has been shown up in the worst light is the chemical industry, an exhaustive study of which has led to substantial criticism being levelled at chemical entrepreneurs:

The shift to a different kind of technical progress than had been achieved ... demanded a substantial change in the organisation of chemical production. This change I have called the shift to knowledge-centred operation, and in Britain it was not forthcoming. Entrepreneurs had the incentives to economise on the use of national resources, but were unwilling or unable to invest in the necessary technical effort, particularly when this involved the systematic application of science.[76]

The industry was dominated by three products – alkali, sulphuric acid and dyestuffs. Recent studies have revealed there was clear evidence of entrepreneurial deficiency in that Britain lagged in the adoption of the contact process of production of sulphuric acid from the late 1890s while the costly conservatism of the Leblanc producers who 'exhibited the early start mentality with its profit-losing attachment to continuity' led to loss of profits in that sector of industry after 1897. The case of synthetic dyestuffs is more complex, 'yielding to either complete absolution of Victorian entrepreneurship for all indictments for passing up profits' or to making 'foregone profits seem enormous in relation to actual output' depending on the yardsticks used.[77] Complete accord has not been reached over the general position in the chemical industry, but in the opinion of one critic 'we are still a long way from a final solution to the vexed question of the inefficiency of British entrepreneurship in the chemical industry', and the authors of the research cited above themselves concede that 'the calibre of entrepreneurship has yet to be quantified satisfactorily'.[78]

Despite the reservation expressed by Aldcroft to the effect that 'any sweeping generalisations regarding British industry are bound to be misleading since the impact of foreign competition and the subsequent variations to it varied from one branch of industry to another', general verdicts as to the performance of British industry overall have been made. Aldcroft himself states that 'it is inaccurate to argue that British industry as a whole was uncompetitive and inefficient since there were some impressive achievements in those years'.[79] Habbakuk, after studying American and English technology, also arrives at a favourable view:

The abundance of entrepreneurial talent in the United States was a consequence rather than the cause of growth and it was the slow expansion of English industry which accounted for the performance of English entrepreneurs. Where market conditions were favourable to the expansion of capacity British businessmen were dynamic. [And] . . . where advanced technology of foreign origin was not incorporated the explanation is more often the limitations of economic circumstances rather than the inertness of British entrepreneurs.[80]

The general opinion produced at a 1970 conference of economic historians was that British entrepreneurs had been found on the whole 'to have been responsive to the opportunities available'.[81] Since then another critic has concluded:

It is not surprising to find careful studies showing that in the economic environment of pre-1914 Britain there were few missed opportunities for individuals acting rationally under constraints beyond their control . . .

With such a large proportion of resources held in the form of foreign fixed interests, the growth potential of the economy was naturally restricted and the behaviour of individual entrepreneurs reflected this restriction.[82]

The main protagonist against the hypothesis of entrepreneurial failure has written that

taken together, the quantitative work is most damaging to the hypothesis of entrepreneurial failure, rejecting repeatedly the presumption of missed opportunities underlying the hypothesis. .
. . . It is fair to say that the late Victorian entrepreneur, who started his histographic career in damnation, is well on his way to redemption.[83]

So it may prove, [writes Payne] though the evidence is not completely convincing. Doubts are entertained by some economic historians about the validity of the assumptions underlying the statistical manipulations involved in the quantitative approach, while case studies sufficiently detailed for quantitative judgements are still all too rare . . . The sheer inconclusiveness of the discussion is challenging, so many questions are as yet unanswered.[84]

Payne raises two interesting objections. Firstly, that it is commonly assumed that entrepreneurs in the early stages of the Industrial Revolution possessed drive, initiative and enthusiasm. Such indeed may not have been the case for 'the eulogistic aura enveloping the pioneers has been somewhat obscuring because earlier assessments have reflected a biased sample. The majority of records concern firms that were sufficiently successful to have a long life. Many who succeeded in the early years may not have fared so well in later decades.' British errors and hesitations, he argues, were always present; they just became more obvious in the period between 1870 and 1914. The second is that it may even be misleading to speak at all of 'the British entrepreneur'. According to Payne 'no such person exists', as managers came from varied socio-economic backgrounds, operated within different institutional frameworks and were concerned with the attainment of different objectives. Payne's judgement as to the loss of British pre-eminence in international trade – which he emphasises is in itself an endlessly debatable proposition – shifts the argument from a possible decline in entrepreneurial activity to 'a surfeit of individual entrepreneurs, a multitude of aggressively independent firms each pursuing its own self-interest when any increase in the rate of economic growth demanded more co-operation'.[85]

One obstacle standing in the way of a resolution of the entrepreneurial failure hypothesis is the lack of availability of the records of industrial firms, and the inadequacy and interpretation of such as do exist. Several commentators remark on this. Particular difficulty has been experienced with the chemical industry in which 'the lack of statistics and the secretiveness of the leading firms make it difficult to assess the performance of the industry'.[86] Hohenberg, in pursuing his comparative study of chemical firms in Western Europe, records regretfully that his attempts to obtain information from important firms about the period before the First World War

met with only partial success. In no case was it possible to gain access to firm's archives. . . . Company histories are commonly available and vary widely both in quality and scope. Though they provide valuable information, they are biased for two reasons. First, they are written by the company or at its invitation and are not critical in the academic sense.[87]

To continue to accept that British industry stagnated in relative terms but at the same time to reject the hypothesis of entrepreneurial failure faces us with 'a new series of problems', writes Payne. In other words:

The British did as well as could be expected: their businessmen behaved intelligently and rationally but still objective conditions prevented the economy from doing as well as that of other industrialising countries. Whatever measure one takes and whether one sees the problem originating around 1870 or 1900, there is *something* to be explained.[88]

Economic factors The principal economic factors which have been advanced include the cheapness of British labour, the availability of capital, unfavourable tariff barriers imposed by other countries and the operation of the patent laws. Commentators have sometimes attempted to explain the differences between England on the one hand and America on the other in terms of the labour problem. The theory is that cheap labour was a disincentive to manufacturers; its consequence was that they were under less pressure to introduce labour-saving devices, technological innovations and modern machinery. Early in the century there was abundant labour in Britain; later this became less true, but employers and workers were still conditioned by attitudes engendered by abundant labour – workers feared the introduction of mechanical methods, seeing them as a threat to their jobs. In Germany and Belgium labour costs were lower than they were in Britain, but this did not prevent them adopting labour-saving devices more widely in the 1890s than did Britain.[89]

Another explanation is based on the assumed high quality of British labour. Harley argues that since Britain at the end of the century had abundant capital and scarce labour one would have expected her manufacturers to use capital-intensive techniques, export capital-intensive products and import labour-intensive products. The fact that many did not suggests that the British choice of techniques was dictated by the high skills of British workmen.[90] Profit maximisation thus was based on skilled labour as opposed to investment in capital equipment.

Labour in America was certainly nearly always dearer than in Britain and this fact may have acted as an incentive for her to introduce labour-saving devices: 'That the dearness of labour played a significant part in shaping American technology could scarcely be denied.'[91] 'For the dearness and inelasticity of American, compared with British labour, gave the American entrepreneur with a given capital a greater inducement than his British counterpart to replace labour by machines.'[92] Thus the evidence seems to suggest that dear labour was a factor in explaining America's willingness to embrace technological innovations, but even so the relative cheapness of labour on the Continent did not deter those countries from behaving likewise. The problem reduces, therefore, to the attitude of management and employees in Britain towards technological innovation. Here perhaps the strength and power of British trade unions was a significant factor, though we have seen in an earlier section that contemporary observers did not find the trade unions obstructionist and resistant to change.

The detrimental effect on the economy of trade union resistance to change remains an unknown quantity at present: 'Precisely how (if at all) did restrictive practices by unions hinder the adoption of new technologies?'[93] The same is true of managerial attitudes: 'How far is it true that British makers held on to labour-intensive techniques, in what sectors and with what justification? This is a huge question but we cannot proffer general explanations until we are in a position to answer it with some degree of precision.'[94]

Yet another unresolved problem appears to be the influence of the availability of capital on Britain's industrial performance. The argument is that too much capital was invested abroad, to the detriment of the growth of British industry. According to McCloskey, 'the common view is that if investors had been restrained from sending abroad one third of the savings available for capital formation Britain would have been better off. It is clear that in this case Britain's domestic capital stock would have grown half as fast again. It is not clear, however, that exchanging domestic for foreign capital would have raised national income.'[95]

McCloskey's arguments have been criticised by Cottrell for ignoring the effect an increase in domestic investment would have had upon the possible structure of the post-1870 economy,[96] and Kennedy concludes firmly that the growth potential of the economy was restricted by the way savings were deployed: 'With such a large proportion of resources held in the form of foreign fixed-interest securities, the growth potential of the economy was naturally restricted and the behaviour of individual entrepreneurs reflected this restriction.'[97]

But if too much capital was invested abroad at the expense of British industry who was to blame? It has been argued that the institutions of the London capital market were biased towards foreign investments and explanations for this have been advanced. One such explanation justifies the bias in terms of Britain's poor industrial performance:

Although the London capital market was often less than forthcoming, reluctance to advance loans was not wholly ascribable to Banks . . . it may be explained by the generally unimpressive quality of Britain's industrial leaders at the time. The reluctance was wholly justified, for the rise in the amount of capital per head invested in industry after 1900 was not accompanied by any increase in productivity.'[98]

An alternative explanation claims that most merchant bankers had little contact with industrialists and had greater knowledge of conditions overseas than they did of the industrial Midlands and North. A further factor was that 'the average firm was a family-based firm and its financial needs were met by the plough-back of profits and bank loans, there was a strong resistance to raising capital externally'.[99]

Another factor which affected Britain's growth of exports, and indirectly productivity, was tariff barriers; in particular the German tariff of 1879 and the McKinley (1890) and Dingley (1897) tariffs in the United States. Temin has argued that tariff barriers could have deprived even the most efficient steel firms of sufficient export markets to prevent the industry matching German and American growth rates.[100] Habbakuk also emphasises that tariffs greatly accelerated the decline in demand for British products in the iron and steel industry – an industry that was heavily dependent upon exports,[101] but Aldcroft concludes that 'it is highly improbable that tariffs were a major factor in Britain's trade losses. . . . The evidence on this matter is far too slight and fragmentary for it to have anything other than a minor factor in Britain's trade losses.' Rather, 'There is much to commend the suggestion that in part Britain's trade difficulties were self-generated, that is they stemmed from internal deficiencies within her industrial structure.'[102]

The role of government Hobsbawm has argued that a positive role of active intervention in support of industry can be ascribed to British governments throughout the late eighteenth century and the nineteenth century because of their policy of wars and colonisation, which provided much needed markets for emerging industries. Unfortunately, no such claim can be justified, nor even advanced, with respect to many other areas affecting industrial progress; in higher education, in the support of science and technology, in promoting research, government intervention was often too little and too late.

In scientific and technical education the major instrument of government policy was the Science and Art Department. Much of the financial support provided through the Department was channelled into promoting museums, collections and geological surveys. In general, astronomy and the biological and geological sciences fared much better than did the physical sciences and engineering. This bias towards activities which could be pursued by cultured amateurs may be partly explained by the composition of British governments in this period.

Between 1868 and the turn of the century English cabinets were headed by Gladstone, Disraeli, Lord Salisbury and Lord Rosebery. The influential and critical post of Chancellor was held by Robert Lowe, Sir

Stafford Northcote, Gladstone himself, Sir Michael Hicks Beach, Sir William Vernon Harcourt, and Lord Randolph Churchill. Whig or Tory, Conservative or Liberal the political complexion of the government of the day made little difference. These were men of similar backgrounds steeped in the same traditions and deeply influenced by the ethos and ideology of the public schools and Oxbridge.

The three Royal Commissions of the 1860s were headed by the Duke of Newcastle, the Earl of Clarendon and Lord Taunton respectively. Whatever 'progressive elements' were included as Commission members the chances were always weighted in favour of a non-radical report. This is exemplified in the Report of the Clarendon Commission which, while critical of the public schools, nevertheless concluded that 'among the services which they have rendered is undoubtedly to be reckoned the maintenance of classical literature as the staple of English education, a service which far outweighs the error of having clung to these studies exclusively'.[103]

That the Commissioners should be so imbued with the value of classics is not surprising for they themselves were successful products of the system. In addition to the Earl of Clarendon (privately educated), the Commissioners included the eleventh Earl of Devon (Westminster and Christ Church, Oxford), the fourth Baron Lyttleton (Eton and Trinity College, Cambridge), the Hon. Edward Turner Boyd Twistleton (Balliol) and Sir Henry Strafford Northcote, first Earl of Iddesleigh (Eton and Balliol). They contrast strongly with the 'apostles' of science and reform such as Lyon Playfair (St Andrews and Giessen) and Thomas Huxley (Charing Cross Hospital).

By the 1860s an influential group of the new men of science had emerged in London, notably Huxley, Playfair, John Tyndall, John Lubbock, Norman Lockyer and Edward Frankland; nine of them came informally together to form the 'X-Club'.[104] These new men were better represented on the Commission set up by the Gladstone administration in 1870 under the seventh Duke of Devonshire. The Duke himself as Chancellor of the University of Cambridge had been closely involved in the reform of the University. Members of the Commission included Kay-Shuttleworth, W. A. Miller and William Sharpey, who had both been active in building research schools at University College, London, and Bernhard Samuelson; the Secretary was Lockyer, two other Commissioners Huxley and Lubbock being members of the X-Club.

Paradoxically Gladstone himself was opposed to science. Lord Morley recalled that Gladstone watched science 'vaguely and with some misgiving – from any full or serious examination of the scientific movement he stood aside, safe and steadfast within the Citadel of Tradition'[105] and W. E. H. Lecky admitted that there 'were wide tracts of knowledge with which he [Gladstone] had no sympathy. The whole great field of modern scientific discovery was out of his range.'[106] Gladstone was backed up by his Permanent Secretary of the Treasury, Ralph Lingen. A strong supporter of Gladstonian finance, he 'deplored the explosive growth of the Department of Science and Art and the soaring costs associated with scientific education'.

Gladstone was against centralisation, state intervention and the idea of a Minister of Science, and all recommendations of the Devonshire Commission. As Gladstone was in power in 1880, 1886 and 1892 there was little chance of reforms being implemented and in any case for most of the period until then the Tories had opposed university reform and the advance of science. Little wonder that 'men of science lost faith in both parties'.[107]

Early in the century the Cambridge mathematician Charles Babbage had written in a work which can only be described as scathing: 'In England, those who have hitherto pursued science have in general no reasonable grounds of complaint; they knew, or should have known, that there was no demand for it, that it led to little honour, and to less profit.'[108] He demanded institutions for the support of science and for active interference by the government. A further twenty years were to elapse before Parliament in 1849 voted a grant of £1,000 for the promotion of original research. In 1876 a further fund of £4,000 was created, to be administered by the Science and Art Department on recommendations of a special Committee of the Royal Society, the Government Fund Committee. 'No-one knew how many would-be men of science were not doing research because they could not afford the time.' In the first year ninety-eight applications for grants totalling £14,500 were received, of which thirty-three accepted. In the next five years £20,000 was distributed between 417 applicants and between 1850 and 1914 government grants assisted 938 men and 2,316 projects with a sum of £180,000.[109] By 1914 there were 170 privately endowed fellowships for scientists in twenty-four institutions outside Oxford and Cambridge.

In 1851 the government grant had constituted about 50 per cent of all parliamentary funds in aid of science. By 1900 it had declined to 5 per cent of all state expenditure on science. But again, as in the case of the Department of Science and Art, much of the money went to the support of astronomy and geology. In the 1870s for instance 'the single most expensive science was astronomy'.[110]

Apart from a reluctance to support science there was a failure on the part of both government and industry to utilise to the full the scientific and technical expert. In Germany scientists took their place in the management structure of industry, and the expert was thus at the centre of the decision-making process in industrial firms. Such was not the case in Britain, where scientists and technologists were largely confined to playing a subordinate role as advisers. The exclusion of the professional scientist and technologist from the essential decision-making processes meant that the last word was with the amateur. 'This may well provide the clue to many failures in British projects that made a promising start.'[111] Professor Allen sees the 'cult of the amateur' and the misuse of the professional expert as being a fundamental fault not only in the industrial world but in the entire structure of society, especially in the system of government. It is his contention that the decline of Britain had its roots in the failure of the governing class, as well as the industrialists themselves, 'to realise as early as their competitors, that the age of the professional in industrial management had dawned and, in particular, to grasp that the future lay with men equipped by systematic training to promote technological innovation'.

Allen firmly assigns the blame for Britain's decline to 'what we now call the "establishment"': political leaders, the Civil Service and those who sat on the boards of the chief industrial companies. They themselves were of course the victims of anachronistic institutions – the English class system and the educational arrangements associated with it.' His final judgement is that 'Britain's industrial progress was gravely hindered by the strong prejudice, in government and many branches of industry itself, against the expert, a prejudice rooted in social and educational tradition, a prejudice which carried into a technological age the prejudices and attitudes of mind inherited from a pre-scientific time.'[112]

Education Sociological, economic and political factors, although contributory, do not appear to account for Britain's relative decline. In any case almost every hypothesis which has been advanced has come in for criticism. In particular no single economic factor taken alone stands up to close examination. The economists use simple models, a constant theme being the need for more sophisticated models. They also criticise the validity both of each other's models and evidence; furthermore some are much less positive in their advocacy than others. This is not to deny that they are right but there is a long way to go before there is universal acceptance of the truth of economic factors:

The range of our ignorance of the influence of entrepreneurship on British economic performance has been narrowed greatly by its intensive study – [but] the process is by no means complete, for nothing less than a full and detailed explanation of late Victorian economic performance would be required for its completion, and that accomplishment is far beyond the horizon.[113]

There remains education. It is our contention that the English educational system was as great an influence as any other factor in explaining industrial performance in the period 1870–1914. But to go beyond the citing of various statistics and pieces of evidence leads one into difficulties. In the final analysis it amounts to no more than a statement of strong belief, for 'the relationship between education and industrial growth is unexpectedly complex. Demonstrated correlation is one thing, proved causation is another.'[114]

Education then is a predominant factor in our view. But we would confine our criticisms to the secondary and higher education fields, particularly that of the higher technical sector. We do not subscribe to the belief expressed by some contemporary observers in the nineteenth century that the answer to Germany's success lay with her primary schools. Likewise, we do not agree with West's statement that 'the belief that education deficiency was an important obstacle to prosperity in the latter half of the nineteenth century has been shown to stem from confusion and mis-information'[115] for West also confines himself to primary education, even more specifically to literacy.

It is not in primary education that the most obvious faults in English education lay, but, as we have attempted to show, in secondary and higher technical education. West argues that it requires a 40 per cent literacy rate for an industrial revolution and that this prerequisite condition was present in England in the late eighteenth and early nineteenth centuries. His main conclusion, which we do not deny, was that 'despite the widespread belief to the contrary education expanded significantly during the periods examined and at least on *a priori* reasoning there is a fair assumption that it significantly assisted economic growth throughout. There was an education revolution as well as an Industrial Revolution and both were inter-related'.[116] But the significance is that West's so-called education revolution was confined to elementary education; it was the absence of an equivalent 'revolution' in secondary and technical education, which had the greatest bearing on Britain's performance in the second half of the nineteenth century. Germany meanwhile had experienced such a revolution and the results were there for all to see: 'Germany began her final stage of growth in 1860 but her educational revolution had already taken place. This enabled her to catch Britain up rapidly.'[117]

The outstanding feature of the English education system was its lack of central direction. Organisation, coherence and integration were lacking. There was no overall plan or blueprint and for this central government is to be blamed. The education found in most German states was in marked contrast to that of England:

The organisation of the German system ensured that the links between the various stages and institutions within the system were good. The curriculum was perhaps prescribed, but at best each stage fitted into the next. Above all the links from the schools to the universities were established early in the nineteenth century. The comparison that immediately stands out is between the organised German system and the haphazard British system.[118]

In trying to arrive at some kind of verdict two key phrases seem to us to encapsulate the problem. The first is by Professor Payne, namely, that 'the whole complex of circumstances that produced British pre-eminence before 1873 was fortuitous'.[119] Britain's pre-eminence was accidental, the outcome of a perhaps never-to-be-repeated conjunction in time of a set of favourable economic, technological and other factors. It was a historical event created by the fortune of circumstances rather than the result of planned policy or human design. As it was not the result of the efforts of entrepreneurs it is wrong to seek a 'failure' in the sense that they behaved differently in the aftermath of the event.

Education played no part in the attainment of this industrial pre-eminence but could have had a key role in the maintenance of the pre-eminence as the favourable circumstances disappeared one by one. It patently did not play such a role in the new era. In asking why, we are led to our second key phrase attributable to Professor Allen, namely, that 'the "establishment" were the victims of anachronistic institutions in the English class system and the educational arrangements associated with it'.[120] The philosophy of the English educational system was class-based as opposed to the meritocratic ethos pervading the German system. The products of the English system were imbued with such attitudes as to reinforce and strengthen the class bias of the central philosophy. This philosophy was inimical to industrial progress in an international competitive situation. The 'English sickness' or 'British disease' was educational in its roots. It could be the inheritance of this attitudinal condition from the nineteenth century which has led to the many ills that assail us at the present time and have bedevilled us since the end of the Second World War. Its realisation was apparent in the Percy Report of 1945: 'The position of Great Britain as a leading industrial nation is being endangered by failure to secure the fullest possible application of science to industry and this failure is partly due to deficiencies in education.'[121]

In emphasising education as being a factor at least as significant as any other in being responsible for Britain's decline, we find ourselves not only in the company of many contemporary observers but also with some modern critics:

There seems little question [writes Professor Payne] that many known cases of neglect have correctly been ascribed to the fact that the Englishman had yet to learn that an extended and systematic education up to and including the methods of original research [was] now a necessary preliminary to the fullest development of industry.[122]

We are happy to be able to quote from Professor Margaret Gowing's Royal Society address (1976) for the final judgement:

Most economic historians seek objective, primarily economic explan-ations ranging from markets and tariff policy to the complexity of Britain's inherited industrial structure. In this interpretation, education is scarcely mentioned, and such views attune with our current disenchantment at the results of recent large educational expenditure. Of course it is impossible to draw a simple cause and effect line between education and economic strength – but a smaller group of historians do accept that Britain's failure in the nineteenth century to develop the educational system essential for national efficiency was a main cause of this decline. I am on their side.[123]

Notes and references

Chapter 1. The national ethos: Britain leads

1. D. Thomson, *England in the Nineteenth Century, The Pelican History of England*, vol. 8 (Penguin Books, 1950) p. 10.
2. J. B. Bury, *The Idea of Progress: an inquiry into its origins and growth* (Macmillan, 1920), p. 324.
3. Thomson, p. 101.
4. *Ibid.*
5. J. D. Chambers in *The Workshop of the World, British Economic History 1820–1880* (Oxford Paperbacks University Series, 1968, p. 1) defines this as the period between the financial crisis of 1825 and the great depression of 1873.
6. E. J. Hobsbawm, *Industry and Empire, The Pelican Economic History of Britain*, vol. 3 (Penguin Books, 1974) p. 13.
7. *Ibid.*, p. 56.
8. Chambers, p. 10.
9. Hobsbawm, p. 56.
10. W. Schlote, *British Overseas Trade from 1700 to 1932* (London, 1952) *p. 71*.
11. G. D. H. Cole, *British Trade and Industry: Past and Future* (Macmillan, 1932) p. 65.
12. *Final report of the First Census of Production* (1907) pp. 39, 93, 285, 387.
13. T. Kelly, *A History of Adult Education in Great Britain* (Liverpool U.P., 1967) (Ch. 7, Science for the citizen) and A. E. Musson and Eric Robinson, *Science and Technology in the Industrial Revolution* (Manchester U.P., 1969) p. 119.
14. Lyon Playfair, 'The study of abstract science essential to the progress of industry', introductory lecture at the Government School of Mines, session 1851–52, printed in *British Eloquence: lectures and addresses*, (London, 1855), p. 1.
15. Lyon Playfair, 'Industrial education on the Continent', introductory lecture at the Government School of Mines, session 1852–53 (London, 1853), quoted in D. S. L. Cardwell, *The Organisation of Science in England* (Heinemann, 1972), p. 88.
16. Thomson, p. 101.
17. C. Thomas, 'Methodism and self-improvement in nineteenth-century Cornwall', *The Cornish Historical Association Occasional Publication*, no. 9 (1965), p. 1.
18. Quoted by A. K. H. Jenkin, *The Cornish Miner* (Allen and Unwin, 1962), pp. 278–9.
20. *Journal of the Cornish Methodist Historical Association*, 3, no. 1 (May 1968), note on John Williams by T. R. Harris, pp. 7–8.
20. Samuel Smiles, *Self-Help with Illustrations of Conduct and Perseverance* (Murray, 1877), p. 369.
21. J. W. Hudson, *The History of Adult Education* (Longman, Brown, Green and Longmans, 1851; New Impression, Woburn Books, 1969), p. 188.
22. Quoted in Cardwell, *The Organisation of Science in England*, p. 98.
23. Matthew Arnold, *Higher Schools and Universities in Germany*, 2nd edn. (Macmillan, 1892), p. 198.
24. *Ibid.*, p. 20.
25. Royal Commission on Scientific Instruction and the Advancement of Science, 8th Report (1874), vol. 3, p. 45.
26. T. H. Huxley, *Science and Education* collected essays, vol. 3 (London, 1902), see 'Science and culture' (Address at the opening of Sir Josiah Mason's Science College, Birmingham 1 Oct. 1880), p. 1.

27. *Ibid.*, p. 2.
28. *Ibid.*, p. 8.
29. T. H. Huxley, *Universities: Actual and Ideal.* Inaugural address as Lord Rector of Aberdeen University, (1874), p. 48.
30. George Gore, *The Scientific Basis of National Progress* (Williams and Norgate, 1882), p. 1.
31. *Ibid.*, p. 7.
32. Royal Commission on Scientific Instruction as the Advancement of Science (Devonshire Commission) *First Report*, vol. 2, p. 75.
33. Huxley, *Science and Education*, pp. 446–7.
34. W. Ashworth, *Economic History of England 1870–1939* (London, 1960), p. 34.
35. *Ibid.*, p. 37.
36. E. K. Muspratt, *My Life and Work* (John Lane, the Bodley Head, 1917), p. 21.
39. *Ibid.*, p. 21.

Chapter 2. Laying the foundations: Elementary education

1. See J. Murphy, *The Education Act 1870* (Newton Abbot, David & Charles, 1972), pp. 10–15, 54–64, and 70–2.
2. E. G. West, *Education and the Industrial Revolution* (Batsford, 1975), p. 78.
3. Parliamentary committee set up in 1816 'to inquire into the education of the lower orders'; the consequent Parish Schools Bill of 1820 was withdrawn.
4. West, p. 77.
5. Quoted in H. J. Tiffen, *A History of the Liverpool Institute Schools, 1825–1925* (published by the Liverpool Institute Old Boys' Association, 1935), p. 17.
6. Roger Smith, 'Social structures of Nottingham and adjacent districts in mid-nineteenth century' (PhD thesis, Nottingham University, 1968), pp. 44, 53.
7. Chadwick *Report on the Sanitary Conditions of the Labouring Population*, 1842, p. 823.
8. *Ibid.*, p. 1053.
9. *Report of the Commission appointed 'to inquire into the State of Popular Education in England'* (the Newcastle Commission, 1861), vol. 6, p. 299.
10. *Ibid.*, vol. 1, pp. 203–4.
11. *Ibid.*, vol. 2, p. 203.
12. J. J. Bagley and A. J. Bagley, *The State of Education in England and Wales, 1833–1968* (London, Macmillan, 1969), p. 17.
13. *Ibid.*, p. 20.
14. West, pp. 38–43.
15. *Ibid.*, p. 42.
16. R. D. Altich, *The English Common Reader* (University of Chicago Press, 1957), p. 171.
17. Newcastle Commission, vol. 2, p. 194.
18. M. E. Sadler, *Continuation Schools in England and Elsewhere,* (Manchester U.P., 1907), p. 3.
19. *Ibid.*, pp. 178, 147, 183, 185.
20. M. E. Sadler, *Report on Secondary Education in Liverpool including the Training of Teachers for Public Elementary Schools*, City of Liverpool Education Committee (1904), Local Record Office, William Brown Library, p. 124.
21. Sadler, *Continuation Schools*, p. 3.
22. *Ibid.*, pp. 70–1.
23. Sir Philip Magnus, *Industrial Education* (Kegan, Paul, 1888), p. 105.
24. *North American Review* (April 1837), p. 507.
25. *Abstract of the Massachusetts School returns for 1840* (1841).
26. Scholarships were founded for the purpose of connecting the public elementary schools with the lower schools of the secondary schools such as Liverpool Institute

High School and Liverpool Collegiate School.

27. Quoted in Bagley and Bagley, p. 20.
28. *Natural Science in Education*, the Report of the Committee on the Position of Natural Science in the Educational System of Great Britain (The Thomson Committee, 1918), p. 11.
29. *Proceedings of the Liverpool School Board, 1873-74* (Jan. 1874); see Local Record Office, William Brown Library.
30. *Proceedings of the Liverpool School Board, 1876-77* (Feb. 1877).

Chapter 3. Science and the secondary schools

1. Board of Education Report (1905-06), p. 49.
2. The term 'secondary education' did not appear at all in the 1902 Education Act, the phrase 'other than elementary' being used. The term was not statutorily defined until 1944.
3. Board of Education Report (1908-09), p. 31.
4. *Ibid.*, p. 32.
5. Royal Commission on Technical Instruction (the Samuelson Commission, 1882), 2nd Report, part 4, pp. 516-17.
6. Royal Commission on Secondary Education (the Bryce Commission, 1895), vol. 1, part 2, p. 101.
7. M. E. Hipwell, 'A survey of the work of the Science Division of the Department of Science and Art, 1853-1899' (MEd thesis, 1964), University of Nottingham.
8. Bryce Commission (1895) vol. 1, p. 326.
9. *Ibid.*, vol. 1, pp. 78-9.
10. *Ibid.*, vol. 3, p. 65.
11. Board of Education Report (1899), p. 35.
12. Report of Her Majesty's Commissioners 'appointed to inquire into the Revenues and Management of certain Colleges and Schools and the Studies Pursued and Instruction Given Therein' (the Clarendon Commission, 1894), vol. 1, p. 56.
13. *Ibid.*, vol. 1, p. 15.
14. *Ibid.*, vol. 1, p. 27.
15. W. E. Bushell, *School Memoirs*, (Liverpool, Philip Son and Nephew, 1962), p. 47.
16. Clarendon Commission, vol. 1, p. 26.
17. *Ibid.*, p. 32 and appendix F, p. 112.
18. *Ibid.*, p. 32.
19. *Ibid.*, p. 146.
20. Sir Francis Darwin, ed., *Darwin's Life and Letters*, vol. 1, chapter ii (Murray, 1887), p. 2.
21. Clarendon Commission, vol. 1, p. 38.
22. The schools examined by the Commission were intended to serve the middle classes. But who were the middle classes? This posed problems to the Commission. One way of looking at it was to include all those living in houses of the assessed annual value of £20; another was to consider only those who married by licence as opposed to those who married over publication of banns. Either way the figure worked out to be roughly three million.
23. Report of the Royal Commission known as the Schools Inquiry Commission (Taunton Commission, 1868) vol. 4, p. 649.
24. *Ibid.*, vol. 9, p. 649.
25. *Ibid.*, vol. 1, p. 285.
26. *Ibid.*, vol. 1, p. 32.
27. *Ibid.*, vol. 1, pp. 56-7.
28. Devonshire Commission, vol. 3, 6th report, p. 5.
29. Somerset Maugham, *Of Human Bondage* (Heinemann, 1952), pp. 75-7, 84.
30. Devonshire Commission, vol. 1, appendix viii, pp. 32-3.

31. *Ibid.*, vol. 1, appendix i, p. 3.
32. *Ibid.*, vol. 1, p. 321.
33. *The Contemporary Review* judged the Church, the Bar and the Army to be the leading professions, medicine, law and engineering were considered to be 'lower' professions.
34. Of 94 appointments at Eton, up to 1840, 52 were in classics and of 107 at Harrow, 68 were in classics, 11 in mathematics, 8 in modern languages and 3 in science.
35. See J. M. Cohen, *Life of Ludwig Mond* (London, 1956).
36. E. K. Muspratt, *My Life and Work*, 1917.
37. *Liverpool Courier*, April, 1902.
38. Memorandum as to the Present Condition of Secondary Education in Liverpool presented by the Secondary Schools and Scholarships Sub-Committee to the Technical Instruction Committee, Minutes of the Technical Instruction Committee, 21.4.1902, vol. 4, p. 329.
39. Sadler, *Report on Secondary Schools in Liverpool* (1904), p. 12.
40. *Ibid.*, pp. 73–4.
41. Bryce Commission, vol. 6, p. 134.
42. Report by H. Lloyd Snape, Director of Education, 'Lancashire County Council Secondary Schools', 1903, Library of Liverpool University Education Department.
43. Bryce Commission, vol. 6, p. 235.
44. Thomson Committee on the Position of Natural Science, Report (1918), p. 2.
45. *Ibid.*, p. 4.
46. *Ibid.*, p. 23.
47. *Ibid.*, pp. 11 and 44.

Chapter 4. Technical education

1. Cardwell, *The Organisation of Science*, p. 138.
2. Third Report of the Directors of the Edinburgh School of Arts for the Instruction of Mechanics, 1824.
3. *Ibid.*
4. See Thomas Martin, *The Royal Institution* (Longmans, Green, 1942).
5. T. Kelly, *A History of Adult Education in Great Britain* (Liverpool U.P., 1962), P. 123.
6. See Kelly, *Ibid.*, p. 128 and his *George Birkbeck* (Liverpool U.P., 1957), p. 244; also J. W. Hudson, *The History of Adult Education* (Longman, Brown, Green & Longmans, 1851; New impression, Woburn Books, 1969).
7. Kelly, *A History of Adult Education*, p. 117
8. *Ibid.*, p. 125.
9. Hudson, p. 57.
10. *Ibid.*, p. 58.
11. Quoted by W. H. Watkinson, *Transactions of the Liverpool Engineering Society*, **34** (1913), 9–10.
12. Sir Henry Cole, *Fifty Years of Public Life* (Bell, 1884), p. 285.
13. Annual Report, 1868, p. 4.
14. M. E. Hipwell, 'Survey of the work of the Science Division of the Science and Art Department 1853–1879' (unpublished MEd thesis, Nottingham University, 1965); see also H. Butterworth, 'The development and influence of the Science and Art Department 1853–1899' (PhD thesis, Sheffield University, 1968).
15. For a description of the early days of the City and Guilds see Sir Philip Magnus, *Educational Aims and Efforts, 1880–1910* (Longmans, 1910), quoted in Michael Argles, *South Kensington to Robbins* (Longmans, 1964), p. 22.
16. D. W. F. Hardie, 'The Musgraves and the British chemical industry', *Endeavour* **14**, (1955), 29–33.
17. D. Hewitt, *Fifty Years of the Geological Society – a Retrospect* (1910); see Local Record Office, William Brown Library, Liverpool.
18. Report of the Royal Commission on Technical Instruction, 4 vols (the Samuelson Commission, 1882–84).

19. Samuelson Commission vol. 1, part iv, p. 515.
20. See Argles, *South Kensington to Robbins*, p. 35.
21. *Ibid.*, p. 35.
22. Parliamentary Papers, 1873–4, Commons Volume 69. Accounts and Papers (20): Education.
23. *Report of the Special Sub-Committee of the Liverpool Education Committee Appointed to Inquire into and Report upon the Receipts and Payments in Respect of Education in Liverpool* (1915), pp. 99–100, Local Record Office, William Brown Library, Liverpool.
24. Liverpool Technical Instruction Sub-Committee Minute Books, vol. 3, 1896, Local Record Office, William Brown Library, Liverpool.
25. Annual report of the Liverpool School of Science, 1887–8, pp. 46–7; Local Record Office, William Brown Library, Liverpool.
26. Annual Report of the Liverpool School of Science, 1890, Local Record Office, William Brown Library.
27. *Trade and Technical Education in Germany and France*, report by J. C. Smail, Organiser of Trade Schools for Boys on Trade and Technical Education in France and Germany, London County Council (1914).
28. *Ibid.*, pp. 8–10.
29. City of Manchester Technical Instruction Committee, Report of the Deputation Appointed to visit Technical Schools, Institutions and Museums in Germany and Austria (1897), pp. 5, 6.
30. Smail, p. 11.
31. Quoted in Smail, p. 7.

Chapter 5. Science and higher education

1. Quoted in Joseph Thompson, 'The Owens College' (J. E. Cornish, 1886), p. 518.
2. Sydney Smith, *Edinburgh Review*, **15** (1810), 46–7.
3. Devonshire Commission, vol. 1, p. 282.
4. T. G. Chambers, *Royal College of Chemistry, Royal School of Mines and Royal College of Science* (Hazell, Watson and Viney, 1896), p. 31.
5. Warren de La Rue, 'Farewell Banquet to Dr Hofmann', 28 April 1864, in Chambers, p. 32.
6. First Prospectus of the Government School of Mines, 1852.
7. Cardwell, *The Organisation of Science in England*, p. 42.
8. W. Whewell, *On the Principles of English University Education* (Parker, 1837), p. 43.
9. According to C. A. Anderson and Miriam Schnaper, 64 per cent of Oxford graduates and 50 per cent of Cambridge graduates during the period 1752 to 1886 became clergymen, see 'School and society in England, social backgrounds of Oxford and Cambridge students', *Annals of American Research* (Public Affairs Press, Washington, 1952), p. 6.
10. T. H. Huxley, *Science and Education*, vol. 3, (Macmillan, 1893), p. 223.
11. Mark Pattison, *Suggestions on Academical Organisation* (Edmonson and Douglas, 1868), p. 157.
12. The Natural Science Tripos instituted in 1848 was not a degree examination. It was open only to graduates and did not become open to undergraduates until 1861. Likewise at the National Science Honours School at Oxford, established in 1850, only those who had previously attained honours in classics or mathematics were allowed to present themselves for study in natural science.
13. Devonshire Commission, vol. 1, pp. 32, 285, 278.
14. *Ibid.*, vol. 3, pp. liv–lv.
15. *Ibid.*, vol. 1, p. 187.
16. *Ibid.*, vol. 1, p. 187.
17. *Ibid.*, vol. 3, p. xxv.
18. *Ibid.*, vol. 1, p. 500.

19. *Ibid.*, vol. 3, p. xxvi.
20. See W. H. G. Armytage, *The Civic Universities* (Benn, 1955).
21. *University College and the University of Liverpool 1882–1907, a brief record of work and progress* (Liverpool U.P., 1907), pp. 4–5, Harold Cohen Library, University of Liverpool.
22. Inaugural Address delivered at the opening of University College, Liverpool, by Principal G. H. Randall, 14 January 1882; see Harold Cohen Library.
23. H. Hale Bellot, *A History of University College, London 1826–1926*, (University of London Press, 1929).
24. J. C. Hearnshaw, *The Centenary History of King's College, London, 1828–1928*, (Harrap, 1929).
25. Joseph Thompson, *The Owens College* (J. E. Cornish, 1886).
26. E. M. Bettenson,*The University of Newcastle-upon-Tyne, a historical introduction 1834–1971* (University of Newcastle, 1971).
27. A. N. Shimmin, *The University of Leeds: the First Half Century* (Cambridge University Press, 1954).
28. A. W. Chapman, *The Story of a Modern University* (Oxford University Press, 1955).
29. E. W. Vincent and P. Hinton, *The University of Birmingham* (Sutton Coldfield: Cornish, 1947).
30. *University of Birmingham Calendars*, 1906–13.
31. *University of Birmingham Calendars*, 1901–13.
32. A. C. Wood, *A History of University College, Nottingham 1881–1948* (Blackwell, 1953).
33. For University College, Liverpool, and Liverpool University see G. W. Roderick, 'Scientific and technical education in Liverpool and its relevance to industrial Merseyside, 1870–1914' (unpublished MA thesis, University of Liverpool, 1971).
34. R. Muir, *The Need for a University of Liverpool* (Liverpool, 1901), Harold Cohen Library.
35. Education Department, *Reports from University Colleges Participating in the Grant of £15,000 made by Parliament for University Colleges in Great Britain* (HMSO, 1894),
36. Muir, p. 64.
37. Moore, *Researches in Biochemistry, 1908–11*, Harold Cohen Library.
38. *Ibid.*, p. 1.
39. *University of Liverpool Calendars*, 1907, 1914.
40. *University of Liverpool Calendar*, 1908.
41. Fortunately the Corporation of Liverpool intervened on behalf of the poorer students and allocated an annual sum of £1,000 for the award of grants to those sons and daughters of poor parents who had failed to secure a scholarship. Of 180 students who received aid from this fund up to 1912 no fewer than 67 graduated with a general degree or an honours degree in science or engineering.
42. *The Yorkshire College Calendar*, 1895.
43. In 1889 government aid to these colleges was £14,000, a sum almost equivalent to the total aid £15,000 shared between all the civic colleges.
44. *University of London Calendar*, 1910.
45. *Ibid.*
46. *The Imperial College of Science and Technology Calendar*, 1910.
47. Chambers, *Royal College of Chemistry*.
48. A. Schuster, *The Physical Laboratories of the University of Manchester*, Manchester University Press (1906).
49. R. Kukula and K. Trübner, *Minerva, Jahrbuch der Gelehrten Welt'*, (Verlag Karl J. Trübner, 1910); also, Board of Education, Reports from Universities and University Colleges participating in the Parliamentary Grant.
50. Devonshire Commission Reports (HMSO, 1872–75). Samuelson Commission First and Second Reports (HMSO, 1882–84).
51. Total Exchequer grants to universities and university colleges in England and Wales during the period 1882–1912 amounted to some £105,000.
52. 'Chemical instruction and chemical industries in Germany', Report by Dr Frederick Rose, HM Consul in Stuttgart, Diplomatic and Consular Reports, Miscellaneous

Series No. 561, Foreign Office, 1901, p. 22.
53. City of Manchester Technical Instruction Committee, Report of the Deputation Appointed to visit Technical School, Institutes and Museums in Germany and Austria (1897), p. 18.
54. Samuelson Commission, 2nd Report, vol. 1 (1884), p. 23.
55. Rose, p. 24.
56. Samuelson Commission, 2nd Report, vol. 1 (1884), p. 192.
57. Rose, p. 25.
58. W. E. Dalby, 'The education of engineers', *Proceedings of the Institution of Mechanical Engineers*, (1903), parts 1 and 2, p. 304.
59. Dalby pointed out that students entering German Technical High Schools were all over eighteen years of age. To obtain his figures for Britain he included all students over the age of fifteen taking a day course for at least twenty hours a week at the technical schools and polytechnics. However, his figures as they stand do not give a true comparison between Britain and Germany for 'probably there are not more than 500 students over 17 years of age in the whole of Britain taking courses in the subjects listed who can fairly be compared with those in Germany' (p. 304).

Chapter 6. Industry, education and training

1. Devonshire Commission, 1st Report, vol. 1, p. 22.
2. See Cardwell, *Organisation of Science in England*, pp. 167–79.
3. F. Versmann, *Alizarin, Natural and Artificial*, New York (1877); quoted in George Gore, *The Scientific Basis of Natural Progress* (William and Norgate, 1882), p. 66.
4. L. F. Haber, *The Chemical Industry, 1900–1930: international growth and technological change* (Oxford University Press, 1971), p. 9.
5. Michael Sanderson, *The Universities and British Industry, 1850–1970* (Routledge and Kegan Paul, 1972), p. 12.
6. *Ibid.*, p. 11.
7. G. W. Roderick, 'Scientific and technical training in Liverpool and its relevance to industrial Merseyside, 1870–1914' (unpublished MA thesis, University of Liverpool, 1971).
8. Sir Swire Smith, Inaugural Address at Dundee Technical Institute, October 1888, p. 20.
9. A. E. Musson, *Enterprise in Soap and Chemicals, Joseph Crosfield and Son Ltd, 1815–1965* (Manchester University Press, 1965), p. 146.
10. Devonshire Commission, 8th Report, vol. 3, p. 45.
11. Sanderson, p. 66.
12. Deed of Foundation of Josiah Mason's Science College, 12 December 1870, quoted in Sanderson, p. 69.
13. Roderick, Thesis.
14. *Minutes of evidence before the Durham University Commission* (1862), Evidence of Rev. J. Cundhill, Q. 480.
15. Muspratt, *Autobiography*, p. 180.
16. Musson, p. 153.
17. Sadler, *Secondary education in Liverpool*, p. 181.
18. D. W. F. Hardie and J. D. Pratt, *A History of the Modern British Chemical Industry* (Pergamon, 1966), pp. 68, 69.
19. P. M. Hohenberg, *Chemicals in Western Europe, 1850–1914; an economic study of technical change* (North Holland Publishing Co., 1967), pp. 104 and 107.
20. Dr Frederick Rose, *Chemical Instruction in Germany and the Growth and Present Condition of the German Chemical Industries*, Diplomatic and Consular Reports Cd 430–16 (1901); Supplementary Report, Cd 787–9 (1902), miscellaneous series (1902), Foreign Office, p. 30.
21. F. Fischer, *Das Studium der Technischen Chemie an den Universitäten und Technischen Hochschulen*, Deutschland (1897), p. 45; quoted in Haber, p. 14.

22. Rose, p. 24.
23. *Ibid.*, p. 75.
24. Ramsay Muir, *the University of Liverpool: its present state* (printed at the Liverpool Daily Post, 1907), p. 27; see Harold Cohen Library, University of Liverpool.
25. W. H. Perkin, 'Research work at the Universities', *Manchester University Magazine*, December 1908.
26. Muspratt, p. 49.
27. Rose, p. 31.
28. Haber, p. 64.
29. Musson, pp. 80–1.
30. Sanderson, p. 18.
31. Samuelson Commission, 1st report, vol. 2, part iv, p. 516.
32. Hohenberg, p. 76.
33. *Ibid.*, pp. 80, 82, 105.
34. *Report on the education and Status of Civil Engineers in the United Kingdom and in Foreign Countries* (published by the Council of the Institution of Civil Engineers, 1870; henceforth referred to as the 1870 Report); and 'The Education and training of engineers' (published by the Council of the Institution in the *Proceedings of the Institution of Civil Engineers*, **166** 1905–6), part iv, pp. 159–82; (henceforth referred to as the 1905–6 Report).
35. 1870 Report, pp. viii–ix.
36. *Ibid.*, p. ix.
37. *Ibid.*, p. xi.
38. 'Young Englishmen and their parents crowd the doors of the offices and workshops, offering premiums of £300 to £500 for the mere permission to pass three years inside the magic gates, which must be passed to gain an entrance into the profession' (1870 Report, p. 201).
39. 1870 report, p. 201.
40. *Ibid.*, p. 204.
41. 1905–6 Report, p. 166.
42. Published in *Proceedings of the Institution of Mechanical Engineers* (1903) parts i–ii, pp. 281–349.
43. *Ibid.*, pp. 281, 282.
44. *Ibid.*, p. 304.
45. *Ibid.*, p. 304.
46. *Ibid.*, p. 327.
47. *Transactions of the Liverpool Polytechnic Society*, 26 (1868), 38–9.
48. *Transactions of the Liverpool Engineering Society*, vol. 34 (1913) p. 10.
49. *Ibid.*
50. Devonshire Commission, 1st Report, vol. 1 (1872) p. 147.
51. *Ibid.*, p. 19.
52. W. Hopkins, Anniversary Address of the President, *Quarterly Journal of the Geological Society*, **8** (1852), p. lxxix.
53. Devonshire Commission, 1st Report, vol. 1, p. 155.
54. Chambers, *Royal College of Chemistry, Royal School of Mines and Royal College of Science*, p. 11.
55. J. D. Bernal, *Science and Industry in the Nineteenth Century* (Routledge, 1953), p. 95.
56. Devonshire Commission, 1st Report, vol. 1, p. 623.
57. Sanderson, p. 21.
58. Haber, p. 13.
59. Cardwell, pp. 105, 175.
60. *Ibid.*, p. 173.
61. D. W. F. Hardie, *History of the Chemical Industry on Widnes* (ICI, General Chemicals Division, 1950), p. 169.
62. *Ibid.*, p. 176.
63. Cardwell, p. 173.
64. 'Within the dyestuffs industry', *Journal of Chemical Industry*, **50** (1931), 254.

65. Cohen, p. 95.
66. Sanderson, p. 87.
67. We are indebted to Mr Malcolm Moore, Public Relations Officer of Unilever, Merseyside Ltd, for this information.
68. Chambers, *Royal College of Chemistry*.
69. A. Schuster, *The Physical Laboratories of the University of Manchester*, Manchester University Press (1906).
70. Whitworth Society, *The Whitworth Register* (London, 1955).
71. Sanderson, p. 100.
72. H. A. Roberts, 'Education in science as a preparation for industrial life', *Journal of the Royal Society of Arts*, 1 March 1912.

Chapter 7. Did Britain go wrong?

1. R. J. S. Hoffman, *Great Britain and the German Trade Rivalry* (Philadelphia, University of Pennsylvania Press, 1933).
2. D. N. McCloskey, 'Did Victorian Britain fail?', *Economic History Review*, second series, 23, no. 3 (1970), p. 459.
3. W. W. Rostow, *The Stages of Economic Growth* (Cambridge U.P., 1960).
4. T. S. Ashton, *The Industrial Revolution 1760–1830* (Oxford U.P., 1948), p. 46.
5. M. W. Flinn, *Origins of the Industrial Revolution* (Longman, 1972), p. 10.
6. E. J. Hobsbawm, *Industry and Empire, Pelican Economic History of Britain*, vol. 3 (Penguin Books, 1974), pp. 44, 54.
7. *Ibid.*, p. 48.
8. S. D. Chapman, 'The cotton industry in the Industrial revolution', in *Studies in Economic History* (Macmillan, 1972), p. 63.
9. H. J. Habbakuk and P. Deane, 'The take off in Britain', in W. W. Rostow, ed. *The Economics of Take Off into Sustained Growth* (Macmillan, 1965), p. 71.
10. Chapman, p. 63.
11. Hobsbawm, p. 69.
12. *Ibid.*, p. 58.
13. *Ibid.*, p. 49.
14. Flinn, p. 93.
15. *Ibid.*, p. 102.
16. *Ibid.*, pp. 93, 14, 18.
17. P. Deane, 'The Industrial revolution in Great Britain', in C. M. Cipolla, ed., *The Emergence of Industrial Societies: The Fontana Economic History of Europe*, vol. 1, p. 164.
18. Ashton, p. 2.
19. In Cipolla, pp. 7–8.
20. Hobsbawm, p. 172.
21. D. S. Landes, 'Technological change and development in Western Europe, 1750–1914', in H. J. Habbakuk and M. M. Postan, eds, *The Cambridge Economic History of Europe*, vol. 6, (Cambridge U.P., 1966), p. 462.
22. Hobsbawm, p. 173.
23. *Ibid.*, p. 174.
24. S. Lilley, 'Technological progress in the Industrial Revolution, 1700–1914', in M. Cipolla, ed., *The Industrial Revolution: Fontana Economic History of Europe* (1975), p. 237.
25. J. D. Bernal, *Science and Industry in the Nineteenth Century* (Routledge, 1953), p. 25.
26. Derek H. Aldcroft, ed., *The Development of British Industry and Foreign Competition, 1875–1914* (Allen & Unwin, 1958), p. 21.
27. D. N. McCloskey, 'Britain's loss from foreign industrialization: a provisional estimate' in *Explorations in Economic History* (Summer 1970), p. 143.

28. G. C. Allen, *The British Disease* (Institute of Economic Affairs), p. 32.
29. Hobsbawm, p. 180.
30. Allen, p. 32.
31. D. N. McCloskey, 'International differences in productivity: coal and steel in America and Britain before World War 2', in *Essays on a Mature Economy: Britain after 1840* (Methuen, 1971), p. 295.
32. D. L. Burn, *The Economic History of Steelmaking, 1867–1939* (Cambridge U.P., 1940).
33. McCloskey, 'International differences in productivity', p. 299.
34. P. W. Musgrave, *Technical Change, the Labour Force and Education: a study of the British and German iron and steel industries 1860–1964* (Pergamon, 1967).
35. Hobsbawm, p. 180.
36. S. B. Saul, 'The market and the development of the mechanical engineering industries in Britain, 1860–1914' in Saul, ed., *Technological change: the United States and Britain in the nineteenth century* (Methuen, 1970), pp. 141–70.
37. Roderick Floud, 'Changes in the productivity of labour in the British machine tool industry, 1856–1900', in McCloskey, ed., *Essays*, p. 313.
38. Hobsbawm, p. 182.
39. D. H. Aldcroft, 'The entrepreneur and the British economy, 1870–1914', *Economic History Review*, 2nd series, **17** (1964), 114.
40. T. G. Orsagh, 'Progress in iron and steel, 1870–1913', *Comparative Studies in Society and History*, **3** (1960–1), p. 230.
41. H. J. Habbakuk, *American and British Technology in the Nineteenth Century* (Cambridge U. P., 1962), p. 180.
42. Hobsbawm, p. 185.
43. D. N. McCloskey, 'Did Victorian Britain fail?', *Economic History Review*, second series, **23** no. 3 (1970), 459.
44. D. N. McCloskey, ed., 'Essays on a mature economy: Britain after 1940', *Papers and Proceedings of the Mathematical Social Science Board Conference on the New Economic History of Britain, 1840–1930* (Harvard University; London, Methuen, 1971), p. 7.
45. W. Ashley, *The Tariff Problem* (P. S. King, 1902), p. 112.
46. *Final Report of the Committee on Commercial and Industrial Policy after the War*, Cd 9035, 1918, **12**, paras. 93–4, 96–9.
47. Arthur Shadwell, *Industrial Efficiency, A Comparative Study of Industrial Life in England, Germany and America* (Longman, Green, 1906), pp. 446, 454.
48. Sir Philip Magnus, *Industrial education* (London, Kegan, Paul and French, 1888), p. 80.
49. Shadwell, p. 426.
50. Sir Swire Smith, *The Real German Rivalry, Yesterday, Today and Tomorrow* (T. Fisher Unwin, 1918), p. 25.
51. Shadwell, *ibid.*, pp. 73, 148, 8.
52. *Ibid.*, p. 331.
53. *Ibid.*, p. 455.
54. *Ibid.*, pp. 14, 15.
55. Magnus, p. 52.
56. Swire Smith, p. 25.
57. Magnus, p. 52. *Ibid.*, pp. 67–8.
58. *Ibid.*, p. 268.
59. Shadwell, p. 468.
60. Magnus, pp. 105, 94–5.
61. *Ibid.*, pp. 106, 195–6.
62. P. H. Lindert and Keith Trace, 'Yardsticks for Victorian entrepreneurs', in McCloskey, ed., *Essays on a Mature Economy*, p. 342.
63. E. G. West, *Education and the Industrial Revolution* (Batsford, 1975), p. 255.
64. Landes, p. 565.
65. Aldcroft, p. 16.

66. 'Some reasons why', in D. S. Lands *Technological Change and Development in Western Europe, 1750–1914* pp. 553–84; also in H. J. Habbakuk and M. Postain, eds, *The Cambridge Economic History of Europe* (Cambridge U.P., 1965), vol. 6, ch. 5.
67. Habbakuk, p. 180.
68. Allen, pp. 33–4.
69. M. M. Postan, *An Economic History of Western Europe 1945–* (Methuen, 1967), p. 281.
70. C. Erickson, *British Industrialists: steel and hosiery, 1850–1950* (Cambridge U.P., 1959).
71. Allen, p. 33.
72. McCloskey, *Essays on a Mature Economy*, p. 6, and S. B. Saul in *ibid.*, p. 393.
73. P. L. Payne, *British Entrepreneurship in the Nineteenth Century, Studies in Economic History* (Macmillan, 1974), p. 58.
74. D. N. McCloskey, 'Economic maturity and entrepreneurial decline. British iron and steel, 1870–1913' (unpublished PhD thesis, Harvard University, 1970), p. 142.
75. Floud, p. 313; Charles K. Harley, 'The shift from sailing to steamships, 1850–1890: a study in technological change and its diffusion', in McCloskey, ed., *Essays on a Mature Economy*, p. 215.
76. P. M. Hokenberg, *Chemicals in Western Europe, 1850–1914: an economic study of technical change* (1967), p. 141.
77. Lindert & Trace, op cit., pp. 265, 264, 267.
78. D. H. Aldcroft in D. N. McCloskey 'Essays on a Mature Economy' p. 275; Lindert & Trace, p. 240.
79. Aldcroft, p. 35.
80. Habbakuk, pp. 213–15.
81. McCloskey, 'Essays on a Mature Economy', p. 7.
82. W. R. Kennedy, 'Foreign investment, trade and growth in the United Kingdom 1870–1915', *Explorations in Economic History*, 11, no. 4 (Summer 1974), p. 416.
83. D. N. McCloskey and Lars G. Sandberg, 'From damnation to redemption: judgments on the late Victorian entrepreneur', *Explorations in Economic History*, 9, no. 1 (1971) esp. p. 108.
84. Payne, p. 12.
85. *Ibid.*, pp. 30–1, 56.
86. L. F. Haber, *The Chemical Industry 1900–1930; international growth and technological change*, (Oxford U.P., 1971), p. 11.
87. Hohenberg, p. 22.
88. Payne, p. 7.
89. Habbakuk, p. 203.
90. C. K. Harley, 'Skilled labour and the choice of technique in Edwardian industry', in *Britain in the World's Economy 1860–1914*, Eliot House Conference, Harvard University, September 1973; reprinted in *Explorations in Economic History*, 11, no. 4, p. 392 (esp. p. 411).
91. Saul, p. 17.
92. H. J. Habbakuk, 'The economic effects of labour scarcity' in Saul, *Technological Change*, p. 26.
93. S. B. Saul, in McCloskey, ed., *Essays*, p. 396.
94. S. B. Saul, *Technical Change: the United States and Britain in the 19th Century*, Methuen, p. 18.
95. D. N. McCloskey, 'Did Britain Fail?', *economic History review*, 2nd series, 23, 1970, p. 459.
96. P. L. Cottrell, 'British overseas development in the nineteenth century', in *Studies in Economic and Social History* (Macmillan, 1975), p. 55.
97. W. R. Kennedy, 'Foreign investment, trade and growth in the United Kingdom 1753–1913', *Explorations in Economic History*, 11, no. 4, (Summer 1974).
98. Allen, p. 33.
99. Cottrell, p. 54.
100. P. Temin, 'The relative decline of the British steel industry, 1880–1913', in Henry Rosovsky, ed., *Industrialisation in Two Systems* (New York, 1966), p. 242.

101. Habbakuk, p. 205.
102. Aldcroft, pp. 22, 23.
103. The Clarendon Commission (1864), Report, vol. 1, p. 56.
104. R. M. MacLeod 'Resources of science in Victorian England: the endowment of the science movement 1868–1900', in P. Mathias, ed., *Science and Society 1600–1800* (Cambridge U.P., 1972), p. 121.
105. John Morley, *Life of Gladstone* (London 1905), vol. 1, p. 209.
106. W. E. H. Lecky, *Democracy and Liberty* (London, 1876), p. xxxi.
107. MacLeod, p. 151.
108. C. Babbage, *Reflections on the Decline of Science* (B. Fellowes, 1820), p. 24.
109 MacLeod, pp. 145, 146.
110. *Ibid.*, p. 356.
111. Allen, p. 49.
112. *Ibid.*, pp. 49, 50.
113. McCloskey and Sandberg, p. 108.
114. West, p. 245.
115. *Ibid.*, p. 256.
116. *Ibid.*, p. 256.
117. Musgrave, p. 255.
118. *Ibid.*, p. 264.
119. Payne, p. 51.
120. Allen, p. 48.
121. Ministry of Education, *Higher technological education*,(The Percy Report:HMSO, 1945), para. 2.
122. Payne, p. 51, Sanderson, p. 17.
123. Margaret Gowing, *Science, Technology and Education in England in 1870*, the Wilkins Lecture, reprinted from *Notes and records on the Royal Society of London*, **32**, no. 1, (July 1977), p. 86.

Further reading

General

W. H. G. **Armytage** *A Social History of Engineering* Faber 1970.
J. D. **Chambers** *The Workshop of the World. British Economic History, 1820–1880* Oxford University Press 1964.
R. C. K. **Ensor** *England 1870–1914* Oxford University Press 1964.
C. P. **Hill** *British Economic and Social History, 1700–1975*, 4th edn, Edward Arnold, 1977.
E. J. **Hosbawm** *Industry and Empire* Penguin Books 1974.
J. T. **Merz** *A History of European Thought in the Nineteenth Century*, 4 vols. London 1869–1914.
G. W. **Roderick** *The Emergence of a Scientific Society in England, 1800–1965* Macmillan 1967.
Samuel **Smiles** *Self-Help with Illustrations of Conduct and Perseverance* John Murray 1877.
E. P. **Thompson** *The Making of the English Working Class* Penguin Books 1963.
D. **Thomson** *England in the Nineteenth Century* Penguin Books 1950.

Education

Michael **Argles** *South Kensington to Robbins* Longman 1964.
W. H. G. **Armytage** *Civic Universities* Benn 1955.
Matthew **Arnold** *Higher Schools and Universities in Germany* Macmillan 1st edn. 1868, 2nd edn. 1892.
D. S. L. **Cardwell** *The Organisation of Science in England* Heinemann 1972.
T. H. **Huxley** *Science and Education; Collected Essays*, Macmillan 1893, 3 vols.
Thomas **Kelly** *A History of Adult Education in Great Britain* Liverpool University Press 1970.
Sir Philip **Magnus** *Industrial Education* Kegan, Paul and French 1888.
Mark **Pattison** *Suggestions on Academical Organisation* Edmonson and Douglas 1868.
E. G. **West** *Education and the Industrial Revolution* Batsford 1975.
W. **Whewell** *On the Principles of English University Education* Parker and Son 1837.

Industry

D. H. **Aldcroft,** ed., *The Development of British Industry and Foreign Competition, 1875–1914* George Allen and Unwin 1968.
G. C. **Allen** *The British Disease* Institute of Economic Affairs 1976.
T. S. **Ashton** *The Industrial Revolution, 1760–1830* Oxford University Press 1948.
J. D. **Bernal** *Science and Industry in the Nineteenth Century* Routledge 1953.
D. L. **Burn** *The Economic History of Steelmaking, 1867–1930* London 1943.
T. H. **Burnham** and G. O. **Hoskins** *Iron and Steel in Britain, 1870–1930* London 1943.
W. H. **Chaloner** *People and Industries* London 1963.

S. D. Chapman *The Cotton Industry in the Industrial Revolution* Macmillan 1972.

Carlo M. Cipolla, ed., *The Emergence of Industrial Societies* Fontana 1973.

Phyllis Deane *The First Industrial Revolution* London 1967.

Charlotte Erickson *British Industrialists: Steel and Hosiery, 1850–1950* London 1959.

M. W. Flinn *The Origins of the Industrial Revolution* Longman 1966.

H. J. Habbakuk *American and British Technology in the Nineteenth Century* Cambridge University Press, 1962.

L. F. Haber *The Chemical Industry During the Nineteenth Century* Clarendon Press 1958.

D. W. F. Hardie *A History of the Chemical Industry in Widnes* ICI 1950.

D. W. F. Hardie and **J. D. Pratt** *A History of the Modern British Chemical Industry* Pergamon 1966.

R. M. Hartwell, ed., *The Causes of the Industrial Revolution* London 1967.

P. M. Hohenberg *Chemicals in Western Europe, 1850–1914. An Economic Study of Technical Change* North Holland Publishing Company 1967.

P. W. Kingsford *Engineers, Inventors and Workers* London 1964.

P. Mantoux *The Industrial Revolution in the Eighteenth Century* 12th edn. London 1961.

Peter Mathias *The First Industrial Revolution. Economic History of Britain, 1700–1914* London 1969.

P. W. Musgrave *Technical Change, the Labour Force and Education; A Study of the British and German Steel Industries, 1860–1964* London 1967.

A. E. Musson *Enterprise in Soap and Chemicals, Joseph Crosfield and Sons Ltd., 1815–1965* Manchester 1966.

A. E. Musson and **Eric Robinson** *Science and Technology in the Industrial Revolution* Manchester University Press 1969.

P. L. Payne *British Entrepreneurship in the Nineteenth Century* Macmillan 1974.

L. S. Presnell, ed., *Studies in the Industrial Revolution* Athlone Press 1960.

L. T. C. Rolt *Victorian Engineering* London 1970.

Michael Sanderson *The Universities and British Industry, 1850–1970* Routledge and Kegan Paul 1972.

S. B. Saul, ed., *Technological Change: the United States and Britain in the Nineteenth Century* Methuen 1970.

Arthur Shadwell *Industrial Efficiency: a Comparative Study of Industrial Life in England, Germany and America* Longmans, Green and Co. 1906.

Samuel Smiles *The Lives of the Engineers* London 1861. *Industrial Biography* new edn. Murray 1889.

Sir Swire Smith *The Real German Rivalry. Yesterday, Today and Tomorrow* Fisher and Unwin 1918.

P. Temin 'The Relative Decline of the British Steel Industry, 1880–1914', in **H. Rosovosky** *Industrialization in Two Systems* New York 1966.

Economy

T. S. Ashton *An Economic History of England: the Eighteenth Century* Methuen 1955.

W. Ashworth *Economic History of England, 1870–1939* Methuen 1960.

J. H. Clapham *An Economic History of Modern Britain (1926–1938)* Cambridge University Press 1926–36 3 vols.

G. D. H. Cole *British Trade and Industry, Past and Future* Macmillan 1932.

P. L. Cottrell *British Overseas Investment in the Nineteenth Century* Macmillan 1975.

W. H. B. Court *British Economic History, 1870–1914* London 1965.

Phyllis Deane and **W. A. Cole** *British Economic Growth, 1688–1959* Cambridge University Press 1965.

H. J. Habbakuk and **Phyllis Deane** 'The take-off in Britain' in **W. W. Rostow**, ed., *The Economics of Take-off into Sustained Growth* Macmillan 1963.

H. J. Habbakuk and **M. Postan**, eds, *Cambridge Economic History of Europe* Cambridge University Press 1965.

R. J. S. Hoffman *Great Britain and the German Trade Rivalry* University of Pennsylavania Press 1933.

D. N. McCloskey, ed., *Essays on a Mature Economy: Britain after 1840* Methuen 1971.

A. E. Musson, ed., *Science, Technology and economic growth in the Eighteenth Century* Manchester 1972.

W. W. Rostow *The Stages of economic growth,* 2nd ed., Cambridge University Press 1971.

S. B. Saul *The Myth of the Great Depression, 1873–1896* Macmillan 1970.

Ingvar Svennilson *Growth and Stagnation in the European Economy,* United Nations Economic Commission for Europe, United Nations, 1954.

Index